e " '' herside

The Media, Culture & Society Series

Editors: John Corner, Nicholas Garnham, Paddy Scannell, Philip Schlesinger, Colin Sparks, Nancy Wood

The Economics of Television
The UK Case
Richard Collins, Nicholas Garnham and Gareth Locksley

Media, Culture and Society
A Critical Reader
edited by
Richard Collins, James Curran, Nicholas Garnham,
Paddy Scannell, Philip Schlesinger and Colin Sparks

Capitalism and Communication
Global Culture and the Economics of Information
Nicholas Garnham, edited by Fred Inglis

Media, State and Nation
Political Violence and Collective Identities
Philip Schlesinger

Broadcast Talk
edited by
Paddy Scanell

Journalism and Popular Culture
edited by
Peter Dahlgren and Colin Sparks

Media, Crisis and Democracy
edited by
Marc Raboy and Bernard Dagenais

Culture and Power
A Media, Culture & Society Reader
edited by
Paddy Scannell, Philip Schlesinger and Colin Sparks

Interpreting Audiences
The Ethnography of Media Consumption
Shaun Moores

Feminist Media Studies
Liesbet van Zoonen

Television and the Public Sphere
Citizenship, Democracy and the Media
Peter Dahlgren

Popular Cultures
Rock Music, Sport and the Politics of Pleasure
David Rowe

DYNAMICS OF MODERN COMMUNICATION

The Shaping and Impact of New Communication Technologies

Patrice Flichy

Translated by
Liz Libbrecht

SAGE Publications
London • Thousand Oaks • New Delhi

English translation © Sage Publications 1995
First published in English 1995

Originally published as *Une histoire de la communication moderne: Espace public et vie privée*, © Éditions La Découverte, Paris, 1991.

This translation has been published with financial support from the Ministère Français de la Culture et de la Francophonie.

 SAGE Publications Ltd
6 Bonhill Street
London EC2A 4PU

SAGE Publications Inc
2455 Teller Road
Thousand Oaks, California 91320

SAGE Publications India Pvt Ltd
32, M-Block Market
Greater Kailash – I
New Delhi 110 048

British Library Cataloguing in Publication data

A catalogue record for this book is available from the British Library

    ISBN 0 8039 7850 2
    ISBN 0 8039 7851 0 (pbk)

Library of Congress catalog card number 95-074573

Typeset by M Rules
Printed in Great Britain by The Cromwell Preess Ltd,
Broughton Gifford, Melksham, Wiltshire

Contents

Preface

The idea of a technologically determined communication revolution with far reaching social consequences has been a recurrent theme in both elite and popular discourse for 30 years or more. Current excitement over Internet and the, so-called, Information Superhighway is merely the latest version of a hype previously attached to cable, the personal computer, satellites and videotext. The failure of each successive technology to deliver on the revolutionary claims made for it by policy-makers and business people does not appear to undermine this deep-seated faith in technological determinism.

This is not to say, however, that technology does not matter. While predictions as to the extent of change may be exaggerated and as to its nature, wrong, technology does, nonetheless, have effects which are not merely random, and technological choices have at times to be consciously made by both businesses and policy-makers. As a result a growing body of work has developed in economics, sociology and policy studies which attempts to understand how technologies develop, why some paths of technological development are followed rather than others and how and why technologies are adopted and used in societies – often in ways that are very different from those the designers and promoters of the technology imagined. Broadly, this line of research tries to replace a simple, a-historical and uni-causal technological determinism, which incorporates a stress on progress and inevitability, and thus predictability – technology as fate, with a historically based study of technological development and its impact as part of a complex economic, social and cultural process of change. Technology both shapes and is shaped by social processes whose very complexity makes the outcomes highly unpredictable.

This book comes out of this tradition. It is an important book which will be of unique value to students of communication because it combines original historical research on the development of communications technology and its social adoption since the late eighteenth century with an analysis based upon the best recent work in the sociology of technological innovation and social use. There are in this book two key messages for both students and policy-makers. First, that the early development of a technology is far from being scientifically determined but is one of struggle and controversy between different potential technological solutions and different visions of future use. Secondly, that the successful social adoption of a technology involves a process of learning and adaption on the part of users which itself shapes the technological solution adopted and determines its social impact.

Because the history Flichy is telling starts in France and the author is French there is a danger that Anglo-Saxon readers, more familiar with such histories told from an Anglo-American perspective, will be tempted to reject the book as being irrelevant to their concerns. This would be a mistake. The analytical approach being taken is essentially historical. It is concerned to explain technological development, adoption and impact as concretely socially situated in the context of a set of related economic, social, cultural and political determinants. Thus the history of each successive development in communications technology and its adoption has to be told where it actually took place. Thus because the story starts in France the book starts there too. As the story moves first to Britain and later to the United States they become successively the focus of the account. The history of technology may be increasingly a global history but technological development has passed and still passes through national and regional levels on its path to global adoption. That passage marks its development and is part of that process of social learning and adaption which we still too often mistakenly think of as the 'impact' of technology.

Nicholas Garnham
Centre for Communication
and Information Studies

Introduction

Over the past 20 years numerous authors have expressed their enthusiasm for the so-called communication revolution (cable TV, satellites, the VCR, videotext, microcomputers etc.). Their writings evoke a blend of technological and social utopia, extolling the abundant supply of television offering live broadcasts of events throughout the world, telematics providing access to the accumulated knowledge of a universal encyclopaedia, or mobile telephones enabling modern-day nomads to be 'switched on' constantly. These new technologies have indeed modified relationships between the public and private spheres, radically changing the organization of work, and transforming the functioning of democracy.

Most of these texts devoted to the new information and communication technologies give the impression that machines for communicating are a late twentieth-century invention. By contrast, this book will take a more objective standpoint, looking at contemporary tools from 'when old technologies were new' – to borrow Carolyn Marvin's expression (Marvin, 1988). Most of its subject matter is therefore situated in 'that long nineteenth century' described by Maurice Agulhon as stretching from the French Revolution to the 1950s. We are thereby able to examine 'the originality of a singular historical cycle, rather than the banality of a perpetual transition to the present' (Agulhon, 1988: 11). Indeed, the nineteenth century saw the birth of those machines on which today's communication systems are based: the telegraph and then the telephone, photography, the gramophone, the motion picture and radio. Contemporary technologies (satellite TV or mobile telephones, for example) should not be studied outside of this historical context.

Whereas the history of all these communication systems has already been written, few authors have looked at the links which existed between each of them. Numerous inventors worked successively on different types of devices and in each period the functions of communication took on a specific form manifested in the various media. A comparative analysis of the different communication devices is therefore particularly fruitful.

A new medium is never the fully fledged product of its inventor's fertile brain. The contribution of many researchers is required before a viable result can emerge from the different possible hypotheses and the combination of numerous preliminary micro-inventions. Historians often tend, in retrospect, to compose a harmonious picture in which each inventor's contribution appears indispensable to the final product. Yet, a detailed genealogy of these inventions brings to light a less consensual situation.

Innovations often grow from violent controversy: technological debates (is an electromechanical or an electronic solution better?); quarrels over technical usage (are Hertzian waves to be used in experiments only, or also for transmitting information?); controversy over social uses (should the phonograph be an office machine or a family tool?); and conflicts concerning the final marketing of the product (how should the user pay for the radio, by subscription or through advertising?).

My goal is to study these different controversies and the ways in which they were settled. While the inventors' skills in gaining support for their devices were of considerable importance, one also has to consider more long-term technological and social developments. In the technological domain, two basic systems were diffused during the nineteenth and twentieth centuries: electricity and electronics. Progress in these two scientifico-technical fields was to be a determining factor in the invention of communication machines. However, since this question has already been covered by the history of technology, it seems unnecessary for us to discuss it in detail here.

'An innovation', wrote Fernand Braudel, 'is conditional upon the social force on which it is based and which necessitates it' (Braudel, 1979: 477). The role of these 'social forces' in the invention of communication machines has enjoyed relatively little attention and is therefore one of the main focuses of this book. Particular emphasis is placed on the following four social movements: the birth of the modern state at the end of the eighteenth century; the development of the stock market during the 1850s; the transformation of private life with the appearance of the Victorian family; and, finally, the individualism of the late twentieth century.

Numerous historical works on the subject all but ignore the uses to which technologies are put; in fact, they implicitly assume that the utilization of machines is a natural result of their technical characteristics. In contrast, certain sociological studies of technology focus solely on the diffusion of a tool and tend to consider it as a 'black box'. The aim of this book is precisely to articulate these two contrasting traditions. The history of an invention is that of a series of technological and social developments, together with interactions between the two spheres. A new communications system is only established at the end of a long process in which each stage warrants attention. When a technical (or scientific) device shifts from one sphere to another, we can consider it captured, in both a military and hydrological sense of the word. When considered in the former sense, the strategies used to seize the technical device should be studied. In the latter sense, the metaphor is that of the flow of water in geological strata, from one river basin into another. The phenomenon appears in unexpected, although not random, places.

This book therefore analyses the development of communication machines by taking into account the major technological and social movements in which they were situated. My twofold ambition led me to reflect upon the origins of different communication systems (the semaphore telegraph, the electric telegraph, photography, the phonograph, the telephone, the radio, motion picture and television), while simultaneously examining their technological and social contexts. I have started at the dawn of the industrial era, with the semaphore telegraph – the first reliable communication device in permanent use – and look at three periods, each corresponding to different types of research work: that of the researcher working alone, that of the small private laboratory and that of the large research centre. The first period (1790–1870) includes the birth of electricity, the concept of a network and the recording of images; it was one of controversy between state-controlled and market-controlled communication. During the second period (1870–1930) another controversy arose between professional and domestic or family use of communication devices. Research on electricity was pursued and Hertzian waves were discovered. The third period (1930 to the present) is that of electronics and the move from family communication to individual communication.

Although all the examples presented in this book[1] belong to the general field of communication (excluding writing), I have nevertheless favoured those which have hitherto received the least attention: telecommunications (telegraph and telephone) and sound technologies (the gramophone and radio). Each study is situated in the country in which the relevant communication device was developed in its established form (France, the UK or the USA, respectively).

Note

1 The original versions of some of these monographs have already been presented in seminars and have been published. However, the corresponding chapters of this book have been rearranged to a large extent.

'L'imaginaire collectif des ingénieurs : le cas des machines à communiquer', *Réseaux*, no. 36, CNET, Issy, 1989.

'L'historien et le sociologue face à la technique : le cas des machines sonores', *Réseaux*, no. 46–7, CNET, Issy, 1991.

'Nécessité sociale et innovation : du télégraphe d'Etat au télégraphe commercial', in François du Castel, Pierre Chambat and Pierre Musso (eds), *L'Ordre communicationnel II* (records of a research seminar 1988–89), La Documentation française, Paris, 1991.

References

Agulhon M. (1988) *Histoire vagabonde. Ethnologie et politique dans la France contemporaine*, Gallimard, Paris.

Braudel F. (1979) *Civilisation matérielle, économie et capitalisme, XVe -XVIIIe siècles*, Armand Colin, Paris, vol. 3.

Marvin C. (1988) *When Old Technologies Were New*, Oxford University Press, Oxford.

PART I
FROM STATE-CONTROLLED COMMUNICATION TO MARKET-CONTROLLED COMMUNICATION (1790–1870)

Introduction

Historians of the industrial revolution have noted that in eighteenth-century England no clear-cut distinction was made between science and technology. Scientists were fascinated by the technological progress made in industry, and technicians took a keen interest in scientific papers. For example, James Watt, one of the pioneers of the steam engine, was a mechanic at Glasgow University and cooperated with both renowned chemists like Black and influential entrepreneurs like Boulton (Musson and Robinson, 1969). In France, the *Encyclopédie* or the *Description des arts et des métiers*, published by the *Académie des sciences*, attempted to draw up an index of all scientific and technological knowledge. The close link between science and technology developed peculiar features in that country with the advent of a new player: the state engineer. The *ancien régime's* policy of establishing institutions for training its engineers (today's *grandes écoles*) was systemized by the Convention when it created the *Ecole polytechnique*. During the Revolution and the Empire, scientists and state engineers worked together in close cooperation.

Thus, scientists in the eighteenth and early nineteenth centuries were well aware of technological developments. In England this link with technology was achieved essentially through industry, while in France it was provided by the state. Constant exchange existed between scientists working alone in their offices or private laboratories, and their colleagues both at home and abroad. Some kept in close contact and compared their work in the large scientific institutions of the day: the *Académie des sciences* in Paris or the Royal Society in London.

In the field of long-distance communication by electricity, studied in this section, the exchange between scientists was all the more important since research remained confined to individual scientists' private laboratories for decades, without resulting in operational uses. Technological progress was thus the result of comparison with peers' work, and of the incorporation of discoveries on electricity.

How did research on long-distance communication move out of these laboratories? Historically, the first case was that of the semaphore telegraph discussed in Chapter 1, which took on a new social meaning with the French Revolution and the constitution of the modern state. In Chapter 2, I look again at the development of the basic principles of a telecommunications network as defined at the time, and examine the progress of research on electricity. Chapter 3 studies the articulation between the new (electric) telegraph and a new social use: the transmission of financial and commercial information.

Reference

Musson A.E. and Robinson E. (1969) *Science and Technology in the Industrial Revolution,* Manchester University Press, Manchester.

1
State-controlled Communication: the Semaphore Telegraph

The idea of long-distance communication appeared in scientifico-utopian literature of the seventeenth and eighteenth centuries. Father Strada, in his *Prolusiones Academicae* of 1616, suggested that 'lovers separated by the severity of their families turn to account the sympathy manifested for each other through two compass needles' to communicate (Cazenoble, 1981: 96–7). The aim of this 'magnetic action'[1] was less to transmit messages than to communicate thoughts or feelings. Long-distance communication was thus telepathic, and the first technical description of a device for transmitting signals by semaphore, presented by the English scientist Robert Hooke in 1684, was entitled 'Method for *making your thoughts* known far away' (Gerspach, 1860: 48, italic added). Several years later, in 1690, the French physicist Guillaume Amontons conducted a first experiment in semaphoric communication in the Luxembourg Gardens. Fontenelle described the device as follows: 'The secret consisted of placing in several consecutive posts persons who, having perceived through a telescope certain signals from the preceding post, transmitted them to the following ones, and so forth' (Gerspach, 1860: 49). In the eighteenth century, several inventors were to perform similar experiments which were hardly more successful and none of which led to an effective device for long-distance communication.

The use for telepathic or telegraphic devices envisaged by literature of that period was primarily that of romantic communication. At the beginning of the nineteenth century a writer in the very serious *Mechanics Magazine* (24 November 1827) suggested that by means of semaphores 'a lover might . . . conspicuously *signalize* his devotion to the fair one of his heart; and the pining mistress might learn from the expanded *arms* of the telegraph how soon she should be restored to the arms of her betrothed' (Wilson, 1976: 71).

Romantic communication was similarly to appropriate another medium in the eighteenth century – the 'string telephone'. This device was also described by Robert Hooke in 1667: 'By using a taut string, I was able to instantaneously transmit the sound over a long distance.' Later, it would often be called the lovers' telephone. In the eighteenth century, long-distance communication devices, whether real or imaginary, were thus for a romantic use. But romantic communication is by nature impulsive, secret and exclusive, and therefore contrary to the idea of a permanent infrastructure. There were two configurations which suited it: the 'string telephone' which allowed for secret communication in a public place (etchings of that period show lovers communicating from one side of a public square to another) and telepathy.

Thus the semaphore telegraph – known and tested from the end of the seventeenth century – was not developed for a century, for lack of an appropriate social structure capable not only of imagining the advantages of long-distance communication, but also of backing the construction of a permanent network. It was first in France with the Revolution and the creation of the modern state that a social agent prepared to take on the establishment of a permanent infrastructure appeared.[2] I shall therefore closely examine the birth of the semaphore telegraph in France, before briefly presenting the development of this medium in other countries.

Communication of Enlightenment Thought

Convincing the Convention

At the start of the Revolution, Claude Chappe was a young physicist who performed several experiments with electricity, of which the results were published in the *Journal de Physique*. In 1790, he defined a new technological project: 'to give the government the means to transmit its orders over a long distance in the shortest time possible' (Chappe, 1840: xii). He was to try several solutions (electricity and sound) but finally visual signs with the aid of a lens seemed to him the most effective system.

Chappe soon realized that he required the assistance of the National Assembly[3] to develop his system. The first message which he transmitted, during his first experiment in the Sarthe on 2 March 1791, a year before presenting his memorandum to the Assembly, was as follows: 'The National Assembly will reward experiments which are useful to the public.' An analysis of his letters and reports presented to the Convention show us how Chappe and the commissaires[4] who supported him obtained approval from the political authorities.

In the petition which he presented on 22 March 1792 to the Legislative Assembly, Claude Chappe insisted that his system be put to use, claiming it to be 'a sure means of establishing correspondence so that the legislative body may send its orders to our borders and receive a reply during the same session' (Gerspach, 1860: 57–8). Two years later (31 August 1794), several months after the first telegraph line had been installed, the use imagined by Chappe was to become a reality:

> *Carnot* [*going up to the tribune*]: Here is the telegraphic message which we have just received. Condé is restored to the Republic. Surrender was at six o'clock this morning.
> *Gossuin*: . . . Condé is restored to the Republic; let us change its name to Nord-Libre.
> *Cambon*: I request that this decree be sent to Nord-Libre by telegraph.
> *Granet*: I request that at the same time as you inform Condé, by telegraph, of its new name, you also inform the fine army of the North that it remains worthy of the homeland.

Later in the session, the chairman read out the following note by Chappe: 'I hereby announce, citizen-chairman, that the decrees of the National Convention . . . have been transmitted to Lille; I received the signal by telegraph.'[5]

We shall see that it was with regard to military news that Chappe's project to govern in 'almost real time' materialized. Gilbert Romme, who was to be made responsible by the Legislative Assembly and then by the Convention for assessing Chappe's proposition on behalf of the Committee of Public Education,[6] was to take advantage of this military demand.

On 12 March 1793, the representative of the Convention in Belgium asked for a regular service of dispatch riders to be organized, so as to have continual contact with the armies. Romme, who was preparing his report on the telegraph, suggested replacing the dispatch riders with Chappe's telegraph.[7] On 1 April, he presented his report to the Convention on behalf of the Committees of Public Education and War.[8] The only use he mentioned was military. The same was true for the Lakanal Report presented on 26 July 1793 to give an account of the experiments proposed by Romme on 1 April and decreed by the Convention.[9] These two reports also insisted on the reliability of Chappe's system and on its capacity to ensure the confidentiality of correspondence.

'The main idea behind the adoption of the telegraph was thus entirely military. Chappe, the Convention and the Committee of Public Safety saw telegraphs, before all else, as instruments of war' (Gerspach, 1860: 334). For Edouard Gerspach, as for most historians of the semaphore telegraph, the conclusion was clear: Chappe succeeded where others had failed, by making use of the demand from the War Department. Indeed, he enjoyed constant support from the Committee of Public Safety in 1793–94 (expropriation, requisitioning of equipment, etc.), and the first telegraphic line was set up in the framework of a war economy.

It was not the first time in the history of the eighteenth century that France was at war. Guillaume Amontons developed his system during the war of the Augsbourg League, and the political authorities took no interest in it. I think that in fact the decision to construct the system was not purely military. In a letter addressed to Lakanal by Chappe, and written after the first experiment had been conducted before the Convention, the latter said of his project's opponents:

> How could they not have been struck by the ingenious idea which you developed yesterday at the Committee [of Public Education] and of which I had not thought? The establishment of the telegraph is, in effect, the best answer to those publicists who think that France is too spread out to form a Republic. The telegraph shortens distances, uniting a huge nation on one single point. (Guillaume, 1891: 7)

On 17 August 1794 Barère (a member of the Committee of Public Safety) informed the Convention of the telegraphic transmission of news on the capture of Quesnoy. He declared: 'By this invention distances between places disappear in a sense. . . it is a means which tends to consolidate the unity of the Republic by the intimate and sudden contact which it gives to all parties.'[10]

The use of the telegraph to ensure national coherence was described by Rabaut-Pommier. He employed the image of instant national mobilization:

> And if in times of peace allied despots wanted to invade our territory, the war cry 'To arms!' would become a decree and would sound throughout the Republic; citizens would leave their occupations to seize their arms, and numerous armies formed suddenly would confront the surprised enemy with barriers which it would not be able to surmount.[11]

Rabaut-Pommier, moreover, had the start of the telegraph line installed on the roof of the Unity Tower of the National Palace (the Tuileries).

A new conception of space

Chappe's innovation was in keeping with an ideological context which went well beyond the targeted uses (military and political) of the device. The Revolution was a period of restructuring the national domain. From July 1789 (when Chappe began to think about his system), the National Assembly debated a new administrative partitioning of France. Thouret imagined a rectangular division, Barère proposed one which would create equal populations. Either way, it was a question of putting an end to regional peculiarities and enforcing national unity by creating divisions based on territorial and demographic equality.

For Barère, the aim of this partitioning was to 'remove all memories of history, all prejudice resulting from the community of interests or origins. Everything must be new in France and we want to date [time] only from today' (Ozouf, 1984: 33). Finally, a partition which mainly took natural borders into account was adopted at the beginning of 1790. This partition into *départements* has scarcely changed for two centuries.

As Mona Ozouf notes, centralization already present under the *ancien régime* 'was worsened further by the link created during the Revolution between the French nation and universal values; peculiarity seemed henceforth not only a hindrance to the national spirit, but also an obstacle to the formation of a universal and generic man' (Ozouf, 1984: 27).

The unity of this homogeneous space had to be constantly strengthened. The telegraph was well suited to the dynamics of territorial coherence. We can thus understand the dispatch published by *Le Moniteur universel* of 6 January 1798 indicating that, thanks to work undertaken by Chappe, Strasbourg could communicate with Paris in 36 minutes. The *Moniteur* also published on 2 September 1794 Chappe's dispatch concerning the capture of Condé (see above). It was signed 'Chappe, engineer-geographer'; what could seem to be a misprint (geographer for telegrapher) was, in fact, a slip of the pen which well illustrated the fact that Chappe's system was part of a reorganization of the national domain.

While the telegraph was well suited to revolutionary rhetoric, it also had a symbolic existence on an architectural level. The dispatch from Strasbourg shows us that 'the telegraphic machine was to replace the cathedral bell-tower.' As for its installation on the roof of the Tuileries, Rabaut-Pommier tells us that 'these constructions will add to the external decoration of the National Palace. By an optical illusion, the poles for supporting the gallery of the telegraph will disappear, so that it will appear to be suspended and without a support'.[12] Thus the scientific works of the Enlightenment were to replace the symbols of royal and religious power. But to celebrate the cult of Reason, science was readily transformed into magic!

The symbolic rather than functional aspect of Chappe's machine had been noted by the German scholar Bergstrasser, the author of several works on the telegraph:

> I fear that the French use their telegraph for nothing other than a political goal; it is used to entertain the Parisians who, their eyes forever riveted to the machine, say 'It's working, it's not working'. They take advantage of this to attract the attention of Europe and so to imperceptibly attain their objective. (Chappe, 1840: 148)

New conception of time

In the second version of his report, Lakanal defined the telegraph as follows: 'It shortens distances. A rapid messenger of thought, which it seems to rival in speed' (Lakanal, 1795: 3). Chappe had, moreover, at first wanted to call his machine a 'tachygraph' ('who writes fast'). In his report to the Assembly, as in those of Romme and Lakanal, the rapidity of transmission was one of the main points of the argument, and very precise transmission times were quoted. For Rabaut-Pommier, 'a decree could be transmitted to the ends [of the Republic] half an hour after being issued, proclaimed forthwith and executed the same day.' Thus, at any place in the nation, the same events could be lived simultaneously.

Bonaparte was one of the first to understand the political value of this new medium. On the evening of the *coup d'état* of *18 brumaire an VIII* (9 November 1799) he had the following dispatch sent by all the telegraphic lines: 'The Legislative Corps has just been transferred to Saint-Cloud by virtue of articles 102 and 103 of the Constitution; the General Bonaparte is named commander of the armed forces of Paris. Everything is perfectly calm and the citizens are content.'

Two days later, Chappe submitted a new dispatch to the Consuls: 'The Legislative Corps has named a three-member *Consulat* to replace the *Directoire*. . .',[13] followed by names and details on the nomination of a legislative commission. The Consuls had the following sentence added: 'Paris is satisfied and public funds have increased by 25 per cent' (Belloc, 1888).

This new telegraphic time, which permitted an almost instantaneous dissemination of information, was in keeping with the revolution of time that members of the National Convention, and particularly Romme (the main author of this reform of the First French Republic), wanted to undertake. When Romme was preparing his report on the telegraph, he chaired a working group on the reform of the calendar with the cooperation of scientists like Lagrange and Monge. Romme wanted to break away from the *ancien régime*, start a new era, make the 'republican calendar' an instrument of ideological struggle against Christianity. These aspects of reform are well known. What is less known is the desire to introduce a rational division of time: months equal to 30 days (plus a special unit of five days), decades, instead of weeks which 'did not divide exactly neither the months, nor the year, nor the lunations', and, in particular, use of the decimal system to divide the day into 10 hours and the hours into tenths and hundredths.

Reform of the calendar was linked to that of weights and measures, although the principle of the latter reform was accepted by the Constituent Assembly. On 21 December 1792 the Committee of Public Education designated a single commission to prepare the two reforms.[14] 'You have undertaken', declared Romme during the presentation of his project:

> one of the most important operations for the progress of the arts and human minds and which could only succeed in a time of revolution. That is, making diversity, incoherence and inexactitude of weights and measures which continually hinder industry and trade, disappear; and taking, even for measuring the ground, the unique and invariable type of all new measures. The arts and history, for which time is a necessary element or instrument, also require new measures of duration, similarly rid of the errors which credulity and superstitious routine conveyed from centuries of ignorance through to us. (Romme, 1793: 1)

As Bronislaw Baczko notes, 'reform of the calendar was in keeping with the framework of a vast enterprise of rationalization which would affect social life as a whole' (Baczko, 1978: 217).

New measures

In 1789 the metrological situation was truly chaotic (Kula, 1984).[15] Different objects were measured with different units; some were in paces, others in cubits or in feet. Certain measures had no physical objectivity, and land was measured according to the number of days' work (in Bourges, for example, an acre was equivalent to 16 days' harvesting). Furthermore, measures varied from one parish to another. At certain markets two or three systems of weights were used simultaneously for measuring wheat. Royal authorities repeatedly tried, in vain, to unify the system of weights and measures. In fact, local metrological particularism was part and parcel of the privileges of the nobility who could always take advantage of it to increase taxes, generally paid in kind. Metrological unification was a significant claim in registers of grievances, but it was only with the upheaval of the Revolution that this was to be realized. As Kula notes, such unification 'was impossible without the Night of 4 August, without the Declaration of Human Rights. Metric reform, the abstract and nationalist work of a few academics, could only become a social reality with the abolition of feudal privileges and the proclamation of equality of all before the law' (Kula, 1984: 210).

Such reform was to be modelled by the rationalism of the Enlightenment. The demands in the registers of grievances were for an end to metrological arbitrariness and for local unification. The academics responsible for implementing this reform, and particularly Condorcet, wanted to give it a universal character and a natural base. Condorcet, as secretary of the

Academy of Sciences, wrote in his report to the National Assembly in March 1791:

> The Academy has tried to exclude any arbitrary condition, anything which could hint of the influence of a particular French interest or a national bias. In short, it wished that if the principles and details of this operation were to be passed to posterity, it would be impossible to guess by which nation it had been ordained and executed. (Kula, 1984: 225)

That is why the Assembly took a quarter of the earth's meridian as the basis of the new metric system.

Under the Convention, reform – like the telegraph – seemed intended more to strengthen national unity. In his report presented on behalf of the Committee of Public Education at the Convention *le 11 vantôse an III*, Prieur de la Côte-d'Or indicated: 'Unity of the Republic demands that there be unity in weights and measures, as there is unity in currency, unity in language, unity in legislation, unity in the government, and unity of interest in defending oneself against outside enemies and for marching together to all kinds of prosperity' (Kula, 1984: 223).

The Enlightenment intellectuals' desire for unification was also at the centre of numerous reform projects for schools examined by the revolutionaries. Condorcet, Romme and Lakanal were the authors of such projects, as were Arbogast and Daunou (the two *commissaires* responsible with Lakanal for supervising Chappe's first experiments). Lakanal wrote in his Report on the establishment of *écoles normales*[16] in October 1794: the springhead of the Enlightenment, 'so pure, so abundant since it will start with the first men of the Republic, of all kinds, and will overflow from reservoir to reservoir, will spread from one sphere to another in all France, without losing any of its purity in its course' (Julia, 1988: 206). His hydraulic comparison was possibly inspired by a machine he had to evaluate for the Committee of Public Education but, whatever the case, this model of diffusion by relays is exactly that of the telegraph.

A universal language

All these reforms in space, time and systems of measures had the same justification: rationality, simplicity, universality. The universal vocation of the Revolution expressed by Lakanal, who spoke of 'the Republic which by its huge population and the genius of its inhabitants is destined to become the teaching nation of Europe', led some to envisage a universal language. This was notably the case with Condorcet, from whom Romme took his main educational ideas (Galante-Garonne, 1971).[17]

The project of a universal language developed by Condorcet was fairly close to that of Leibniz. It was a matter of discovering the intellectual operations at the base of all reasoning. This project was initially applied to the sciences but its ambition was broader, since it was essentially a linguistic analysis of knowledge (Granger, 1954: 197–219). Other revolutionary intellectuals wanted to construct an artificial universal language, an Esperanto before its time. Delournel, for example, presented a 'universal language project' to the Convention in 1795.

Themes such as these were adopted by an intellectual movement called the Ideologists (of which Daunou was a member), which prevailed at the time of the *Directoire* and the *Consulat*. Some of them considered changing the language. For Lancelin, 'the uniform division of the French territory, uniformity of legislation and administration for all *Départements*, and finally the establishment and introduction of a uniform system of weights and measures for the entire Republic are new steps towards this goal' – a general analysis of ideas.[18] His project 'did not only seek to determine the common foundations of all languages; [it] was also animated by the dream of finding the lost universal language whose restoration would ensure perfect communication, the true base of understanding and social communication' (Branca, 1982: 59–66).

Such universal language utopias are a reflection of the concrete difficulties which the revolutionaries experienced in trying to get their political message across. The Directoire of the Corrèze (*département*) indicated, for example, that 'the translator from the Juillac canton did not have the accent of the other cantons which differed more or less, particularly at a distance of seven or eight leagues' (de Certeau et al. 1975: 162). In the face of such linguistic fragmentation, a means of communication had to be found to constitute a public sphere. Thus Pierre Bernardeau wrote to Abbé Grégoire: 'The knowledge I have of the country surrounding me made me think of translating, into the most common language out of all the jargon of its inhabitants, the blessed Declaration of Human Rights.'[19]

Such projects for a universal language soon proved to be impractical. Reforms envisaged were rather relative to vocabulary and spelling, and a principle for the multiplication of words was sought. For Degérando, French multiplied meanings rather than words: 'The language therefore suffers from the vice of extreme indetermination with the result that men living in the same country and using the same words, often understand one another as little as if they were talking in a foreign language.'[20] It was thus a question of rationalizing the construction of vocabulary. Furthermore, the reform of spelling, like that of weights and measures, was to allow for the definition of a rational system, so that the sounds of words could be noted in a universal fashion, and the use of the language standardized. 'It was necessary to try to have a single elocution in a single and indivisible Republic.'[21] In the end the universal language was simply the diffusion of French across the Republic as a whole. Like the reform of weights and measures, which in 1790 Talleyrand had envisaged could be led jointly with England so as to be truly universal, it became national and Jacobin.

In January 1794 (when Chappe was building his first telegraphic line), Grégoire and Barère presented a report to the Convention which concluded with the necessity of making French compulsory in all public acts. But as Renée Balibar indicates, the real linguistic revolution was less the diffusion of French as opposed to patois, than that of writing 'the Republican language'. This language, considered 'universal' in the nation, was 'founded on the grammaticization of the French language and appeared explicitly as the expression of popular sovereignty. [It represented] the condition of "communication" between citizens and with the State, in the debates of assemblies, the reports of commissions, the laws, and in the organization of the new school system' (Balibar, 1988).

Ignace Chappe, who was the ideologist of the family,[22] related their project to the idea of a universal language. 'We were strangely wrong' he wrote:

in saying that the telegraphic language was a universal language or a plausible language as Leibniz conceived it. This philosopher wanted to introduce a new method of reasoning founded on formulae similar to those used in algebra . . . but they could only be universal for rules of logic and they would not have served to indicate . . . The telegraph thus only writes languages which are already formulated; but its language becomes almost universal in that it indicates combinations of numbers instead of words, and that the manner of expressing these numbers is generally known and can be applied to the words which compose all dictionaries. His aim is not to find a language which is *easy to learn without a dictionary* (Leibniz's expression in his letter to M. Renard) but to find the means to express many things with few signs. (Chappe, 1840: 135–6)

Numerous innovators

All these utopian conceptions of space, time and communication were produced not only by the intelligentsia and politicians but also by unknown persons who sent letters to the Convention or the Committee of Public Education. Some of this literature is still accessible today in the French national archives. From 1792 to 1798 there was one invention project per year for a long-distance communication system. Some of these projects were completely impracticable, such as Julien Chapus' cannon-ball mail, whereby a letter introduced into a cannon-ball was shot from cannon to cannon in a relay system.[23] Some were very rudimentary, such as that of Labarthe which coded messages by means of cannon shots.[24] Others, such as Bréguet's and Bethencourt's systems, proposed alternatives for semaphore telegraphs.

My intention in this chapter is, however, not to write a technical history of telegraphic inventions, but a history of the representations of the technology. The amateur inventors of this period are of interest to me because of their discourse. The idea of instant communication was part of the utopianism of the era. Favre discovered a system which permitted 'the transmission in a few seconds of a mind's image from one end of the Republic to another', but he was careful not to reveal his method.[25] A 'citizen of Angely-Boutonne' sent two notes, one on the telegraph, the other on 'Directions on the French Calendar', preceded by 'Reflection on chronology in relation to the people's freedom'.[26]

This twofold interest in the revolutionary calendar[27] and communication was also to be found in Morin's memorandum. He proposed a system of phonetic writing 'which gives an accurate image of speech' and 'reduces it to its most basic simplicity'. He hoped to 'make France and all peoples of the earth enjoy this great advantage which should contribute to the progress of the Enlightenment and make French a language of communication with all peoples'.[28] To illustrate his phonetic writing he used the example of the republican calendar. Morin, steeped in Enlightenment ideology, was so convinced that one needed only a little simplicity and universality to understand nature, that he described in a second note another discovery: the 'mechanism of nature', the matrix of all sciences.

All these scholarly or spontaneous representations of space, time, measurement systems and communication constitute the prevailing outlook in which Chappe was able to develop his innovation. He was not content to convince the military lobby of the Convention alone. Moreover, his project was adopted by Romme and Lakanal not only because it was reliable (it was not unique in this respect) but because it was in keeping with the new perception of space and time which had appeared under the Revolution. Chappe's advantage over Amontons was that he proposed a project which corresponded to the way of thinking of his era.

If we look further at this idea of correspondence between a technology and an outlook, we see that the semaphore telegraph did not correspond to any significant technological development. It was situated in a technological paradigm which had been stable for the preceding two centuries. One could therefore consider at one level that we are dealing with a latent innovation which the movement of ideas resulting from the Revolution had allowed. Yet, the histories of the telegraph, the calendar and systems of measurement reveal an interpenetration between technological and social dimensions.

Chappe was a product of the Enlightenment and the Revolution. In his account to the Legislative Assembly, he stated:

> The most difficult obstacle to conquer will be the spirit of prevention, with which creators of projects are normally received. I would never have been able to get beyond the fear of being associated with them, had I not been supported by the persuasion that every French citizen owes to his country, now more than ever, the tribute which he believes will be useful to it.

Two years later, Barère gave his reply in his speech to the Convention:

> In spite of the Enlightenment which characterizes the end of the eighteenth century, modern inventions are not shielded from the ridiculous accusations which also struck brilliant ideas in other centuries. It is up to the legislators to stop the clamours of ignorance or the agitation of curiosity; it is for the National Convention to encourage the arts and sciences.

Chappe was thus persuaded that he was participating in the progress of the Enlightenment. On the other hand, earlier inventions were considered as mere curiosities.[29]

State communication

Diffusion of innovation

Diffusion of the telegraph was largely related to that of the republican calendar and the metric system. All three seem to have resulted from the

Revolution and they spread with the movements of the French armies. The telegraph was to be extended towards northern Italy (Turin–Milan–Venice then Trieste) and Flanders (Antwerp–Amsterdam and Brussels).

Diffusion of Chappe's telegraph, in particular, was linked to the extension of the Republic. It was only implanted in those territories annexed by France and in certain sister republics. Kula notes that in other European countries, conquered later by Napoleon, it was not republics but kingdoms which were created, and no attempt was made to introduce the metric system. 'The time of exporting the republican régime, the metric system [I could add Chappe's system], in short, the Revolution, had already passed' (Kula, 1984: 206). In 1814, the Italian and Flemish parts of the telegraphic lines were closed, as pro-French Europe abandoned the metric system.

The republican calendar was abandoned in 1806 after 12 years. In retrospect, it seems hardly surprising that the most purely ideological reform did not survive the Revolution. We should not forget that, as Kula (1984) has demonstrated so well, there was also considerable resistance to the metric system. If the registers of grievances requested the unification of weights and measures, it was more a question of harmonization on a local level than creation of an abstract universal measure which used the decimal system. The 'Republican' system of measures was as ideologically weighted as were the calendar and the telegraph.

The reason for the calendar's failure has been clearly explained by Baczko. While there existed considerable diversity of weights and measures, the Christian world had unified its measurement of time on the Gregorian calendar. The need for universality was thus far less obvious. Similarly, the English who had unified their system of measures were hardly interested in the metric system. The latter was finally to be adopted in Italy, in Germany and in Russia (along with the Gregorian calendar) at the time of the 1917 Revolution.

Baczko concluded his research on the Enlightenment utopia by indicating that social imagination 'goes through "heated" phases characterized by a particularly intense exchange between the "real" and "fantasy", by a greater pressure by the imaginary on daily living, by explosions of passions and desires. This is notably the case of revolutionary crises' (Baczko, 1978: 218). We recall the May 1968 slogan in France: 'Let's indulge in wishful thinking';[30] that intensity of desire, that force of social imagination, was one of the conditions for the birth of the telegraph. It was common to Chappe and other inventors of the telegraph alike. While Chappe triumphed thanks to the reliability of his system, he did not hesitate to use ideological arguments to fight his most serious competitors. He thus wrote to the Convention, attacking Bréguet's and Bethencourt's projects: 'Irrespective of the perfection of their machine, the government must not permit that the telegraph, born French, passes to posterity disfigured by the rags of foreign livery.'[31] Indeed, Bethencourt was Spanish!

The Chappe brothers worked not only on the technical, but also on the social and political aspects of their invention. This was shown notably by the fact that their system survived changes of régime, from the Convention to the July Monarchy. In 1832, during his retirement, Abraham Chappe alerted the Minister of the Interior to the necessity for laying the legal foundations of the telegraphic monopoly. According to Antoine Lefébure, this intervention played a decisive role in the preparation of the 1837 Act (Lefébure, 1984: 11–21).

Use of the telegraph

There was of course a discrepancy between society's idea of the telegraph and its effective uses. Rabaut-Pommier declared in 1795: 'One day, when peace permits the perfecting of useful inventions, the telegraph applied to trade, physics, politics, even agriculture, will multiply means of communication and make them more useful by their speed. The author of this fortunate invention has already used it to warn of storms.'[32] In fact, the extension of the telegraph's use outside the military field was very limited. In 1799, Chappe suggested to the *Directoire* using the telegraph for transmitting exchange rates and announcing the arrival of ships in ports. In 1801, under the *Consulat*, he renewed his proposition by extending it to the diffusion of national lottery results and the transmission of an official information bulletin approved by the First Consul. Only the lottery project was accepted. Several historians see in this the refusal by the state to open its communication networks to the private sector. It was, however, not the only reason; these projects necessitated the extension of the network towards ports, while the First Consul had just cut the telegraphic services' budget by a third (Gerspach, 1860: 29–31).

Other reasons for the failure of attempts to extend the use of the telegraph are to be found in the lack of demand. The industrial revolution was still in its infancy in France and the demand for rapid transmission of industrial and commercial information was limited. During the Revolution and the Empire, uses of the telegraph were essentially military; under the *Restauration* they were rather for the police.[33] Abraham Chappe described in a letter of 23 August 1832 the role of the telegraph after the Empire:

> [telegraphic lines] carry to the centre of government, at the speed of thought, all political feeling . . . This communication verifies all administrative reports, it gives more unity of action . . . When the government has to be ready to defend itself against attacks, when each minute must be efficiently used . . . a similar means must be considered, rightly, as one of the most powerful administrative means and one of the most worthy of interest. The telegraph is thus an element of power and order.[34]

The construction of lines was most often linked to a specific request related to current events. The first Paris–Lille line was built under the Convention for communicating with the army in the North. The *Directoire* requested the installation of the Strasbourg line to be able to communicate with its plenipotentiaries during the Rastadt Congress. Napoleon, to improve his communication with Italy, wanted to build the Lyons–Milan line in 15 days. After the Russian campaign, he also requested the urgent construction of a

Strasbourg–Mayence line. Under the *Restauration* a Paris–Bayonne line was similarly built in preparation for the Spanish expedition of 1823.

Such principles for building the network did not allow for an effective response to the development of the military/police demand. In 1829, wanting to argue for the construction of a coherent network, Abraham and René Chappe recalled that news of Napoleon's landing in the Juan gulf in 1815 did not reach Lyons until three days later, and from there a telegram was sent to Paris (Chappe and Chappe, 1829). The Lyons–Toulon line was to be built only in 1821.

Other European networks

In other countries the semaphore telegraph was also being developed according to the demands of military activity.[35] The British Admiralty built telegraphic lines between London and four coastal ports in 1796 and 1808. In 1814, these lines were closed. Similarly, in The Netherlands a telegraph was built in 1831 during the Belgian War of Independence and was closed as soon as the war ended. Except in France, the installation of a permanent transmission device for the needs of the state was developed later. Britain installed a network of semaphores in the 1820s for the Admiralty's needs. It is interesting to note that the Admiralty closed the lines which served during the Napoleonic wars and declared in 1816 to Ronalds, an inventor of the electric telegraph, 'telegraphs of any kind are now totally unnecessary, and no other than the one now in use will be adopted' (Wilson, 1976: 33). Yet it had a new semaphore system built to cover the same areas (Deal, Portsmouth and Plymouth) with slightly different alignments.

Some historians, such as Jeffrey Kieve (1973), are surprised by the Admiralty's lack of insight when it failed to grasp the opportunities offered at that time by the electric telegraph. I think, on the contrary, that it proves the real demand for a permanent communication system. The semaphore telegraph, already running smoothly, seemed to the Admiralty more reliable than an electric telegraph still in its infancy.[36]

It was only in the 1830s that the other European states built telegraphic links. In 1832 Prussia built a Berlin–Coblenz line and Sweden installed a network around Stockholm. In 1839, Russia established a line between St Petersburg and Warsaw. In Spain, a real network was installed: Madrid–Irun in 1845 and then, from Madrid, links with Barcelona, Valencia and Cadiz. These networks were, however, short-lived. The English network was to be replaced by the electric telegraph in 1847, while on the Continent the transformation was to take place later, in the 1850s.[37]

All these telegraphs belonged to the state and were managed by the military (England, Prussia) or by state civil engineers (Spain, Sweden). They were instruments intended to strengthen national unity and consolidate the power of the state. For Prussia, the telegraph which crossed the independent states of central Germany constituted in the strict sense a link between the two parts of the country (the Rhineland and Eastern Prussia). For Russia, the

Warsaw line enabled it to consolidate its annexation of Poland. In Spain, the construction of the telegraph came in a period when the monarchy had to fight the Republicans and Carlists. In Sweden, the main function of the network was to ensure communication between the continent and the islands. These different networks were to retain their national character. The Spanish Irun line, for example, ended just a few miles from the French (Béhobie) line; yet, in spite of this proximity, they were never connected.

Operation of the semaphore telegraph would have lasted around half a century. The seeds of this system's technical potential had existed since the seventeenth century, but the telegraph became a reality only because it accorded with a major change in attitudes: that of the French Revolution prepared by the Enlightenment. A French utopia seemed at the time of the Revolution that of universality; redividing space evenly, measuring it with a new unit based on nature, counting time in a new way, creating a universal language so as to ensure perfect communication.

The universality of 1789 was rapidly reduced to the French nation. The Revolution created the modern nation-state, a nation where citizens all had the same rights, a state where territorial units all enjoyed equal status. In order to guarantee its coherence and unity, this nation-state needed a system of rapid communication, and behind the transformation of outlook it generated a demand for such a system. Under the Revolution and the Empire, this demand was essentially military; under the *Restauration*, it also became that of other sectors of the state apparatus, notably the police.

This association between the telegraph and the creation of the nation-state was not solely French; it was equally present in other European countries. But if the semaphore telegraph was largely associated with France, to the point where numerous histories of telecommunications ignore the English, German or Spanish systems, this is undoubtedly because it was created by a Frenchman during the Revolution and because the idea of a nation-state was largely a product of the revolutionary model. In conquering Europe, under the pretext of awakening liberty, the republican and then imperial armies were to arouse national sentiment in Prussia, Spain and Russia (Gusdorf, 1987).

Impossible trade communication

In 1836 an affair of telegraphic fraud sparked off debate again on the use of this means of communication. Two bankers from Bordeaux had bribed a telegraph employee to add signals to official dispatches. This system permitted them to be informed of the development of the rate of government stocks before the arrival of the press which was sent by post. The device was rather rudimentary and made this affair seem incredible. To avoid transmission errors, inevitable in Chappe's system, each dispatch was decoded half-way by the director of the local office in Tours. The message was then retransmitted to Bordeaux. The pirates introduced additional signals after Tours, indicating

stock market developments. To inform their 'stooges' carrying out the operation, the fraudsters sent them, by post from Paris, white or grey gloves
depending on whether the rate of the stocks was going up or down. The
fraud lasted for two years. When it was discovered, the protagonists were
detained for trial but then released. Since the state telegraphic monopoly was
not defined by law, they could not be convicted.

From de facto *to* de jure *monopoly*

The two Bordeaux bankers were not the first to discover the value of information in the establishment of stock market rates. Under the *Restauration*,
the Rothschilds had already set up a system of private mail which permitted
them to know, before anyone else, the main political events and rates on
other markets. Thus the 'assassination of the Duke of Berry, in February
1829, was known in Frankfurt by the House of Rothschild well before everyone else. It then made necessary arrangements and only announced the news
after having sent its mail and its orders' (Gille, 1959: 262). Regarding French
intervention in Spain, the Prime Minister Villèle noted in his mémoires: 'The
Rothschild mail again caused our government funds to rise. It is spreading the
rumour that there will be no intervention. Misleading increases which prepare
new fluctuations in prices and high losses tell me nothing good'(quoted in
Gille, 1959: 262).

Those bankers who did not have the means to set up private postal systems
across Europe also thought of using the telegraph, and other clandestine
operations took place between Paris and Lyons. At the start of 1832,
Alexandre Ferrier launched a subscription to constitute the capital of a private telegraph company which was to link the main European towns.[38] He
envisaged an essentially commercial use. His telegraph offered 'the immense
advantage of having an idea, at a glance, of all the markets, of being present
at all the stock markets and giving their operations more supply at the same
time than safety stock' (Ferrier, 1832). The demand for stock market information in the provinces rose sharply in the 1820s. According to Bertrand
Gille (1959: 178), it was at this time that people in the provinces began sub-
scribing on a large scale for government stock.

Ferrier obtained the support of Casimir-Perier (President of the Council
and Minister of the Interior), who wrote to him: 'I have seen in this question
of public usefulness, progress in civilization which promises real advantages
for industry, and I am pleased to be able to encourage it with my approval.'[39]
Ferrier could similarly give about 40 deputies as a reference: liberals of the
(left-wing constitutional monarchy) movement's party like Laffitte,
LaFayette or Odilon Barrot, bankers like Benjamin Delessert, jurists, and so
forth. He also assured his future subscribers of 'the approval of the traders
consulted on the utility of the project'. He was finally surrounded by the
advice of several lawyers who concluded that, without a law on the telegraph
'the powerless administration will have to respect the property rights and
freedom of industry'.[40]

In the full assurance of this support, Ferrier built a Paris–Rouen line and prepared the installation of a national network. He was convinced that he would obtain government backing, and wrote to several prefects asking them to indicate 'trustworthy persons whom he could appoint as managers of the lines he was to create'.[41] Negotiations were moreover initiated with the Minister of the Interior to study possible cooperation.[42] Then in June 1833, the administration broke off the negotiations and decided to have a law voted on telegraphic monopoly.[43]

This about-turn by the political authorities is interesting. At first the position of the liberal business bourgeoisie (Casimir-Perier, Laffitte) prevailed, then finally a position of affirmation of the state monopoly was adopted in the bill which was voted by Parliament in 1837. Furthermore, the opponents of the bill in the Chamber of Deputies, as in the *Chambre des Pairs* (the Upper House), were fewer than the petitioners in 1832.

The defenders of private use of the telegraph presented two options: either the creation of private lines, or the opening of state lines to the public. Vatimesnil, with the aid of a post/telegraph comparison, summarized these two options very well:

> The post office monopoly of mail can be justified, firstly because it is a source of government revenue, and secondly because it does not disadvantage private persons, since the administration undertakes to have their dispatches transported. On the contrary, state monopoly of telecommunications earns nothing for the government and would rather harm citizens' interests by preventing them from using this mode of correspondence which is so rapid, and consequently so fitted to imparting a new activity to trade relations. For matters to be otherwise, it would be necessary for the government to establish telegraphs on all important communication lines and put them at the service of private persons, in return for a charge fixed by the law.[44]

The two options envisaged corresponded to the two forms of liberalism – political or economic. Political argument maintained that state monopoly over use could be envisaged only under a despotic government, while the conquest of freedom guaranteed by the revolution of July 1830 implied the possibility for citizens to communicate in all possible ways. From an economic viewpoint, the state could not confiscate for its own use technology required for economic activity.[45]

To support their argument, the liberals referred to the press which was not a government monopoly, affirming: 'A law on telegraphs, like a law on the press, must be limited to regulating the use and curbing abuse.'[46] Nevertheless, during debate on the 1837 law, the opposition fought less against a state monopoly than in favour of private use. It thus took the suggestions of the Count of Montureux who in April 1830 had published in a Montpellier journal, 'reflections on the possibility of making the telegraph a branch of government revenue and facilitating commercial operations by putting this means of correspondence at the disposal of merchants'.

The liberal thesis, which seemed strong in 1831, was largely in the minority in the vote on the 1837 law which provided for a prison sentence for 'whosoever transmits, without authorization, signals from one place to another'. Debate on this law is essential for an understanding of how French society in the 1830s perceived communication. There were two opposed communication projects: that of free communication necessary for the development of a market economy, and that of state communication where 'the telegraph is an indispensable complement of our governmental centralization'.[47] This vision of communication has often been presented as thoroughly reactionary, as the last outburst before the liberalization of the 1850s. Such an analysis is, however, content to gather a few speeches in its favour and misunderstands the conceptions of the July Monarchy. The debate must, on the contrary, be studied in all it richness.

Justifications for the law presented by the Minister of the Interior Adrien de Gasparin and the two rapporteurs of the Chamber of Deputies and the *Chambre des Pairs*, Joseph-Marie Portalis and the Duke of Plaisance, were based on their ideas of non-governmental use of communication. They saw two possible uses: political agitation and stock market speculation. The fear of insurrection was not only a fantasy of the Minister of the Interior, the July Monarchy had been confronted right up till 1835 by a series of social movements of considerable magnitude both in Paris and in the provinces, notably in Lyons. The authorities could thus legitimately fear that the telegraph might become an instrument in the hands of conspirators. As for its stock market use, it was seen by many deputies as a means of 'immoral and spoliatory speculation'.[48] The deputy Fulchiron could thus declare: 'Until now I have never seen telegraphic lines established by private persons with good intentions'; they serve to 'establish a brigandage, so as to rob those who do not have news of the Paris Bourse'. This scorn for financial activity and, more broadly, for economics was shared by most of the political class under the July Monarchy.[49]

Fear of insurrection, lack of interest in the economy, refusal to liberalize telegraphic communication, appear easily understandable. But the defenders of the bill could not stop at that; they faced genuine opposition. A large number of deputies supported Ferrier's project, so their refusal had to be more thoroughly argued. They therefore attempted to prove that the telegraph could not be included in the Post Office. The argument ran as follows: the mail could transport a considerable number of dispatches all arriving at the same time, so that it was difficult to manipulate information. A letter could be contradicted by another one which arrived at the same time. 'But the telegraph does not lend itself to such freedom, that equality, that simultaneous action. In itself it excludes such competition and the telegraph is, necessarily, a monopoly.'[50] At the time it was not feasible to install several competing lines. The economic difficulties of the Paris–Rouen line built by Ferrier confirmed Gasparin's thesis: if a single private line seemed hardly profitable, this was even more true for a second line.

The monopolistic aspect of the telegraph was due mainly to the conditions of transmission. Potential traffic on a line was limited and nothing guaranteed that a dispatch sent half an hour or an hour after another one would arrive the same day.[51] 'Will the first one not enjoy an immense, exorbitant, inadmissible privilege?'[52] All these monopolistic tendencies meant that 'the lines would certainly fall into the hands of parties . . . or into those of the richest speculators who would thus remove any chance of success from the least opulent merchants and thereby obtain an exclusive privilege to the poorest merchants' detriment.'[53] The Rothschild's private mail system shows that this latter hypothesis was altogether realistic.

To preclude 'a monopoly in the service of private interests, of commercial, jealous, exclusive, demanding interests using their immense advantage to crush rivals, without any doubt to speculate',[54] the only solution was state control. Thus Gasparin could affirm, 'without paradox, that the only way of preventing the telegraphic monopoly' was 'to attribute it to the government'.[55]

In short, one finds the same governmental and centralized conception of the telegraph which had taken shape under the Empire and the *Restauration*, but the conception of monopoly had changed. It was no longer a police and military instrument which found its own legitimacy within itself, but an instrument of general interest. The Duke of Plaisance envisaged the government being responsible for diffusing stock market information and thus guaranteeing its objectivity. Private use implied certain operating conditions for a telegraphic correspondence service: the obligation to accept all dispatches irrespective of their origin, by following the order of registration, at a moderate tariff. It was because Gasparin considered that the semaphore telegraph could not meet these conditions that he would not allow it to be applied to private use. His argument was of a socio-technical nature. The July Monarchy was certainly not inclined to liberalize the telegraph, but the limits of the semaphore technique strengthened it in its opposition.

This law closed a socio-technical cycle, that which associated the Chappe telegraph with the state. The association was finally broken during the following 10 years, giving birth to a new socio-technical entity: electric commercial telegraphic communication.

The liberal telegraph

The English situation was radically different. In the liberal British view, regulation of society was largely guaranteed by the market. Communication infrastructures were part of private initiative, and in the second half of the eighteenth century there was an increase in the number of canals and roads with turnpikes constructed on this principle.

Private initiative also manifested itself in respect of the telegraph. A royal act in 1825 devoted to the improvement of Liverpool Harbour authorized the dock administrators 'to establish a rapid means of communication between Liverpool and Wales, to warn fitters and merchants of the arrival of ships'. Two years later, a telegraphic line was opened, and run by Watson. The *Shipping and Mercantile Gazette* of 4 January 1842 assessed this telegraphic link and emphasized its efficiency and 'the commercial significance of this communication mode'. From 1839 to 1842, Watson opened four other lines, to Hull, London, Southampton and Dartmouth.

Even though it owned its own lines (see above), the Admiralty also used Watson's telegraph (Wilson, 1976: 68-93) which had received the support of the East India company and Lloyd's. If we can believe the account of a contemporary, J. Humphery, this telegraphic link offered great benefits to ship-owners since certain boats could spend several weeks blocked by cross-winds, unable to sail up the Thames (Wilson, 1976: 93). The risks of maritime transport had consequences on the availability of goods and the movement of prices. David Landes recalls that:

> traders and bankers of nineteenth-century London and Paris waited eagerly for the first word of sails off Land's End or l'Ouessant bringing golden cargoes from the Pacific. The amounts involved were a tiny fraction of debts outstanding in the money and securities markets; but they made all the difference between easy and hard liquidation at month's end (Landes, 1969: 205)

Watson also envisaged other uses for his telegraph: information for managing the railways (in particular he drew up a plan for a telegraph along the Liverpool–Manchester line in 1836), and stock market information between Paris and London.

Commercial use of the telegraph thus existed in the 1830s in England as in France. It gave rise to the installation of networks distinct from those of the state.[56] In France, the government blocked the development of private networks; in England, it left them to be created. Commercial liberalism was to constitute a framework favourable to the development of the telegraph. Innovation, in the form of electricity, was to find a new field for development.

Notes

1 The English poet Mark Akenside, in *Pleasures of Imagination* (1744), gave an interpretation of this magnetic action: 'Two faithful needles – from the informing touch of the same parent stone, together drew its mystic virtue; – And though disjointed by kingdoms . . . yet preserved their former friendship and remembered still the alliance of their birth.'

2 Because of the close ties between the construction of the first telegraphic network and the appearance of the new French revolutionary state, resulting from Enlightenment thought, reference will be made to political facts with which the reader may not be familiar. In such cases he or she might find the explanatory notes given here useful.

3 *Translator's note*: During this period in France legislative and executive power lay successively with the National Constituent Assembly (1789–91), the Legislative Assembly (1791–92) and the Convention (1792–5).

4 *Translator's note*: Commissaries, or peoples' representatives.

5 *Le Moniteur universel*, 1 and 2 September 1794.

6 *Translator's note*: This Committee was responsible for education but also for the arts and science in general.

7 *Le Moniteur universel*, 14 March 1793, p. 33.

8 Ibid., 4 April 1793, pp. 30–1.

9 *Procès-verbal de la Convention*, 26 July 1793.

10 *Le Moniteur universel*, 18 August 1794, p. 516.

11 Ibid., 22 July 1795, vol. XII, pp. 265–6.

12 Ibid., 22 July 1795, vol. XII, p. 266.

13 *Translator's note*: From 1795 to 1799 the régime in France was that of the *Directoire*.

From 1799 to 1804 Bonaparte was First Consul. In 1804 he became Emperor Napoleon I, until 1814.

14 The two reforms were soon to be led by different men, at a different pace. Prieur de la Côte-d'Or was to lead the commission on the reform of weights and measures, together with Arbogast who was also to form part of the commission responsible for evaluating Chappe's first experiment.

15 On this point, the reader is referred to the excellent book by Witold Kula, *Les mesures et les hommes* (1984), from which I have borrowed all my information.

16 The *écoles normales* (teachers' training colleges) were an essential link in the imparting of knowledge because teachers were trained there in contact with academics.

17 On Romme's educational ideas, and more generally on his activities within the Committee of Public Education, see Allessandro Galante-Garonne, *Gilbert Romme: histoire d'un révolutionnaire* (1971).

18 Lancelin, *Introduction à l'analyse des sciences*, 1801, quoted by Branca (1982: 59–66).

19 Augustin Gazier, *Lettres à Grégoire sur les patois de la France (1790–1794)*, 1880, p. 292, quoted by Braudel (1986).

20 Degeranda, *Des signes et de l'art de penser*, quoted by Branca (1982).

21 Sigard, *Débats de l'Ecole normale*, quoted by Branca (1982).

22 Claude Chappe built and managed the telegraphic network with the cooperation of his four brothers, Ignace, Pierre, René and Abraham. After Claude's death (1805), his brothers Ignace and Pierre succeeded him. When they retired, Abraham and René took over until 1830.

23 *Archives nationales*, F17–1137.

24 Ibid.

25 Ibid., F17–1281.

26 Report by the Committee of Public Education, 3 January 1795.

27 Gilbert Romme popularized the republican calendar by having an almanac published, the *Annuaire du cultivateur*, which gave day-by-day advice to farmers.

28 *Archives nationales*, F17–1009A.

29 In a letter to the Polish king's secretary, Fénelon described Amontons' experiment and judged his invention as 'more curious than useful', quoted by Belloc (1888).

30 *Translator's note*: '*Prenons nos désirs pour des réalités*', literally, 'Let our desires be our reality.'

31 *Le Moniteur universel*, 29 April 1798.

32 Ibid., 22 July 1795.

33 *Translator's note*: With the *Restauration* in 1815, royalty was reinstated until the July 1830 revolution. Thereafter a constitutional monarchy (the July Monarchy) ruled until 1848.

34 *Archives nationales*, F90–1427.

35 For an exhaustive presentation of semaphore telegraphs in the world see G. Wilson's book *The Old Telegraphs* (1976).

36 Transmission difficulties caused by fog were less frequent than is often thought. According to *The Times* of 4 April 1830, the semaphore telegraph was only interrupted for 29 days in 1839.

37 Germany: 1852; Russia: 1854; Spain 1855; Sweden: 1858 (Wilson, 1976).

38 During a visit to Paris, O'Etzel, director of the German semaphore telegraph, met Ferrier who presented his project for a European network to him (see Herbath, 1978: 21).

39 Quoted in *Consultation pour M. Alexandre Ferrier, gérant de l'entreprise des télégraphes publics*, by Me Ad. Crémieux et al., *Archives nationales*, F90–1456.

40 Ph. Dupin in *Consultation*, *Archives nationales*, F90–1456.

41 *Archives nationales*, F90–1456.

42 Manuscript note from the Minister of the Interior's office on the breaking off of negotiations, 4 August 1833, *Archives nationales*, F90–1456.

43 Circular from the Minister of the Interior to the prefects, 29 June 1833, *Archives nationales*, F90–1456.

44 de Vatimesnil in *Consultation*, *Archives nationales*, F90–1456.

45 For more details on the arguments of the defenders of telegraphic freedom, see Lefébure (1984).

46 Jollivet, consultant for A. Ferrier, quoted by Delespaul, debate in the Chamber of Deputies, 14 March 1837, in *Archives parlementaires*, vol. 108.

47 Adrien de Gasparin, speech to the Chamber of Deputies, 6 January 1837, in *Archives parlementaires*, vol. 106.

48 Tesnière, debate in the Chamber of Deputies, 14 March 1837, in *Archives parlementaires*, vol. 108.

49 On this point see Pierre Rosanvallon's book, *Le moment Guizot* (1985).

50 Gasparin's speech to the Chamber of Deputies, 6 January 1837, *Archives parlementaires*, vol. 106.

51 Weather conditions could delay a dispatch. A statistic obtained in 1842 and 1843 gave the transmission speed as 50 kilometres per minute. However, only 64 per cent of the dispatches arrived the same day and this figure dropped to 33 per cent in winter (Ministry of the Interior statistic). Lardner also describes how, during the Napoleonic wars, a message was sent from Plymouth to London. Only the first part arrived: 'Wellington defeated . . .'. The rest of the message was blocked by thick fog and was only sent the next day. It profoundly modified the meaning: '. . . the French at Salamanca' (Lardner, 1867: 40).

52 Gasparin's speech to the Chamber of Deputies, 6 January 1837, *Archives parlementaires*, vol. 106.

53 J-M. Portalis, Chamber of Deputies, 28 February 1837, *Archives parlementaires*, vol. 107.

54 A. de Gasparin, *Chambre des Pairs*, 21 March 1837.

55 A. de Gasparin, speech to the Chamber of Deputies, 6 January 1837, *Archives parlementaires*, vol. 106.

56 The same was true in Germany where private networks were built in Hamburg and Bremen.

References

Baczko B. (1978) *Lumières de l'utopie*, Payot, Paris.

Balibar R. (1988) 'Parlez-vous français?' in *L'Etat de la France pendant la révolution*, La Découverte, Paris.

Belloc A. (1888) *La Télégraphie historique*, Firmin Didot, Paris.

Branca S. (1982) 'Changer de langue', in *Histoire, épistémologie et langage*, pt 1, Presses universitaires de Lille, Lille.

Braudel F. (1986) *L'Identité de la France: espace et histoire*, Arthaud-Flammarion, Paris.

Cazenoble J. (1981) *Les Origines de la télégraphie sans fil*, CNRS, Centre de documentation des sciences humaines, Paris.

Chappe A. and Chappe R. (1829) *Mémoire sur la télégraphie*, Imprimerie Béthune, Paris.

Chappe I. (1840) *Histoire de la télégraphie*, Richelet, Le Mans.

De Certeau M., Julia D. and Revel J. (1975) *Une politique de la langue: la Révolution française et les patois: l'enquête de Grégoire*, Gallimard, Paris.

Ferrier A. (1832) *Etablissement de télégraphes publics de jour et de nuit*, prospectus of 24 January, Bibliothèque historique de la ville de Paris.

Galante-Garonne A. (1971) *Gilbert Romme: histoire d'un révolutionnaire*, Flammarion, Paris.

Gerspach E. (1860) 'Histoire administrative de la télégraphie aérienne en France', in *Annales télégraphiques*, vol. 3.

Gille B. (1959) *La Banque et le crédit en France de 1815 à 1848*, Presses universitaires de France, Paris.

Granger G-G. (1954) 'Langue universelle et formation des sciences: un fragment inédit de Condorcet', in *Revue d'histoire des sciences*, vol. 7, no. 3, PUF.

Guillaume J. (1891) *Procès-verbaux du Comité d'instruction publique de la Convention nationale*, vol. 2, Paris.

Gusdorf G. (1987) 'Le cri de Valmy', in *Communications*, no. 45: *Eléments pour une théorie de la nation*, Le Seuil, Paris.

Herbath D. (1978) *Die Entwicklung der optischenn Telegrafie in Preussem*, Rheinland Verlag, Cologne.

Julia D. (1988) 'L'école: un gigantesque effort pédagogique', in *L'Etat de la France pendant la Révolution*, La Découverte, Paris.

Kieve J. (1973) *The Electric Telegraph: a Social and Economic History*, David and Charles, Newton Abbot.

Kula W. (1984) *Les mesures et les hommes*, Editions de la Maison des sciences de l'homme, Paris.

Lakanal J. (1795) *Rapport sur le télégraphe*, Imprimerie Nationale, Paris, August.

Landes D (1969) *The Unbound Prometheus: Technological Change and Industrial Development in Western Europe from 1750 to the Present*, Cambridge University Press, Cambridge.

Lardner Dr (1867) *The Electric Telegraph*, James Walton, London.

Lefébure A. (1984) 'L'invention du monopole', *Bulletin de l'Association internationale d'histoire des télécommunications et de l'informatique*, no. 1, Paris, May.

Ozouf M. (1984) 'La Révolution et la perception de l'espace national', in *L'Ecole de la France: essais sur la Révolution, l'utopie et l'enseignement*, Gallimard, Paris.

Romme G. (1793) *Rapport sur l'ère de la République*, Convention national, 20 September.

Rosanvallon P. (1985) *Le moment Guizot*, Gallimard, Paris.

Wilson G. (1976) *The Old Telegraphs*, Phillimore, London.

2

Networks and Electricity

Before looking at the history of electricity, which made another form of long-distance communication possible, the telegraph must be placed in a different technological perspective – that of the evolution of transport and the genesis of technological networks.

The invention of networks

The Chappe telegraph was part of a tradition which we have not yet mentioned, that of the reorganization of road networks. In *Lire et écrire*, François Furet and Jacques Ozouf note: 'The school is a marvellous example of the main paradox of the French Revolution – rupture and continuity' (Furet and Ozouf, 1977: 97). While the semaphore telegraph was a significant novelty and represented a definite break in representations of time and space, it was also part of the continuity of an evolution, that of the transport of messages.

During the 40 years preceding the Revolution, France experienced what some historians have called a transport revolution. New techniques were used to build a network of main roads on which it was possible to travel 'at a gallop'. Postal networks also multiplied and in 1775 the creation by Turgot of the state-controlled stagecoach and messenger service made regular traffic possible. These major improvements had the significant effect of increasing the speed of traffic which had remained unchanged since the Middle Ages. Fernand Braudel, who analysed the transport of mail to Venice between 1500 and the mid-eighteenth century, shows that there was no fundamental change during that period. A letter from Paris took two to three weeks to reach the city of the doges. In short, as Paul Valéry said, 'Napoleon moved no faster than Julius Caesar' (Braudel, 1979: 374–5).

From the end of the eighteenth century the speed of traffic was doubled, so that a journey from Paris to Marseilles, for example, took only a week instead of a fortnight (Braudel, 1986: 238–9). Chappe's telegraph continued this evolution but also introduced a break, since the average message took 15 minutes from Paris to Valenciennes in the North. With this quasi-instantaneous means of transmission, the aim was to conquer space, rather than time. It is therefore hardly surprising that the tachygraph (the first name imagined by Chappe) became the telegraph. From 1793 the network spread out from certain main axes and was to be extended to other European countries during the Empire. While their network never comprised more than five main lines, the Chappe brothers' goal was to link all important towns so as to 'cover the kingdom with a telegraphic network linking all areas to one another and to a common centre. The French . . . [would] thereby benefit from the considerable social advantages provided by frequent and rapid communications' (Chappe, 1840: 133).

It is interesting to compare this telegraphic network, imagined and partially realized by the Chappe brothers, with transport networks built during the same period. Bernard Lepetit shows that, until the eighteenth century, French roads were merely earth tracks, all more or less the same, and that traders used or abandoned a particular road depending on its state. While the 'memorandum on the reparation of roads' in 1738 introduced a first hierarchical classification of roads,[1] the attempt to plan an ordered and articulated network was not to materialize. Improvements were carried out on sections of roads only, and although towns were well aware of the advantages in being situated on an important road, their main concern was their connection with neighbouring cities. The situation was to differ with the first railways which were built on a line-by-line basis, even though multiple local and regional interests had to be taken into account.[2]

The engineers of telegraph lines were subjected to far fewer constraints. Telegraph installations were not of the same size and local authorities' intervention was insignificant since the central government was the sole user of the telegraph. When Chappe launched a line, he had a global view of it and carried it through to completion. The Chappe brothers' network (as we have seen, Ignace used the term in his book of 1840) nevertheless remained a group of lines from Paris to the provinces, with no connection between them.

In a memorandum in 1829 Abraham and René Chappe presented their 'general telegraphic communication system'. To the lines which spread out from Paris and between which there were no links, they suggested adding 'junction lines' so that a message leaving a given point could take several different routes (Chappe and Chappe, 1829: 7–8). A few years later, a text written by the Chappe brothers' successors referred to this same notion of junction lines (the principle of a multiconnection network):

> There is no relation between the five lines from Paris. They are isolated, so that each of them has to be self-sufficient and can expect no help from any of the others . . . The causes for a suspension or slowing down of transmissions (bad weather or heavy traffic) are reduced when the lines are linked . . . so that each telegraphic direction has at least two alternatives for corresponding with the centre.[3]

The Toulon and Bayonne lines were first linked in 1835 and in the following year 10 per cent of the traffic from Toulon used the Bayonne line (via Montpellier–Toulouse). A systematic connection between lines was then envisaged. The discovery was an important one, since a network was no longer conceived as a juxtaposition of lines, but as a coordinated set in which the optimization of transmission time did not necessarily imply use of the shortest route.

The concept of a multiconnection network appeared in the telegraph at the same time as in other urban networks. Networks built at the beginning of the nineteenth century for the distribution of water had a branching structure, with several independent networks in each large town. In 1820 engineers started envisaging the interconnection of the branches or trunks of this structure and the construction of a 'circumvallation' canal to allow for a more balanced flow. This reticular design for the distribution of water may have been based on work on the human circulatory system.[4] Doctors and engineers had the opportunity of comparing their network designs at the *Ecole polytechnique*.[5]

To return to the semaphore telegraph, one of its main drawbacks was that it could not function perpetually and was interrupted during rainy or misty weather and particularly at night. Chappe made several attempts at adapting the telegraph to night use, and up till the 1840s a number of other inventors proposed a variety of systems with the same objective in mind. These telegraphs were often called universal, although none of them functioned perfectly. In a note on this question, Alphonse Foy, the general administrator of telegraphs, wrote in 1842: 'A nocturnal telegraph [achieved] by means of lighting the machine would certainly be a beneficial extension since it would increase available time for the work. However, it would not free telegraphic transmission from the precarious state in which it is placed by the weather.' He therefore wanted a detailed examination of whether the electric telegraph 'did not allow for the perfection of the telegraphic systems – the continuity of transmissions'.[6] Beyond technical choices, this telegraph operator had thus clearly defined his goal.

Chappe contributed another significant innovation when he discovered that for information to be transmitted efficiently, it had to be coded with a universal code used in every network. He examined several alternatives. First, he used a code based on the decimal system and then, in 1800, switched to a system with 92 elementary signals which made it possible to define a ciphering system similar to that used by diplomats. He thereby constituted a vocabulary of 8,464 words. Each word was identified by its page number and its order on the page. The system ensured an economy of signals and confidentiality of messages. Competing telegraph systems used other codes: an alphabetic code was used in England, while Bergstrasser in Germany used a binary code.

Whatever the technical system proposed, each inventor imagined a universal code. In the 1820s F. Sudre, for example, developed a 'universal musical language' consisting of four notes transmitted by means of a bugle. The army experimented with this rudimentary system in 1829 and called it 'telephone' (Libois, 1983: 13).

Thus, the semaphore telegraph was the starting point for telecommunications systems. Even though it was an almost outdated technical system, it included the four basic characteristics of telecommunications, which other systems were to reorganize:

1 Although not instantaneous, transmission was extremely fast. Chappe increased the speed by improving the coding system.

2   A permanent network was constituted which spread further and further afield.
3   A specialized technical body took over the operation of the network.
4   Information was coded in a 'universal language'. Chappe had integrated operational constraints in the communication system by defining operation signals (start, end, interruption, station number, etc.) which were distinct from correspondence signals.

In order to understand fully the highly innovative aspect of the telegraph as an integrated system, it is interesting to compare it again with the railway. In 1802 the Englishman Edgeworth suggested establishing railways for public transport. As W. Schivelbusch (1977) points out, the railway was in this case seen as a road equipped with rails, rather than as an autonomous transport system. Twenty years later, railways were conceived of as distinct from the road network, yet they were based on the same principle as toll roads which could be used by private vehicles. Schivelbusch, who studied the constitution of the system of railway machines, indicates that in 1848 there were still private vehicles using the Manchester–Liverpool line (Schivelbusch, 1977). Individualism in the use of railways naturally posed a number of traffic coordination problems and was consequently abandoned. The operator of each line was granted an absolute monopoly of traffic. This technical option was, however, opposed to the liberal economic spirit of the day and was not enforced immediately. The final stage in the construction of a railway system was the interconnection of lines designed independently of one another, on a purely local basis.

The beginnings of electricity

'Parlour' electricity

While a permanent communication network for the transmission of coded information was being set up at the turn of the eighteenth century, a new technology was being developed: electricity. Until the first third of the eighteenth century, electrical phenomena were a mere curiosity. It was found that light bodies could be attracted by rubbing together certain substances, and sparks were obtained from an electrostatic machine. Around 1730, the British physicist Stephen Gray showed that electricity was propagated along a wire. With certain bodies called conductors, it was possible to obtain the propagation of a charge over a few hundred feet (Taylor, 1879: 6; see also Shiers, 1977). A few years later, Petrus van Musschenbroek of Leyde in The Netherlands and Ewald Kleist in Pomerania found a device for accumulating electricity. The 'Leyde bottle'[7] (called the 'Kleist bottle' in Germany) was to serve as a basic tool in the 'amusing', commonplace scientific experiments carried out in small private physics laboratories.

In an age when the distinction between science and technology had not yet been defined, scientists were to envisage both the hypothesis of a link between vital energy and electrical fluid, and the use of electricity as a medical instrument. Abbey Nollet wondered, in 1746, whether an electric shock could be used to 'revive more or less inhibited movement in a sick part' (Zelbstein, 1985: 297). Electrical therapy was used by the English theologian John Wesley (mainly known as the founder of Methodism) and by Marat, the future French revolutionary (1782), while Bichat studied muscular contractions by 'galvanizing' the bodies of executed prisoners.

Another research field – the study of the propagation of electric fluid – was also to gain importance. By using a Leyde bottle, Louis Le Monnier, in France, Watson, Folkes and Cavendish, in England, and Father Joseph Franz, in Austria, managed to attain distances of several miles. Johann-Heinrich Winkler already thought that 'electricity could be transmitted to the ends of the earth' (von Klinckowstroem, 1967: 220). Certain observers of these experiments imagined transporting information in this way. In 1753 an article signed C.M. in *Scot's Magazine* proposed sending messages by electricity, with a system of 26 wires each connected to a letter of the alphabet.[8] Georges-Louis Lesage, professor of mathematics in Geneva, designed a similar project in 1760. In 1774 he built an experimental device. At the transmitting end a wire linked to a letter was touched by a wax stick electrified by friction. At the receiving station the electric spark pushed an elderberry corresponding to the letter being transmitted. This experiment attracted the attention of the scientific community. The Swiss physicist Louis Odier considered that the procedure should make it possible to 'converse in less than a half an hour over four or five thousand leagues, with the Great Mogul or the Emperor of China' (von Klinckowstroem, 1967: 221). Similar experiments were carried out by other inventors: Lomond (1787) and Jean Alexandre (1802) in France, and Cavallo (1795) in England. The Spaniard Francisco Salva is said to have conducted a larger experiment, over 40 kilometres, from Madrid to Aranjuez.

These diverse instruments, based on the use of static electricity, were interesting objects for playing around with in private laboratories, but they remained too rudimentary to be used for a regular telegraphic service. Hence, the Spaniard Bethencourt,[9] who conducted an experiment on electric telegraphy in 1787, abandoned this technical solution in favour of a semaphore telegraph which he developed with Bréguet to compete with Chappe's system (see above). In fact, Chappe himself was already studying the electric solution. 'Electricity first held the attention of this hard-working physicist' Lakanal (1795: 4–5) tells us:

> he imagined corresponding by using two identical clockworks to electrically mark time corresponding to the same values. He placed and isolated conductors at certain distances, but the difficulty of insulation, the lateral expansion of the fluid in a long space and the intensity that would have been required – subjected to the state of the atmosphere – made him see his project of communication by means of electricity as chimerical.

The rudimentary nature of all these experiments does not, however, adequately explain why the electric telegraph was not developed. Within the context of technical knowledge at the time, significant improvements could be made. In 1816 Francis Ronalds, for example, developed a system with a single electric wire. In each of the two stations a small wheel, driven by a clock, successively displayed the letters of the alphabet in an aperture. The two clocks were synchronized. If an electric charge was emitted when a letter appeared on the transmitting end, this charge could be detected on the receiving end. Yet, as we saw in Chapter 1, Ronalds received a dilatory response from the British Admiralty when he proposed his system to it.

Why were inventors discouraged? The main reason was that the model of commercial communication had not yet appeared, while the state's limited communication needs were fulfilled by the semaphore telegraph. This is what the chemist Chaptal, Minister of the Interior, explained with respect to Jean Alexandre's invention: 'Besides the fact that his machine would leave much to be desired even if it were created on a workable scale, what he announces as a discovery is no more than the varied and well-known art of transmitting by signs or figures. The [semaphore] telegraphs used until now are far better and simpler' (Stourdzé, 1987: 191). Yves Stourdzé who reports this event is shocked by the short-sightedness of the French government which tended to 'imagine that mechanics alone constitutes a reliable universe'. Was this behaviour so typically French? In Britain, the Admiralty refused Ronalds' propositions in 1816 and, two years earlier, it had replied to similar propositions by Ralph Wedgwood that 'the war being over and money scarce, the old semaphor system is altogether sufficient.' Thus, both major states at the beginning of the nineteenth century refused the innovation of electricity. And, as Stourdzé rightly points out, 'there was no recourse possible . . . what the inventors did not manage to get from the government they did not either manage to wring out of the banks and commercial institutions' (Stourdzé, 1987: 191).

Electric action and magnetic action

While inventors waited to find an alternative to state support, scientific knowledge on electricity progressed. In 1800, the Italian Volta managed to set up a regular source of electricity by means of the chemical action of copper and zinc discs separated by cloth. His famous voltaic battery opened new possibilities to telegraphy even though a way still had to be found to make the electricity effective over a distance. In 1809, the German physicist Soemmering imagined a device based on the electrochemical decomposition of water. An electrical circuit corresponding to each letter of the alphabet, with the extremity immersed in a basin of water, was set up. When a charge was sent through one of the circuits the water decomposed and vapour appeared. Soemmering circulated models of his telegraph in Paris and Vienna. In Philadelphia, John Coxe imagined a similar device in 1816 (Taylor, 1879: 13–14; Jarvis, 1956: 135).

From 1820, with the discovery of electromagnetism, another device for signalling information became possible. The Danish physicist OErsted showed, in 1820, that electric current had an influence on magnetic needles. As soon as he became aware of its existence, Ampère took an interest in his colleague's work. In a memorandum to the *Académie des sciences*, he suggested that the action of an electric current on the magnetic needles could constitute a telegraphic device. But Ampère never implemented his idea; he preferred devoting himself to the theory of electrodynamics. In the same year, Arago's work on the temporary magnetization of iron by an electric current made the creation of electromagnets possible.[10]

The needle-telegraph device described by Ampère was realized by a Russian diplomat, Baron Schilling. He witnessed several experiments by Soemmering, with whom he corresponded regularly. In 1825 he created a device with five wires connected to five magnetic needles. The combination of the respective positions of the needles enabled him to represent all the letters of the alphabet. He presented his device several times to the Emperor, who nevertheless opted for a semaphore line between St Petersburg and Warsaw (see above). In parallel with Schilling's research, the physicist Gauss – who had also seen Soemmering's device – and his young colleague Weber also designed a needle telegraph. They used this at Göttingen from 1833 to 1838 to communicate between the observatory which Gauss directed and the university situated 1,500 metres away. However, Gauss and Weber preferred devoting themselves to their scientific work and therefore suggested that one of their colleagues, Steinheil, develop their invention. Steinheil improved the device in several ways. He used two stylets to transcribe the codes corresponding to each letter on a strip of paper. He, moreover, discovered that the current could return through the earth and he built a permanent line of about 5 kilometres between the Royal Academy, the observatory and his home in Munich.

From the middle of the 1820s the electric telegraph became an object of scientifico-technical debate. In 1825 Peter Barlow challenged Ampère, proving that beyond 200 feet a telegraph based on the deviation of a magnetic needle was not only unfeasible but also impossible for theoretical reasons (King, 1962: 281; see also Shiers, 1977). William Richtie, however, responded to Barlow's objections in 1830 by presenting the Royal Society with a prototype corresponding to Ampère's description.

In central Europe, debate first crystallized around Soemmering's device in the 1810s. In 1833 Schilling visited Gauss. Two years later he returned to Germany to a congress where one of the participants, Muncke from Heidelberg University, asked him for a copy of his device to present to his students. A young Englishman, William Cooke, witnessed such a demonstration in 1836 and his ensuing enthusiasm led him to build a first prototype even before returning home.[11]

In the United Kingdom various research projects were developed concurrently during the second half of the 1830s. The physicist Wheatstone measured the speed of electricity in 1834, concluding that electricity was the best solution for transmitting information over a distance. He then developed a first model of such a device. Cooke, who had difficulties in making his device reliable, met Wheatstone in 1837 and they decided to cooperate. It seems that the difficulties in transmitting over a long distance, which neither of them had until then managed to overcome, were solved after a meeting with the American physicist Joseph Henry when he was in Europe. In 1831 Henry had already published his works on electromagnetism and long electric circuits (King, 1962: 289; Taylor, 1879: 81). Independently of Cooke and Wheatstone, Davy started working on the telegraph in 1835 and presented a prototype two years later. In the same year, the Scot William Alexander demonstrated a device based on Ampère's principles (Kieve, 1973: 23–4).

The year 1837 was not only one in which electric telegraph projects flourished, it also saw a shift from purely scholarly research to the desire to exploit the invention commercially. Cooke and Wheatstone patented their five-needle six-wire apparatus; a year later, Davy patented one with two wires, while Alexander limited his patent to Scotland. When the US federal government put out a call for tenders for the construction of semaphore telegraph lines, Samuel Morse, Professor of Art at New York University, who had been working on an electric telegraph prototype in his free time, immediately saw the opportunity for having his invention recognized. He intensified his research and started working with a mechanic, Vail, and one of his colleagues, Gale, who used Henry's research results on electromagnetism. In February 1838 Morse was able to demonstrate his device to federal government representatives in Washington. A few months later he travelled to Europe in search of support and with the hope of filing a patent. Although the precedence of Cooke and Wheatstone's patent prevented him from doing so in London, he was able to patent his device in Paris in 1838 and again in the United States on his return in 1840.

Unlike the first inventors of the telegraph, Morse, like Cooke, was not a scientist. He was interested in a simple and practical device. Rather than moving needles on a dial to indicate letters, as in the European instruments, his telegraph executed coded signals by means of a manually activated lever. By opening or closing a circuit, it stimulated identical signals in the receiving device. The code was composed of only two elements – a short and a long signal – and a combination of only four of these sufficed to represent the letters of the alphabet.

France was largely absent from this period of invention in electric telegraphy. After Ampère's article, French inventors had kept in the background. Yet, in 1838 the French government organized an official comparison between Cooke's, Morse's and Steinheil's telegraphs on the one hand, and a local system developed by Bréguet on the other. No decision was forthcoming from these tests, but the operation amply illustrated the changing trend. Until then comparisons had been limited to the scientific community itself and scientists visited and wrote to one another. As soon as the commercial exploitation of a system was envisaged, the various prototypes were compared in order to determine the most effective one.

Circulation of the invention

To conclude this brief technical history, we can but support the view of Robert Sabine the English historian who in 1867 wrote that 'The electric telegraph did not, strictly speaking, have an inventor. It grew little by little towards perfection, with each inventor adding his bit' (Sabine, 1867: 40). This cumulative technical progress (which did not exclude work carried out simultaneously – for competitive reasons or through ignorance) was only possible because ideas and prototypes could circulate thanks to the personal contacts of scientists and to the institutions which facilitated this exchange of knowledge: the press, the academies and exhibitions.

It was chiefly in the academic press that the first publications appeared. Ampère's report was published in the *Annales de chimie et de physique* (1820) and Barlow wrote in the *Edinburgh Philosophical Journal* (1825). The *American Journal of Science* (January, April and July 1831) described Henry's experiments, while the *Philosophical Transactions of the Royal Society* reported Wheatstone's experiments on the speed of electricity. Demonstrations were also performed before recognized scientific bodies: Schilling presented his prototype to the congress of German physicists in 1835; Richtie, Wheatstone and Alexander demonstrated their invention to the London Royal Society in 1830 and 1838, and Morse was invited to the *Académie des sciences* in Paris in 1838.

From 1837 the debate started to move beyond the scientific community and articles appeared in the general press. *The Times* of 8 July 1837 presented Alexander's system, while the American *Journal of Commerce* spoke of Morse's telegraph in September of the same year. The popular press, which a scientist like Wheatstone did not scorn (*Magazine of Popular Science of March 1837*), also took an interest in the subject, and the first field experiments received general press coverage. *The Times* of 2 September 1839 and the *Railway Times* of December 1839 both reported on the opening of Cooke and Wheatstone's experimental line along a railway track. A detailed description of the telegraphic machine was, however, presented in several issues of the technical journal *Mechanics Magazine* in 1838 and 1839. Furthermore, these inventors also held public presentations: Alexander at the Royal Gallery of Practical Science in 1839 and Davy at Regent's Park in 1837.

This diffusion of technical ideas also promoted the capitalization of technological progress, with each inventor re-using certain ideas or systems developed by his peers. Thus, around 1843, Morse decided to change his system of telegraphic wires. Until then he had buried them but, because of imperfect insulation, transmission of the signal never exceeded 10 miles. When he read in the English press that Cooke and Wheatstone attached their wires to poles, he adopted the same method (Bidder, 1944; Shiers, 1977).

A universal system

In 1843, four years after the installation of the first line, Cooke organized public demonstrations of his telegraph. The main point emphasized in public posters (see Jarvis, 1956: 588) was the transmission speed which was that of electricity: 280,000 miles per second (according to Wheatstone's measurements). With that kind of performance, the telegraph promised to reach the whole world, crossing oceans and continents. The first inventors thus strove to realize Winckler's forecasts a century earlier. In 1840 Wheatstone suggested a Dover–Calais line to the special railway committee in the House of Commons. He had already mentioned the idea in 1837 in a letter to friends. The cross-Channel link was finally established in 1850. Eight years later the first transatlantic cable was laid.[12] In 1860 another line linked London to India.

In the United States, Samuel Morse set up a first inter-urban line between Washington and Baltimore in 1844. New York was linked to San Francisco 15 years later. In 1866 Western Union had unified the American network which was 37,000 miles long and included 22,000 telegraphic offices. Morse was able to write that the telegraphic network was 'very much as . . . I wished them to be at the outset . . . making one great whole like the Post Office system' (Winston, 1986: 303).

This desire for universality, found at the birth of both the semaphore and the electric telegraphs, steered the different systems towards standardization – one of the conditions of a truly universal communication system. Communication was, moreover, the industrial sector in which standardization was achieved the fastest. According to David Landes (1969), it was only in the 1830s in Great Britain that the systematic standardization of parts within the same company was introduced,[13] and this was moreover only generalized in the latter half of the nineteenth century. 'If standardization within a firm was difficult, how much harder was it to persuade manufacturers throughout an industry to accept a national norm!' (Landes, 1969: 315).

In the United States national standards only started to appear in the 1880s, while England set out on this path much later with the creation of the Engineering Standards Committee in 1901. In newer industries, such as electricity, standardization was more rapid, although the current provided in each country was often different. Despite the difficulties involved, standardization in industry was always necessary because it was a significant source of economy of scale. In the communications sector, in particular, the universal nature of the activity made standardization all the more essential. It was therefore in this field that national and international standardization first became indispensable and was introduced almost immediately.

The Morse alphabet was to be used 15 years after the invention of the electric telegraph by all the countries that installed the technology. The interconnection of national networks was begun in 1849 (or 10 years after the installation of the first network in England) between Prussia and Austria. In the following year the agreement was extended to Saxony and Bavaria. We thus witness the telegraphic unification of German-speaking countries at a time when political unification had not yet been realized. In 1855 Belgium, Switzerland, Sardinia, Spain and France created the Telegraphic Union of Western Europe. These different international agreements led to the creation of the International Telegraphic Union in Paris in 1865 (Codding, 1972). It was the first international body of a technico-administrative nature.[14]

Standardization of the railways, another network where a universal system offered numerous advantages, took more time than that of the telegraph. The standardization of gauges in Great Britain was instituted by parliament through the Gauge Act in 1846. This legislative decision, taken 25 years after the opening of the first railway line to the public, solved a conflict over two different gauges. The English standard was adopted on the Continent, with the notable exceptions of Spain and Russia (Daumas and Gille, 1968). The international interconnection of railways was simultaneous with that of the telegraph; in 1850 a first line crossed the Franco-Belgian border.

Notes

1 See Bernard Lepetit, 'L'impensable réseau: les routes françaises avant les chemins de fer', in Dupuy (1988: 21–2).

2 See Georges Ribeil, 'Au temps de la révolution ferroviaire, l'utopique réseau', in Dupuy (1988: 57–8).

3 Ministère de l'Intérieur, *Exposé des motifs à l'appui du projet de loi relatif au complètement des communications télégraphiques*, handwritten text 1830 (?), *Archives nationales*, F90–1456.

4 See André Guillerme, 'L'émergence du concept de réseau (1820-1830)' in Dupuy (1988: 41–7).

5 The Saint-Simonians played an important role in developing the concept of a network. On this question, see Musso (1988: 11–30).

6 Alphonse Foy, handwritten note on a night telegraph, 12 January 1842, *Archives nationales*, F90–1456.

7 The Leyde bottle is a capacitor, an instrument which makes it possible to accumulate significant quantities of electricity on limited surfaces. A set of capacitors forms a battery.

8 Historians of electricity attribute this to either Charles Morrison or Charles Marshall (see Taylor, 1879: 6; Jarvis, 1956: 130).

9 His name is also spelled Bettancourt.

10 Louis Figuier gave an accurate description of the role of electromagnets in telegraphy: 'In Paris there is an active cell. The conducting wire of this cell stretches right to Calais, for example. There it is wound around an iron vane and led back to the cell in Paris. The electric current leaving Paris magnetizes the iron vane in Calais and, if we place a moving iron disc in front of the vane, this disc, when it is attracted, will touch our artificial and temporary magnet. Now, if in Paris we cut the contact between the conducting wire and the cell, the iron vane in Calais is demagnetized; it no longer holds the mobile iron disc, which returns to its original position. Thus, by successively connecting and interrupting the current in Paris, we obtain a back and forth movement of the iron disc in Calais. This movement, made possible over long distances by temporary magnetization, is the fundamental fact on which the construction of the electric telegraph is based' (Figuier, 1873: 358).

11 William Cooke's father was a friend of Ronalds, whose telegraph he often handled in his garden. The young Cooke probably observed these experiments (Kieve, 1973: 18).

12 This cable only functioned for a month. A permanent link was established in 1866 (Kieve, 1973: 109–15).

13 Landes was referring here to the systemization of standardization. The first examples of standard parts appeared in the United States at the end of the eighteenth century in the armaments industry.

14 The Universal Postal Union was created in 1874, and the International Railway Conference in 1882.

References

Bidder H.W. (1944) 'The centenary of the Morse telegraph', *Electrical Engineering*, vol. 63, New York.

Braudel F. (1979) *Civilisation matérielle, économie et capitalisme XVe-XVIIIe siècle*, vol. 1, Armand Colin, Paris.

Braudel F. (1986) *L'Identité de la France: les hommes et les choses*, Arthaud-Flammarion, Paris, pp. 238–9.

Chappe A. and Chappe R. (1829) *Mémoire sur la télégraphie*, Imprimerie Béthune, Paris.

Chappe I. (1840) *Histoire de la télégraphie*, Richelet, Le Mans.

Codding G. (1972) *The International Telecommunication Union: an Experiment in International Cooperation*, Arno-Press, New York.

Daumas M. and Gille P. (1968) 'Les chemins de fer' in Maurice Daumas (ed.), *Histoire générale des techniques*, vol. 3, Presses universitaires de France, Paris.

Dupuy G. (1988) *Réseaux territoriaux*, Paradigme, Caen.

Figuier L. (1873) *Les Grandes Inventions*, Hachette, Paris.

Furet F. and Ozouf J. (1977) *Lire et écrire: l'alphabétisation des Français de Calvin à Jules Ferry*, Editions de Minuit, Paris.

Jarvis M. (1956) 'The origin and development of the electric telegraph', *Journal of the Institution of Electrical Engineers,* London.

Kieve J. (1973) *The Electric Telegraph: a Social and Economic History*, David and Charles, Newton Abbot.

King J. (1962) 'The development of electrical technology in the 19th century: the telegraph', *Contributions from the Museum of History and Technology*. Bulletin 228, Washington DC, p. 281.

von Klinckowstroem C. (1967) *Nouvelle histoire des techniques*, Editions du Sud, Paris.

Lakanal J. (1795) *Rapport sur le télégraphie*, August.

Landes D. (1969) *The Unbound Prometheus: Technological Change and Industrial Development in Western Europe from 1750 to the Present*, Cambridge University Press, Cambridge.

Libois L-J. (1983) *Genèse et croissance des télécommunications*, Masson, Paris.

Musso, P. (1988) 'Aux origines de concept moderne: corps et réseau dans la philosophie de Saint-Simon', *Quaderni*, no. 3, Paris.

Sabine R. (1867) *The Electric Telegraph*, Virtue, London.

Schivelbusch W. (1977) *Geschichte der Eisenbahnreise. Zur Industrialisierung von Raum und Zeit im 19. Jahrhundert*, Munich/Vienna.

Shiers G. (1977) *The Electric Telegraph: an Historical Anthology*, Arno-Press, New York.

Stourdzé Y. (1987) 'Le gouvernement de la mécanique', in *Pour une poignée d'électrons*, Fayard, Paris.

Taylor W.B. (1879) *An Historical Sketch of Henry's Contribution to the Electro-Magnetic Telegraph*, Washington.

Winston B. (1986) *Misunderstanding the Media*, Routledge and Kegan Paul, London.

Zelbstein U. (1985) 'Médecine et électricité', *Culture technique*, no. 15, CRCT, Neuilly, November.

3

Market-controlled Communication: the Electric Telegraph

Among the numerous inventors of the electric telegraph, those who wanted their device to be more than just a scientific plaything adopted the same approach as Chappe; they turned to the state. We have already mentioned Alexandre who wrote to Chaptal to obtain an audience with Bonaparte, and Wedgwood and Ronalds who appealed to the British Admiralty, but there are other examples. Schilling never got effective support from the Russian government, and although Parodi – who continued Schilling's research after his death in 1837 – received an order from the Czar, this was merely for an experimental line linking two imperial residences. Steinheil in Bavaria managed to convince the government to finance a Munich–Augsbourg line but the funds were never made available (King, 1962: 284–6). Finally, in England in 1837, Alexander addressed a proposition to the Home Secretary, Lord Russel, for the construction with state aid of a telegraphic line between Edinburgh and London (Kieve, 1973: 24). In spite of support from a member of the Royal family, the Duke of Sussex, who let him set up a model of the telegraph at his residence Kensington Palace, Alexander received no order from the state.[1]

Cooke, on the other hand, was truly innovative in that he tried to find a commercial use for his telegraph and contacted potential investors. Unlike his predecessors and Wheatstone, it was not academic renown that interested him; he wanted to become an entrepreneur in telegraphs. Cooke's system was probably not of the most advanced, but he was the first to take out a patent. While his machine is sometimes presented as the technical conclusion of research in the late eighteenth and early nineteenth centuries, this is an erroneous interpretation of his role. Cooke was in fact a 'pirate' who had found in Germany a device which had until then remained confined to a laboratory, and modified its use. The Cooke–Wheatstone alliance was particularly representative of the change that took place at the end of the 1830s when telegraphic technology left the private laboratories of individual scientists to form the basis of new enterprises. Whereas Chappe was part of the nascent tradition of state engineers, Cooke was one of the first Schumpeterian entrepreneurs.

While Alexander was wearing himself out in his negotiations with the state, Cooke was approaching the railway companies and presenting his system as suitable for facilitating security – particularly in tunnels – and generally improving the running of their lines.[2] He demonstrated his system to the

directors of several railway companies and signed an agreement in 1838 with
the Great Western Railway for the installation of a first line of 13 miles. Thus,
Cooke was taking advantage of the latent demand from railway companies, to
which Watson had also tried to respond and which Ferrier had similarly perceived when he wrote in 1832: 'The discovery of new accelerated means of
transport demands greater rapidity in written communication . . . The railway
lines need to be complemented by telegraphic lines.' The telegraph was first
used as a security device to avoid collisions on single tracks; it provided the
possibility of controlling traffic since it could be used to anticipate the arrival
of trains.

But, whereas the electric telegraph network was originally built for the
individual needs of the railway companies, it was to be opened to private use
at the end of 1842. Other uses appeared during the following years. In 1845 a
line replaced Watson's semaphore telegraph between Liverpool and the Welsh
coast. In the same year the Admiralty signed an agreement with Cooke
(Wilson, 1976: 60) for its exclusive use of two specialized wires on the
London–Portsmouth telegraphic line.[3] Two years later, the Admiralty closed
all its semaphore lines. In 1850 a telegraph was installed at the Central Post
Office in London. Thus, the English telegraphic network was developed by
private enterprise, without the intervention of the state which abandoned its
own network and used a private one.

In the United States, Morse made the same choice as most of his
European emulators: he tried to obtain federal government backing. After
lengthy discussions, Congress financed a first line between Washington and
Baltimore in 1844. In the following year, the telegraph was handed over to
the Post Office which employed Morse to manage it. But Congress's inabil-
ity to provide the investments needed to develop the network led it to sell the
first telegraphic line to a private company. Growth was extremely rapid. In
1850 there were already 12,000 miles of telegraphic lines, compared to 2,200
in Britain (Kieve, 1973: 51). Two years later, the American lines measured
22,000 miles. The network was developed by a few large companies which
merged in 1866 to become Western Union, the first American firm with
activities spanning the entire continent (Chandler, 1977: 197). In the 1870s it
had the telegraph monopoly. The telegraph played an essential role as a
social and economic link in a nation-in-the-making, and in its territorial
expansion. The state, although outside this development, provided financial
and military support for the lines used in conquering the West. In 1860
Congress passed a bill for 'facilitating communication between the States of
the Pacific and the Atlantic by means of the electric telegraph'. Western
Union obtained a 10-year deficiency grant for the operation of this line.
When the line was opened on 24 October 1861, on the eve of the War of
Secession, Abraham Lincoln received the following message at the White
House: 'The Californian people desire ... to express their loyalty to the
Union and their determination to stand by its government on this, its day of
trial' (Barett, 1941: 60).

A state electric telegraph

In France the 1840s were a decade of twofold evolution: that of the change from the semaphore to the electric telegraph, and that of the abolition of state monopoly over its use. In 1838 the telegraph administration examined the possibilities offered by the application of electricity in its communication system. On the occasion of the vote in 1842 for funds to experiment with a night semaphore telegraph proposed by Dr Guyot, the Chamber of Deputies debated the question of telegraph technologies. In spite of Arago explaining that the semaphore solution was obsolete and that the state should invest in the electric telegraph, funds were voted for the former. This debate on the choice between two technologies provides some insight into the political classes' representation of the telegraph. They saw it solely as an administrative instrument for controlling territory and communicating rapidly with government officials. An instrument of control, the telegraph had to be closely guarded. Since it was easier to protect a few hundred Chappe towers than several thousand kilometres of wire, the Assembly naturally preferred the semaphore technology. Behind this technical choice lay another choice, that of the function of the telegraph which was consistent with the one made in 1837. If the Assembly financed Guyot's innovation, it was not because it was more reliable than the numerous other night telegraphs which had been envisaged over the preceding half-century, but because the inventor had the same representation of communication as its own. Guyot wrote: 'No, the electric telegraph is not a feasible invention . . . A single man could, without being seen, cut all the telegraphic wires leading to Paris . . . in contrast, the semaphore telegraph has its towers, its walls, its gates guarded by strong men with guns' (IRIS, 1978: 38–9).

The debate was not, however, closed. In November 1844, the government appointed a commission of enquiry into the electric telegraph, comprising the physicists Arago, Becquerel and Pouillet, the administrator of telegraphs, Foy, and a Saint-Simonian economist,[4] Michel Chevalier, author of a report on the means of communication used in the USA. In less than a fortnight the commission had come to the conclusion that, in view of the extent to which the electric telegraph was being developed in England, the USA and Germany, it was essential that an experimental line be built in France. The government took an immediate decision and the Paris–Rouen line was tested in the spring. In the following year construction of the Paris–Lille line was begun.

The electrico-semaphore telegraph

The French telegraph authorities soon had to control a mixed network of semaphore and electric lines, in which the electric telegraph was to execute the ordinary signals of the semaphore telegraph. The Chief Administrator, Alphonse Foy, asked Bréguet to have this type of device built. The Foy-Bréguet electric terminal used two needles to reproduce the movements of the

Chappe telegraph. 'Its performance was perfect', wrote Ludovic Ternant in 1884, 'but the idea was so strange that the transmission of messages by electricity remained altogether unsatisfactory and the use of this "electrico-semaphore" telegraph had to be abandoned' (Ternant, 1884: 15).

In fact, the device was more than just a passing whim of the authorities, and a large-scale controversy broke out around it. *L'Illustration* of 26 June 1847 spoke of 'the defective system of electric telegraphs that the French authorities have maintained'. Abbey Moigno also attacked the electric telegraph in his treatise in 1852, but admitted that 'it is impossible to formulate a definite judgement'. Some experts strongly opposed the device, while others recognized its merits. Bréguet and the telegraph engineer Gounelle were persuaded of its qualities: 'speed, easy crossing of questions and answers, simplicity and convenient manipulation'.[5]

A hundred and thirty years later, Yves Stourdzé (1979) was to consider the Foy-Bréguet telegraph as an archetype of the half-measures and makeshift solutions that the French telecommunications authority adopted for a century. Consistently reticent with regard to new technologies, it opted for hybrid systems when it could no longer refuse innovation. Parliament was certainly not inclined to vote funds for the construction of electric lines, and Stourdzé was therefore right in noting the political classes' resistance to electricity. Nevertheless, Alphonse Foy's position was less clear cut than it seemed (see Chapter 2), and Gounelle's interest in electricity could not be denied. He performed experiments on the speed of electricity and was responsible for the construction of the first Paris–Rouen electric line. His defence of the Foy-Bréguet system was certainly not due to his technical incompetence. Should one not rather consider, as Michel Atten does, the system to be 'one of the first examples of the compatible development of two technological systems' (Atten, 1988: 71).

With hindsight, the 'electrico-semaphore' telegraph appears as an aberration without any technological merit. It was, nevertheless, a socio-technical compromise which allowed it to be appropriated more easily by its users (telegraph operators). It was what development specialists today call an 'appropriated technology'. With the Foy-Bréguet device, we have an example of a situation where controversy around two technological systems did not consist only of opposition between engineers, but also of a general debate. Like any compromise, it was debatable, but respectable.

Opening up to private communication

The advent of the electric telegraph in France did not prevent the state from steadfastly clinging to its monopolistic use of the lines. In July 1847 the Minister of the Interior declared (Kieve, 1973: 46): 'telegraphy must be a political and not a commercial instrument.'[6] The state did nevertheless extend its use of the electric telegraph. News reports sent every day by Havas to the prefects by carrier pigeons were henceforth sent by electric telegraph when lines existed.[7] In the following year, the 1848 Revolution[8] was to intensify the state's telegraphic activities; traffic doubled in a year and remained constant in 1849.[9]

However, contradictions between the potential of the electric telegraph and the idea of a state-monopolized telecommunication system became more and more marked. The government decided to create new electric links in the framework of an agreement with the railway companies for the construction of lines on railway territory. In exchange, the latter would be able to use the telegraph for their own purposes. The deputy Marchal noted, in a question put to the Minister of the Interior in April 1849, that 'electric telegraphs are occupied at the most one-tenth of their potential working time.' The other nine-tenths could be used for industrial and commercial business and 'ordinary relations'. This would provide the state treasury with a means for obtaining returns on its investments. Finally, he noted that the privilege enjoyed by the railways seemed totally unwarranted. Change became inevitable. On 1 March 1850 the government presented the Assembly with a bill on 'private telegraphic correspondence'. Thirteen years after the 1837 law, the state finally acknowledged that the telegraph could be used for private communication. Yet a striking feature of National Assembly debates at the time is the continuity in attitudes regarding the telegraph.

The rapporteur Le Verrier considered, as he had in 1837, that 'it would have been impossible to place the semaphore telegraph at the disposal of private interests' not for political reasons, but because of material obstacles. 'Semaphore telegraphs could at the most meet official needs; no part of available time could have been ceded to the public without compromising the state's service.' As for private telegraph lines, 'they have always been at the sole disposition of speculators.' Change was finally prompted by technology; owing to the use of electricity, 'the number of dispatches that could be transmitted in a given timeframe was suddenly multiplied a hundred-fold.'[10] Furthermore, this technological innovation became 'the inevitable complement to the existence of the railways', and most foreign countries opened their telegraph lines to private individuals. 'Faced with such a general movement, it seems impossible', concluded the Minister of the Interior, 'that the French government refuses to let commerce and industry in our country share the wonderful facilities of correspondence which saves time – the most precious element in business.'[11]

Like the Saint-Simonians, Louis Napoléon Bonaparte's government saw in the telegraph an instrument likely to benefit commerce and industry. He wanted to see its use spread, but the Assembly remained reticent. Some deputies 'viewed this measure with regret and would have preferred to postpone its application'. By losing its monopoly over the use of the telegraph, they said 'the government will no longer have any privilege, and private persons will be informed at the same time as it of events throughout the territory. For the government, the result will be roughly the same as if the telegraphic invention was reduced to nothing.'[12] However, to allay the Assembly's fears of commercial communication overwhelming state communication, the priority of government dispatches was protected by law.

Similarly, to prevent criminal elements from 'using the telegraph to hatch their detestable plots with more ease and rapidity',[13] the law demanded that private dispatches be sent uncoded and signed, and that the user declare his or her identity. This constraint was added by the Assembly which changed the government's wording ('any person is allowed to correspond') to 'any person whose identity has been established'. The Director of Telegraphs could refuse to send or to distribute messages. This form of censorship was not specifically French; similar regulations existed in Prussia, Austria and The Netherlands. In England, even though the telegraph was private, the state could, in exceptional circumstances, interrupt use of the network.

Thus, the model of state communication remained largely present in the 1850 law. Moreover, the state rapporteur suggested taking advantage of the new possibilities offered by the electric technology to create a government news bulletin. 'By thus guaranteeing the authenticity of documents which often arrive altered or mutilated, one could produce in the press a widespread moral revolution in favour of the truth.'[14] In the mind of French legislators, commercial communication remained secondary.

The stock market operator

The quasi-police surveillance of private use of the electric telegraph at the start of the Second Empire has provided historians with detailed statistics on the subject. From the outset the network was used extensively and, during the first year, with fewer lines than the semaphore telegraph, the traffic showed a 50 per cent increase over official messages sent the preceding year. It quadrupled in the second year (1852) and by 1858 it had multiplied fifty-fold.[15]

Distance, or more precisely the difficulty in communicating, was one of the main reasons for using the telegraph. In France, international traffic accounted for 47 per cent of all traffic in 1851.[16] In North America, where transport difficulties were far greater than in Europe, the telegraph's success was striking. During its first year of use (1847) the Toronto–Quebec line carried no less than 33,000 messages (Foreman-Peck, 1989), twice as much traffic per mile as in Britain in 1851 (Kieve, 1973: 68).

The main use of the electric telegraph was the transmission of stock exchange information (see Tables 3.1–3.3).[17] In the first months after the French network had been opened to the public, it accounted for half of the traffic, before stabilizing at around 40 per cent. In Britain, the stock market similarly accounted for half of the traffic on the network and in Belgium this number was even higher (Table 3.1). If one separates national and international traffic, it becomes clear that stock exchange use predominated in the international sector. Its share in the national network increased significantly from 1851 to 1858 (see Tables 3.2 and 3.3).

Use of the telegraph in stock exchange activities introduced a greater degree of rationality into investors' transactions. Until the mid-nineteenth century, stock exchange information circulated essentially in the form of

Table 3.1 *Nature of dispatches on the telegraphic network by country*

	Stock market (%)	Trade (%)	Family (%)	Other (%)
France (1851)	38	28	25	9
France (1858)	39	33	20	8
Britain (1854)	50	31	13	6
Belgium (1851)	60	19	10	11

Sources: *France*: 1851, Ministry of the Interior statistics, *Archives nationales*, F90–1468; 1858, Pélicier (1859) (I have taken a weighted average of national and international statistics); *Britain*: Kieve (1973: 119); *Belgium*: Vercruysse and Verhoest (1991)

Table 3.2 *Nature of dispatches on the international telegraphic network in France*

	Stock market (%)	Trade (%)	Family (%)	Other (%)
1851	62	17	11	10
1858	48	20	20	12

Sources: Ministry of the Interior statistics, *Archives nationales*, F90–1468; Pélicier (1859)

Table 3.3 *Nature of dispatches on the domestic telegraphic network in France*

	Stock market (%)	Trade (%)	Family (%)	Other (%)
1851	17	38	37	8
1858	34	40	20	6

Sources: Ministry of the Interior statistics, *Archives nationales*, F90–1468; Pélicier (1859)

rumours. Peter Mathias (1969: 235) describes this speculative activity as follows: 'On the Stock Exchange the sharks moved in with bogus companies, patents for perpetual motion and other fraudulent schemes. Persons came into the market to play for capital gains, ready to jump out again as soon as prices showed any hesitation.' Charles-Albert Michalet (1968: 31) comments on the 'poor financial information [available] to the public'.

The telegraph made it possible to supply up-to-date and reliable information on prices of other markets. The English Telegraph Company, moreover, set up news rooms in the main stock exchanges in the provinces, thus making political and economic information more readily available. Interestingly, a first attempt at creating news rooms in public places had been unsuccessful (Lardner, 1867: 237); only stock exchange activities gave fast information its true value. In the United States, the Gold and Stock Telegraph Company, established in 1867, provided its subscribers (of whom there were 729 in

1871) with instantaneous information on gold and stock market prices (Tarr, 1987: 44).

The predominance of stock exchange news in telegraphic activities explains why traffic decreased or stagnated, depending on the market, after economic crises. An analysis of the evolution of the main English telegraph company's traffic (Electric and International Telegraph Company) from 1851 to 1868 shows that the number of messages sent per mile of network rose sharply, by 15 per cent on average every year. The two lowest growth rates appeared after the depressions in 1857 (minus 9 per cent) and 1866 (1 per cent) (Kieve, 1973: 66).

Hence, the stock exchange and the electric telegraph were closely linked. In the 1840s, in England, the railway boom led to a surge of activity on the London stock exchange and a dozen new stock exchanges were created in the provinces (Crouzet, 1978: 267). The circulation of information between these different places was, of course, provided by the fledgling telegraph. In France, the railway boom took place during the 1850s, when the electric telegraph was opened to commercial use. Stock market activity (which can be measured by market capitalization) was rising steeply: from 1851 to 1860 market capitalization increased seven-fold. If we take 1853 as a reference point (the year in which capitalization was identical to that before the 1848 Revolution), growth over a period of seven years remained at around 150 per cent. From 1860 to 1870 the growth rate was 100 per cent (Saint-Marc, 1974).

In order to compare prices on the different stock exchanges, and to transmit purchasing or selling orders rapidly, the telegraph became indispensable to investors. Kieve considers that the telegraph enabled the industrial and commercial world to provide 'enormous subscription of English capital to foreign loans' (Kieve, 1973: 238). The telegraph was also a key player in crises on the stock market. In 1879 Jules Verne described an imaginary crash as follows: 'Telegraphic dispatches started flowing in from all corners of the globe. Hardly a minute passed without a strip of blue paper, shouted out over the din of voices, being added to the collection of telegrams posted on the north wall by the stock exchange guards.'

Commercial use of the telegraph accounted for 30 per cent of all traffic. Le Verrier's report provides details of such activity in the United States. Shipowners and traders had information sent to them on the departure and arrival times of ships or the prices of wheat and cotton in the different towns. Shippers followed the progress of their products along the Mississippi, the Great Lakes and other waterways. Thus, the electric telegraph appeared as being linked to other means of transport in the creation of modern distribution during the second half of the nineteenth century. It made it possible to fit local trade into a broader regional or national context. Traders on the East Coast could order cereals from the West, resulting in a rapid increase in trading activities. Wheat could be sold while it was still in transit and even before it was harvested (Chandler, 1977: 210). According to Kieve (1973: 237), 'It made the world market a possibility. Its most efficient use was between the cotton and corn markets of Liverpool and the New York cotton and Chicago corn markets.'

Use of the telegraph by the general public, qualified as 'family use' at the time, remained minimal. In France, it only accounted for 20 per cent of both domestic and international traffic. In England and Belgium, where distances were shorter, this figure was even lower.

Other users of the telegraph were mainly the press and the railway companies. Kieve has evaluated the traffic of each of these users at 5 per cent in England in 1868. As for official dispatches, they were not included in French statistics, but a British report estimates them at 10 per cent of all French traffic in 1869 (Brown, 1870: 6; Foreman-Peck, 1989). Thus, at the end of the 1860s, the telegraph was no longer the instrument of state communication; it had become that of market communication. The use originally imagined by Cooke (service information for the railways), and which enabled him to develop his invention, had become marginal. We note in this respect that, as in the case of the Chappe telegraph, a discrepancy existed between the initial use – which allowed the inventor to be recognized – and the final use of the telegraph. The former was a response to an imperative demand related to current events of the day – the war for Chappe and management of the railways for Cooke – but was not sufficient to enable the new medium to develop significantly. In England, the Admiralty's semaphore network was abandoned after the Napoleonic wars and then reconstructed on a more modest scale.

In France, the Chappe system had been developed because it was a party to the project to centralize the state and thereby strengthen national unity. The same was true of the electric telegraph which was part and parcel of the development of the capitalist market in the mid-nineteenth century. This dominant use was no mere coincidence; a latent demand had already manifested itself in several semaphore telegraph projects, whether successful (Watson) or not (Ferrier). In particular, it matched prevailing economic theories at the time: liberalism in England and the Saint-Simonian movement in France. On both sides of the Channel, it was part of the current of ideas in favour of free trade.

Economists and the flow of information

The question of markets played an essential role in the construction of the classical economy; they provided both a system for adjusting supply and demand and a condition for the division of labour. Classical theoreticians have examined the conditions of the development of such markets. Adam Smith (1723–1790) showed the determining role played by transport. For example, with transport on waterways, the product of each kind of work had the whole world as its market (Smith, 1776). The importance of maritime transport was thus one of the main contributors to the wealth of nations and in particular that of England. Three-quarters of a century later, Jean-Baptiste

Say (1767–1832) spoke of the same question and remarked that 'the industries and population of the town of Manchester have tripled since the Duke of Bridgewater's canals linked it to the port of Liverpool' (Say, 1840: 177). He defined the notion of market in its original sense, that is, a place where transactions take place. The advantage of a permanent market as opposed to fairs, he said, is that it 'provides meeting points for all those who have goods to sell and those who want to acquire them, and serves to *fix the rates*' (Say, 1840: 175). Auguste Cournot (1801–1877) gave a different definition of the market in 1838: 'For economists the market is not a determined place where sales and purchases are accomplished, but an entire area where all parties are linked by free trade relations, so that prices are levelled out quickly and easily' (Cournot, 1838: 93).

To fix a price, to level it quickly, information has to circulate fast. That is precisely what Alexandre Ferrier proposed in 1832 with his semaphore telegraph which 'made it possible to know the state of every market at a glance'. Cooke made a similar proposition in 1836, suggesting that one of the potential uses of the electric telegraph might be to supply daily information on the state of different markets (Kieve, 1973: 18). The neo-classical economist William S. Jevons (1835–1882) was one of the first to show the role of information in the constitution of markets. Chapter 4 of his *Theory of Political Economy* (1871) dealt with the theory of trade. For Jevons, a market can exist without any fixed locality, if there is close communication between the partners of the transaction. For example, the expression 'Money Market . . . is applied to the aggregate of those bankers, capitalists and other traders who lend or borrow money, and who constantly exchange information concerning the course of business.' More generally, he considered that 'it is of the very essence of trade to have wide and constant information' and defined the theoretically perfect market as that in which 'all traders have perfect knowledge of the conditions of supply and demand, and the consequent ratio of exchange' (Jevons, 1871: 84–7). Thus, for Jevons, full information was one of the conditions for pure and perfect competition, the core of neo-classical theories.

Alfred Marshall (1842–1924) similarly considered the market 20 years later in his *Principles of Economics* (1890). When he wanted to quote a market that functioned on an international basis with rapid adjustments between supply and demand, he quoted the main international shares listed on a number of stock exchanges.

> For stock of this type, the telegraph maintains prices at roughly the same level on all the stock exchanges of the world. If the price of one of them climbs in New York or Paris, London or Berlin, the news of this is enough to provoke the same trend on other markets. If for some reason the rise is not immediate, that particular category of stocks will most probably be sold shortly on the market where the increase took place, following telegraphic orders from other markets. On the other hand, speculators on the first market will buy stocks on other markets by telegraph. (Marshall, 1890)

Thus, the telegraph was the technical agent of the international stock market.

The liberal state, telegraph operator

For liberal economists, state intervention in the economy had to be limited. In particular, it was not to intervene in production. Besides the exercise of monarchical functions (the army, justice, police), the state, according to Adam Smith in 1776, could develop public utilities (roads, bridges, canals): 'The expense of maintaining safe and practical roads and of facilitating communications is without a doubt beneficial to society as a whole and, consequently, one can in all fairness finance it by a general tax.' Nevertheless, in so far as these expenses only benefited a small minority, Adam Smith considered it preferable to finance them by the users in the form of toll charges.

John Stuart Mill (1806-1873) also discussed this question in 1848 in his *Principles of Political Economy.* He reasserted that 'laissez-faire should be the general rule: every deviation from it, unless it is absolutely necessary to achieve something great and good, is certainly harmful.' Neverthless, he did consider that for community services which became monopolies to a greater or lesser degree, it was the state's responsibility to control the quality of the service and to ensure that 'in the long run profits from the monopoly benefit the public.' John Stuart Mill nevertheless envisaged a few exceptions, notably the Post Office: 'This service is one of the few that a government can provide without any drawbacks' (Mill, 1848).

The position of French economists, and notably Jean-Baptiste Say, hardly differs from that of the English classical economists. Yet, the Saint-Simonians attributed a very important role to the state, due to the influence it could have on economic activity as a whole. In this movement it was Michel Chevalier (1806-1879) who considered the question most fully. After being the spokesman for the Saint-Simonian school, he became a Professor at the Collège de France in 1840, occupying the chair that had formerly been created for Jean-Baptiste Say. He developed a synthesis between liberal doctrine and Saint-Simonian thought. Jean Walch, a specialist on Chevalier, considers that 'he provided the "practical" Saint-Simonianism of the Pereires, the Talabots . . . and later of Napoleon III, a theoretical instrument on which they could lean' (Walch, 1975: 260).

For Chevalier, 'the government is the manager of the national association . . . Wherever the public interest is at stake, the government must intervene' (Chevalier, 1842: 69; Walch, 1975). This state intervention must take place in three domains: the development of means of communication, of money-lending institutions, and of professional training (Chevalier, 1844). Nevertheless, direct state responsibility for an economic activity must remain exceptional. In the field of communication, it is justified by the fact that this is a sector which:

1   'permanently affects all transactions';
2   requires an administrative unit;
3   requires an 'elite staff'.

Chevalier considered, for example, 'that canals could provide . . . trade with the advantages one could reasonably expect it to' only if the state formed a regular body of lock-keepers, personnel for towage and probably even boatmen. We note that for the telegraph, this technical team was created by Chappe and his successors and that it later took over operation of the electric telegraph. Like all Saint-Simonians, Chevalier attributed a significant role to the railways in the advent of the industrial era. In 'the Mediterranean system', he qualified the railway as 'the most perfect symbol of a universal association'. More generally, means of communication were, according to him, an essential factor not only in economic growth, but also in the happiness of the people. Upon his return from a trip to the United States, he wrote:

> Improving communications is . . . working for true, positive and practical freedom . . . it is extending this liberty to the greatest numbers as far and as well as is possible by the laws of election. I would even go so far as to say it is a way of practising equality for all and democracy. Efficient means of transport reduce distances not only between different places, but also between different classes. (Chevalier, 1836: 3; quoted by Walch, 1975: 152)

Saint-Simonian thinking had a profound influence on political leaders of the time. In France, the state played a significant role in favouring the development of the railways. We have seen that it also provided considerable funds for the construction of the telegraphic network (in 1853, for example, when there were only 5,000 kilometres of telegraph lines, the government planned the construction of a further 9,000 kilometres during the same year).[18] It is, moreover, interesting that in parliament in 1851, unlike in 1837, no deputy proposed leaving it up to the private sector to build a telegraphic network for commercial use.

Nationalization of the telegraph in Britain

In England state intervention in communication systems was far weaker. The railways were developed solely by private initiative and the state limited itself to supplying authorizations and imposing a few rules, primarily in security matters. We have already seen that the same was true of the telegraphic network. These choices corresponded to the thinking of liberal economists, although they did not rule out state intervention in the communications field. Indeed, it was traders and industrialists that were to demand the nationalization of the telegraph. In 1861, John Lewis Ricardo, nephew of the renowned economist David Ricardo (1772-1823), ex-president of the main English telegraph company and a member of parliament, sent a report to the Chancellor of the Exchequer Gladstone, suggesting that the Post Office buy the telegraph from the private companies that owned it. He compared the position in Great Britain with that on the Continent where, he concluded, the telegraph was 'a powerful engine of diplomacy, an important aid to civil and military administration, and an efficient service to trade and commerce' (Kieve, 1973: 121). This standpoint seems very surprising in a man who was known to be an advocate of free trade, who had fought in parliament for the abolition of the Corn Laws and, in particular, who had created, with Cooke and Wheatstone, the Electric Telegraph Company and had presided over it until 1858.[19]

Yet his proposition was not totally incongruous. Despite the dominance of 'laissez-faire' theories, the British civil service had become stronger and had extended its ambit. In 1855 the creation of the Civil Service Commission put an end to the system of recommendations which provided access to employment in the civil service. The United Kingdom gradually enhanced the quality of its civil service (Checkland, 1964: 313). In the 1840s, the Post Office was reorganized and became an efficient service. The 1844 Railway Act provided for the possibility of buying out certain companies at the end of their concession, although this facility was in fact never used (Mathias, 1969: 288). In 1859 the government granted subsidies to maritime traffic in the north Atlantic for the transport of mail (Checkland, 1964: 361).

This context was, however, insufficient for J.L. Ricardo's ideas to be accepted and the government rejected his propositions. In 1863 a law on the telegraph, defining the regulatory role of the state, was voted. The debate was resumed in 1865 by the Edinburgh Chamber of Commerce, which severely criticized the telegraph companies. It accused them of high tariffs for a very poor service, including insufficient lines, excessive delivery time of telegrams, long distances between telegraphic offices and business centres, and limited office opening hours. To remedy these shortcomings, it proposed the nationalization of private companies and management of the network by the Post Office. The latter had, over the preceding 20 years, developed an efficient and inexpensive mail service.

The same stance was taken by other chambers of commerce. The press, which was similarly dissatisfied with telegraphic tariffs, also supported this campaign. Petitions were subsequently sent to parliament, presenting nationalization as 'essential to the progress of the mercantile and manufacturing interests of the country' (Kieve, 1973: 128). This wave of opinion was furthermore taken up by the directors of the Post Office who wanted to increase the scope of their activities. The economist J.S. Jevons also supported the proposition in favour of nationalization (Kieve, 1973: 136).

In 1868 a law nationalizing the telegraph was voted in parliament by both Conservatives and Liberals. The preamble clearly states the grounds for nationalization:

> Whereas the Means of Communication by Electric Telegraphs within the United Kingdom of *Great Britain* and *Ireland* are insufficient, and many important Districts are without any such Means of Communication: And whereas it would be attended with great Advantage to the State, as well as to Merchants and Traders, and to the Public generally, if a cheaper, more widely extended, and more expeditious System of Telegraphy were established in the United Kingdom . . . (Kieve, 1973: 231)

While the bill was being voted, the question of monopoly was debated. Was the Post Office to be given a monopoly on the telegraph? The majority felt that it would block technical progress and thereby the improvement of the service. The government, however, defended the principle of a monopoly for two reasons. It believed that private competitors would operate on the more profitable lines, so reducing profits which the Post Office could otherwise reinvest in less profitable links. Furthermore, if the Post Office did not have a monopoly, it might not buy out all the private companies, thereby creating a situation of inequality with respect to nationalization. The monopoly bill was finally passed, but only for national lines. International lines, and particularly the main submarine lines to America and India, were to be built by private companies.[20] At the end of the nineteenth century these companies controlled two-thirds of all international cables. The network was used by the British state which finally subsidized certain strategic links – and by other major powers. When conflicts of colonial expansion became too intense, the British government censured telegrams between Europe and Africa or Asia, although this rarely occurred. As Daniel Headrick (1989) says: 'during a period of forty years, this technology which was the monopoly of a single power, contributed to the development of international trade and to the colonial expansion of all Western countries.'

By the end of the nineteenth century a European model of public management of the telegraph had been established. In France, it consisted of the opening of a state network to commercial use. This opening was concomitant with the abandoning of the semaphore technique in favour of the electric technique and rapid growth of the network. In England, limited development of the commercial telegraph led to nationalization (the first in the history of the nineteenth century) and management of the network by the Post Office (in France this was to take place in 1873). While the state developed and operated a communication network intended for the stock exchange and the market, private British capital created an international network for commercial and state use. A century after Chappe's invention, a balance was established between state-controlled communication and market-controlled communication. Although the latter played a preponderant role, it was the state that was chiefly responsible for its development.

Notes

1 It should, however, be pointed out that the British government did on occasion finance inventions to do with information machines. In 1823, Charles Babbage obtained public funds to develop a machine capable of automatically compiling various kinds of mathematical tables. State intervention was justified by the unprofitable nature of such an invention and its general interest (Hyman, 1982).

2 Cooke had also thought of state use of his telegraph. In a memorandum in 1836, he wrote that by means of the telegraph the government would be enabled 'in case of disturbance to transmit orders to the local authorities and if necessary to send troops to their support; whilst all dangerous excitement of the public might be avoided' (Kieve, 1973: 18).

3 In 1839, negotiations had been initiated for the opening of the Navy's London–Portsmouth semaphore line to private use.

4 *Translator's note*: The Saint-Simonians were disciples of the philosopher Claude-Henri de Rouvoy (known as Saint Simon), who believed that science and technology would solve most social problems and that the state should play a major role in industrial development. The ideas of the Saint-Simonians had a pervasive influence on the intellectual life of nineteenth-century Europe.

5 Quoted by Michel Siméon, 'Adoption du télégraphe Morse par la France (1850-1860)', in report of the *6e colloque international de FNARH*, Montpellier, May 1989.

6 This was not only a French point of view, since the first semaphore telegraph line built in Germany was at the initiative of the state. It linked Berlin, the seat of the Prussian government, and Frankfurt where the first German government was located. Siements built this line (Michel and Longin, 1990: 28).

7 Havas Agency archives, *Imprimerie nationale*, Paris, 1969 (quoted by Mattelart and Mattelart, 1979: 25).

8 *Translator's note*: In 1848 a new revolution put an end to the July Monarchy. The Second Republic lasted from 1848 to 1852, after which Napoleon III ruled the Second French Empire until 1871.

9 Number of dispatches sent in a year (a circular sent to several places counts as one unit): 1847: 4,787; 1848: 9,504; 1849: 8,902 (Ministry of the Interior statistics, *Archives nationales*, C1002).

10 Report by M. Le Verrier to the Chamber of Deputies on 18 June 1850 in *Le Moniteur universel*.

11 Ferdinand Barrot, speech to the Chamber of Deputies on 1 March 1850 in *Le Moniteur universel*.

12 M. Le Verrier's report, *Le Moniteur universel*.

13 Ibid.

14 Ibid.

15 Ministry of the Interior statistics. Since the network was opened in March, I have taken data from March 1851 to February 1852, for the first year. *Archives nationales*, F90–1468.

16 Statistics for eight months (March to October 1851) (Ministry of the Interior statistics, *Archives nationales*, F90–1468).

17 On 1 May 1849, even before the law liberalizing use of the telegraph was voted, the Second Republic had authorized the transmission of stock exchange rates on the Paris–Lille line (letter from the Minister of the Interior of 1 April 1849, *Archives nationales*, F90–1456).

18 *Archives nationales*, C1036.

19 According to certain sources, the memorandum was drawn up in 1858.

20 Nevertheless, the English state did intervene economically abroad since in 1875 it bought a 46 per cent stake in the Suez canal.

References

Atten M. (1988) 'Quand les télégraphes français font traverser la Manche à Maxwell (1860-1890)', *France Telecom*, no. 67, December.

Barett R.T. (1941) 'The conquest of a continent', *Bell Telephone Quarterly*, vol. 20, February.

Brown M.J. (1870) *Report on the Workings of the French, Belgian and Swiss Telegraphic Systems*, HMSO, London, Post 83/66: 6.

Chandler A.D. (1977) *The Visible Hand: the Managerial Revolution in American Business*, Harvard University Press, Cambridge, Mass.

Checkland S.G. (1964) *The Rise of Industrial Society in England (1851–1885)*, Longmans, Green and Co., London.

Chevalier M. (1836) *Les lettres sur l'Amerique du Nord*, vol. 2, Gosselin, Paris.

Chevalier M. (1842) *Cours d'économie politique fait au Collège de France, année 1841–1842*, Capelle, Paris.

Chevalier M. (1844) *Cours d'économie politique fait au Collège de France, année 1842–1843*, Capelle, Paris.

Cournot A. (1838) *Recherches sur les principes mathématiques de la théorie des richesses*, Calmann-Lévy edn, Paris, 1978.

Crouzet F. (1978) *L'Economie de la Grande-Bretagne victorienne*, SEDES, Paris.

Foreman-Peck J. (1989) 'The state and the development of the early European network', *UIT*, *Colloque de Villefranche-sur-Mer*, June.

Headrick D. (1989) 'Le développement des empires et des télécommunications', *UIT, Colloque de Villefranche-sur-Mer*, June.

Hyman A. (1982) *Charles Babbage: Pioneer of the Computer*, Oxford University Press, Oxford.

IRIS (1978) *Communications et Société, Elements d'analyse, 1*, Université de Paris–Dauphine.

Jevons W.S. (1871) *The Theory of Political Economy*, Macmillan, London.

Kieve J. (1973) *The Electric Telegraph: a Social and Economic History*, David and Charles, Newton Abbot.

King J. (1962) 'The development of electrical technology in the 19th century: the telegraph', in *Contributions from the Museum of History and Technology*, Bulletin 228, p. 281.

Lardner Dr (1867) *The Electric Telegraph*, James Walton, London.

Marshall A. (1890) *Principles of Economics*, Macmillan, London, 9th edn, 1961.

Mathias P. (1969) *The First Industrial Nation: an Economic History of Britain (1700-1914)*, Methuen and Co, London.

Mattelart A. and Mattelart M. (1979) *De l'usage des médias en temps de crise*, Alain Moreau, Paris.

Michalet C-A. (1968) *Les Placements des épargnants français de 1815 à nos jours*, Presses universitaires de France, Paris.

Michel A. and Longin F. (1990) *Siemens – trajectoire d'une entreprise mondiale*, Institut, Paris.

Mill J.S. (1848) *Principles of Political Economy*, University of Toronto Press edn, Toronto, 1965.

Pélicier E. (1859) 'Statistiques de la télégraphie privée en France (1858)', *Annales télégraphiques*, July–August.

Saint-Marc M. (1974) 'Introduction aux statistiques monétaires et financières françaises (1807-1970)', *Revue internationale d'histoire de la banque*, no. 8, Librairie Droz, Geneva.

Say J-B. (1840) *Cours complets d'économie politique*, vol. 1, Guillaumin, Paris.

Smith A. (1776) *An Inquiry into the Nature and Causes of the Wealth of Nations*, Penguin edn, Harmondsworth, 1970.

Stourdzé Y. (1979) 'Généologie de la commutation', *Collogue Bernard Gregory*, CNRS-MIT, February.

Tarr J.A. (1987) 'The city and the telegraph', *Journal of Urban History*, November.

Ternant A.L. (1884) *Les Télégraphes*, vol. 2, Hachette, Paris.

Vercruysse J.P. and Verhoest P. (1991) 'Le structuration du rôle de l'Etat dans le secteur des télécommunications en Belgique au cours du XIXe siècle', *Réseaux*, no. 49, CNET, Issy. (English trans. in *French Journal of Communication*, no. 3.)

Verne J. (1879) *Les Cinq Cents Millions de la Bégum*, Hetzel, Paris.

Walch J. (1975) *Michel Chevalier économiste saint-simonien*, Vrin, Paris.

Wilson G. (1976) *The Old Telegraphs*, Phillimore, London.

PART II
FAMILY COMMUNICATION
(1870–1930)

Introduction

'Mr Watson, come here, I want you'; tradition has it that this sentence was the very first telephone conversation. Moreover, it is probably the reason for Watson still being known as Bell's assistant. If history granted some renown to a research assistant, it was because research itself changed, from an activity practised by solitary scholars in the eighteenth and early nineteenth centuries, to an activity undertaken by small teams. Bell started with a single assistant in 1874, after which his team grew. Edison set up a small laboratory at Menlo Park in 1876, which was later expanded and considered the first modern technological research centre. The 1870s were thus a period of transformation in the organization of inventions.

Another change appeared sooner. In the 1840s most inventors were no longer considered scientists as in the past, but self-taught technicians who created their own enterprises developing and marketing their inventions. Cooke and Morse were typical examples of this technician-entrepreneur model and we shall meet others in this section. Bell, Edison, Berliner, Eastman and Marconi all had these similarities: no basic scientific training and the desire to market their respective inventions.

This change from scientist to technician-entrepreneur also appeared in a geographical shift from Paris around 1800 to the East Coast of America around 1880. Most mathematicians and physicians (Serres, 1989) in the 1800s lived in Paris and were also engineers and politicians. Chappe was part of this tradition, as were Carnot and the Monges. Three-quarters of a century later the innovators of communication were American, or at least lived in the United States. That was where the telephone, the phonograph, the cinema and amateur photography were born.

At the end of the nineteenth century, the inventors of communication devices had diverse interests. They often worked on several media simultaneously. Despite technical differences, a certain unity in the communications field appeared. At the centre of this research was Edison, who quickly gained prominence. He played a role in the beginnings of the telephone, by inventing the coal microphone, and particularly in the recording of sound and the development of animated images. But Edison was by no means the only 'multi-media inventor'. Wheatstone, in conjunction with his work on the telegraph, also worked on images in relief. Bell, after his research on the telephone, became interested in recording sound and conducted experiments in wireless transmissions. Berliner oriented his work towards the telephonic microphone and the recording of sound. In France, Charles Cros was not only interested in sound machines, he was also the inventor of a multiplex telegraph and the development of colour photography. The inventors of communication devices sometimes had a fervent interest in other media. Thus Morse showed great enthusiasm for the daguerrotype which he had discovered during a trip to Paris and which he promoted in the USA.

In this section we study the origin of most of the innovations leading to what were later to be called telecommunications and the audiovisual media. Other innovations in the communication field also appeared during this period. The mecanograph (tabulator-sorter of punched cards) was developed in 1884 by the American Herman Hollerith (Ligonnière, 1987: 127–39) and was the first electromechanical information-processing system. This machine was adopted on a large scale in major firms for both statistics and accounting until the advent, after the Second World War, of modern computers. Moreover, the firm established by Hollerith was, after a number of transformations, to become the present day International Business Machines (IBM).

If the turn of the nineteenth century saw the birth of the audiovisual media (photography, records, motion picture and broadcasting), another medium was already well established: the press. Until the 1830s it was essentially, to borrow Yves de la Haye's expression, 'a correspondence-press which included readers of the *Constitutionnel*, the *Journal des débats*, the *Moniteur* . . . in intimate but limited communion' (de la Haye, 1984: 12). This press flourished in revolutionary situations; it was not only the means of expression of a political movement but also a rallying point. With the Constitution, it was a fundamental element of the bourgeois public sphere studied by Habermas (1962). Moreover, the development of the press was in a sense similar to that of the semaphore telegraph. The latter was not linked to any eighteenth-century technological innovation, but far more to the spread of the Enlightenment,[1] to the emergence of public opinion through the game of reasoning publicly.

The first change in the press appeared on the eve of the launching of photography and the electric telegraph. In 1836 Emile de Girardin with *La Presse* and Dutacq with *Le Siècle* simultaneously introduced a new formula. They sold their newspapers for 10 centimes (50 per cent cheaper than other newspapers), financed them chiefly by means of advertisements and attracted readership with novels in serial form. Circulation shot up from a few thousand to 20–30,000 copies. At the same time the penny press appeared in the United States and was even more successful.

A further development in the press appeared in 1863 when Moïse Millaud launched the *Petit Journal*, a daily in which political information occupied very little space and which was sold at 5 centimes (1 sou). Six years after being launched it had reached a circulation of 350,000 copies; it was thus the first popular newspaper. This transformation of the press into a mass media was to be facilitated by technological developments: invention of the rotary printing press by the Frenchman Hippolyte Marinoni (1865), then a new typesetting machine, the Linotype (1884) by the American engineer Ottmar Mergenthaler.[2]

This second stage in the development of modern communication was also influenced by the transformation of private life, the emergence of the Victorian family, and withdrawal into the domestic sphere. The nascent media were to find a niche in which to develop. The inventors of communication machines fiercely debated whether their new instruments were intended for the professional or domestic world. This controversy was not unlike the one we witnessed during the preceding period, between state-controlled communication and market-controlled communication. The debate between professional use and public use took place among innovators of the phonograph and telephone, while in the case of the wireless the state was also involved. In 1920, for example, the British government interrupted Marconi's experiments in radio broadcasting. It was pressured by radiotelephone manufacturers and the army who complained 'that this use for entertainment of what was primarily a commercial and transport-control medium was frivolous and dangerous' (Williams, 1974: 32).

This second part of the book contains three chapters. Chapter 4 is devoted to the birth of image and sound recording technologies (photography, phonograph, motion picture). In particular, I emphasize the appearance of a new family sphere, the place in which photo albums were kept and recorded music listened to. In Chapter 5 I study the birth of the telephone and the shift from professional use, similar to that of the telegraph, to telephone conversations which become one of the components of family sociability. Chapter 6 is devoted to the wireless. It looks at how scientific discoveries were transformed to give birth to a telecommunications system originally intended for maritime links but finally transformed into a form of mass media.

Notes

1 On the role of publishers and printers in the spread of the Enlightenment, see Eisenstein (1986).

2 *Histoire générale de la presse*, vol. 2, PUF, Paris, 1972.

References

Eisenstein E. (1986) 'Print culture and enlightenment thought', Rare Book Collection, University of North Carolina, Chapel Hill.

Habermas J. (1962) *Strukturwandel der Offentlichkeit*, Frankfurt am Main.

de la Haye Y. (1984) *Dissonances, critique de la communication*, La Pensée Sauvage, Grenoble.

Ligonnière R. (1987) *Préhistoire et histoire des ordinateurs*, Robert Laffont, Paris.

Serres M. (1989) 'Paris 1800', in *Eléments d'histoire des sciences*, under the direction of Michel Serres, Bordas, Paris.

Williams R. (1974) *Television, Technology and Cultural Form*, Fontana/Collins, London.

4

Collection and Souvenir: Photography and the Gramophone

The discovery of sound recording was preceded by that of image recording by about 40 years. I will, however, discuss these two inventions in the same chapter, since the example of images was often quoted by inventors of the sound machine and since these two media, in particular, were to have an impact on the private sphere. Although the discovery of photography was contemporaneous with that of the telegraph, their social functions were fundamentally different. We shall also see that there were similarities between the use of photography and that of the phonograph. Finally, I conclude this chapter with a presentation of the discovery of the motion picture.

Images revealed

In 1802 an article appeared in London entitled: 'Description of a procedure for copying paintings onto glass and for making silhouettes by the effect of light on silver nitrate.' The author, Wedgwood, thus defined the objectives of the inventors of photography. He did not achieve his goal, but 15 years later Nicéphore Niepce, who had just learned lithographic techniques (then new in France), tried to automate the copying and reproduction of drawings or engravings. By means of the effect of light in a camera obscura, he developed a procedure which he called 'heliography' and described it as follows:

> Light in its state of composition and decomposition reacts chemically on bodies. It is absorbed, it combines with them and communicates new properties to them. Thus, light increases the natural consistency of some of these bodies; it even solidifies and renders them more or less insoluble, depending on the duration or the intensity of its action.[1]

He soon discovered that he could also copy scenes from real life and produced his first 'photograph' in about 1816.[2]

Single or multiple copies

In a letter to a member of the London Royal Society, Niepce defined his system as one which: 'fixes the image of objects by the chemical effect of light; it fixes this image precisely, except for the diversity of its colours and . . . transmits it by means of printing, with procedures known in engraving.'[3] In a memorandum written a few months later, also for the Royal Society, he indicated: 'I had set myself an important problem for the drawing arts and engraving.'[4] However, under the influence of Louis-Mandé Daguerre with whom he worked, Niepce abandoned his work on the reproduction of images in a camera obscura. Daguerre advised him to strive for 'perfection rather than multiplicity' and Niepce's sole aim became that of 'replicating views offered by nature without having recourse to an artist'.[5]

After Niepce's death in 1833, Daguerre improved his partner's invention and gave it his name; the heliograph became the daguerrotype. Daguerre had first been a painter who knew how to 'represent nature with prodigious accuracy' (Figuier, 1888: 23), hence he strove to produce unique copies on a copper plate coated with iodine-sensitized silver. These highly precise photographic images could not, however, be reproduced. We see here how Daguerre's 'piracy' was twofold. Daguerre, like Cooke, appropriated someone else's invention (and to avoid any misunderstanding gave it his name), and proposed a use for it which corresponded to an immediate market: the copying of important buildings, scenery and still lifes, and the realization of portraits. As soon as the Daguerre system was revealed to the public in 1839:

> one could see at their windows, at the first signs of dawn, a large number of experimenters tentatively trying to put the image of the neighbouring gable window, or the perspective of a population of chimneys, onto a specially prepared plate . . . After a few days, in all the squares in Paris, one could see daguerrotypes aimed at the prominent buildings. (Figuier, 1888: 44)

Daguerre was not the only inventor to opt for the uniqueness of photographic documents. In the same year another Frenchman, Hippolyte Bayard, developed a procedure of positive photography directly onto paper (as opposed to the daguerrotype which used silver-plated copper). However, all the other inventors at the time were primarily interested in the question of reproduction. In 1839 the Englishman, William Fox Talbot, invented the development of positive proofs on paper from a negative: the 'calotype'.[6] He also worked on a photo-engraving device in 1853. Two French inventors, A. Poitevin (1848) and Niepce de Saint-Victor, Nicéphore's nephew (1853), each developed similar devices: the photolithograph and the helio-engraver (Colson, 1898). Photographic publishing was to develop very rapidly in the 1850s.

Like the inventors of the telegraph, the inventors of photography cannot be placed along a straight road of technological progress. They developed projects concurrently, borrowing ideas from their fellows as they went along. Both technologies and applications circulated. By favouring the single proof, Daguerre and, to a lesser degree, Bayard (whose procedure was not diffused) made of photography an instrument of expression for both professionals and amateurs. In contrast, interest in multiple copies oriented other inventions towards photographic publishing. These two options were developed simultaneously until George Eastman invented mass photography and turned it into the most prevalent use of the technology.

The state as a promotor of photography

If it was possible to see daguerrotypes all over public squares, this was because the state had promoted the new invention – strange as it might seem for a liberal régime. On 3 July 1839 the Chamber of Deputies voted a law authorizing the state to buy Daguerre and Niepce's photographic procedure. The intention was not to turn it into a state monopoly, but to 'provide society with the discovery which it wants to enjoy in the interests of all'.[7] An enthusiastic legal rapporteur, Arago, claimed that: 'France adopted this discovery from the first moment. It took pride in being able to offer it freely to the whole world.' Daguerre was presented with a sum which was not as 'petty as an annuity' but which was identical to a pension. He was considered a national hero: 'It is with a pension that you reward the warrior who was mutilated on the battle fields . . . that you honour the families of Cuvier, Jussieu and Champollion.'[8]

State intervention was justified in legal terms: 'It is impossible – for the authors of this discovery – to make of it an industrial object . . . Their invention is not apt to be protected by a patent. As soon as it is known, anyone will be able to use it.' This justification seems most strange, since all the inventors who improved the photographic procedure, and notably Fox Talbot, patented their device. During the same period Cooke protected his electric telegraph (a machine which was also easy to copy) with a patent. Daguerre, however, had no intention of creating an industry. Like Chappe half a century earlier, he offered his invention to the nation in 'the interest of the sciences and the arts'. Moreover, Arago saw in this new technology an instrument to be used by archaeologists (for copying hieroglyphics), astronomers and physicists, or by painters to rapidly build up a collection of studies.

As Gay-Lussac was to say in the Upper House,

> everything that contributes towards the progress of civilization, to the physical and moral well-being of Man, must be the constant object of an enlightened government's concern, on a level with the destinies entrusted to it; and those who by their efforts assist in this noble task, should receive honourable rewards for their success.[9]

These words of Gay-Lussac echo those of Barère when he supported Chappe's project. On that occasion he had declared: 'It is up to the National Convention to encourage the arts and the sciences. It has always seen citizens who contribute towards enhancing knowledge or using all the results of the sciences, as benefactors of the fatherland.'[10]

The July Monarchy, like the Convention, considered it legitimate for the state to support major inventions and to put them at the disposal of the nation. Although Daguerre expected an annuity, while Chappe had been satisfied with the National Assembly's recognition, in both cases the inventor did not envisage exploiting his intellectual property. Both asked the state to make their invention available to the nation.

This altogether exceptional choice of making industrial property a collective good had an impact on the other inventors of photography. In particular, Talbot never managed to have his patent rights respected in France. In England, his homeland, these patent rights soon lapsed. On the other hand, the diffusion of daguerrotypes was extremely rapid. In 1846 (seven years after Daguerre's publications) annual sales in Paris amounted to 2,000 cameras and 500,000 plates (Freund, 1974: 30). The absence of a patent thus seems to have made wide diffusion of the innovation possible. Moreover, this choice corresponded to the position adopted by the Saint-Simonians at the time. Michel Chevalier, for example, wrote: 'Inventions, to reach a practical state, are realized in successive stages, often in different countries, with the care and initiative of several persons. Why and by what right should the last person in this series of inventive minds appropriate the benefits of all the others' effort?'[11]

'You press the button, we do the rest'

The photographic technique was finally established in the 1850s with the appearance of the negative on collodion-covered glass plates. The photo-sensitivity of this solution disappeared as soon as it dried, so that the photographer had to prepare his negative just before taking the photo. He was thus not only an artist, but also an artisan who produced his own photo-sensitive materials.

During the 1870s plates of dry gelatine that could be kept for several months began to appear in England and France and then in the United States. These plates were later produced industrially. In the US, Eastman's new business managed to establish a sound reputation in this market from 1881. A few years later it developed flexible film in a spool to be used by photographers. However, in spite of improvements which yielded results comparable to those on photographic plates, by 1887 failure was obvious. Eastman wrote:

> When we started our scheme of film photography we expected that everybody that used glass plates would take up films, but we found that the number that did this was relatively small and that in order to make a large business we would have to reach the general public and create a new class of patrons. (Jenkins, 1975)

To reach this goal, he had to transform his product.

Eastman began to market a device that was easy to handle, together with film, and offered the service of industrially developing the film – a process that was too complex for amateurs. This new system was aptly illustrated by the famous slogan: 'You press the button, we do the rest.' At the end of 1888 Eastman launched a new product which he called Kodak (a name which seemed to him easy to remember in a number of languages). It was immensely successful. Like Morse, who had shifted his innovation 40 years earlier from state-controlled to market-controlled communication, Eastman changed ground, moving into the trend of mass consumption emerging in the United States.

Recorded sound

In 1856 Nadar, who was one of the main photographers of his era and highly enthusiastic about technological developments at the time, imagined an 'acoustic daguerrotype which faithfully and tirelessly reproduces all the sounds subjected to its objectivity'.[12] A few years later he described this machine, which he called a 'phonograph', 'as a box in which melodies could be caught and fixed, like the camera obscura captures and fixes images'.[13] This technical conceptualization could obviously not lead to a concrete result, but it showed that research on the recording of images and sound was underway simultaneously.[14] The aim was the same: preserving the memory of that which had disappeared. As Jacques Perriault (1981: 133) so rightly said, 'socially, the phonograph is the camera obscura of sound'.

It is to Léon Scott de Martinville that we owe the first technical result in this domain. In 1857 he built a device for graphically recording sound. His aim was to realize 'natural stenography' and to study speech mechanisms. The machine on which Thomas Edison, in the USA, and Charles Cros, in France, worked concurrently 20 years later, added another function: the restitution of sound.

Edison had set up a research laboratory at Menlo Park in 1876. There, with just over a dozen assistants, he conducted research on telegraphic and then telephonic systems. His laboratory notebooks provide us with detailed information on the genealogy of this research (Charbon, 1991). On 3 February 1877, Edison patented a telegraphic repeater in which a disc covered with paper turned on a turntable and an engraving stylet suspended on an arm marked a series of dots and dashes in a spiral. On 17 July, the research team discovered that if the table turned faster than a certain speed, the reading stylet transmitted vibrations similar to the human voice. The next day Edison noted the idea of a telephonic repeater and then remarked: 'Speech vibrations are recorded exactly and there is no doubt that I will soon be able to record and reproduce the human voice.'

A new research project had been defined. On 12 August a first sketch of the phonograph appeared in the laboratory notebooks. On 4 December a first prototype was created. A few weeks later Edison included a description of the phonograph in his patents on improvements to the telephone, which were being registered in Paris and London.

During the same period, the French poet and inventor Charles Cros was working on a talking machine. Unfortunately, we have very little information on the development of his research. On 10 October 1877 an article on his projects appeared in the science section of *La Semaine du clergé*. Having heard about Edison's research, he sent a note to the Académie des sciences on 3 December.[15] However, lacking financial resources and no doubt also the taste for producing technological devices, Cros never built a prototype.

Despite their differences – on the one hand, an inventor-entrepreneur with the first research laboratory of the time and, on the other hand, a solitary inventor, a bit of a dreamer – Edison and Cros had the same conception of a talking machine. In *Scientific American* of 17 November 1877, Edison wrote that he had just developed 'a wonderful invention, capable of repeating speech countless times by means of automatic recordings' (Charbon, 1989: 35). Charles Cros expressed the same idea in verse (Perriault, 1981: 153).

The machine imagined by Cros was called a 'paleophone'; it was thus, before all else, a machine for memorizing. This conception was shared by Cros's contemporaries. Louis Figuier, the main popularizer of science at the time, wrote about Edison's phonograph in an article in the 1889 Exhibition's journal: 'The French Academy is, without delay, going to attend to equipping a sort of library with devices for recording its members' voices. It will not be one of the lesser prodigies of the future, that of making the dead speak' (Figuier, 1889; Perriault, 1981: 184–5). Jacques Perriault, who quotes Figuier, compares this project with that of Nadar who captured the image of celebrities of his time by means of photographs. The desire to preserve a trace of the present, the challenge to time which enables one to see and hear the dead, was a fundamental element in people's image of communication at the end of the nineteenth century.

Office machine or domestic machine

We have seen that the research which spawned Edison's machine was originally focused on the telegraph and then the telephone. Edison was thinking of linking the telephone to the phonograph when he wrote:

> A telephone subscriber can connect his phone to a phonograph which, with each call, will inform the exchange that he is out and that he will be back at a certain time. Similarly, one subscriber who calls another and finds him out, will be able to say what he wants to and have this recorded on a phonograph. (IRIS, 1978: 30)

Bell also took an interest in the 'telephone recorder' and, together with his assistant Tainter, he built the 'graphophone'. He replaced the tin foil cylinders in Edison's machine with cylinders covered with a blend of wax and paraffin. This machine could also serve as an office dictaphone. In another text Edison wrote: 'The phonograph is particularly useful for writing letters, for dictating texts. It was built with this aim in mind.'[16] It was no doubt on the basis of this use that Edison organized the – largely unsuccessful – marketing of the phonograph, and Graham Bell that of the graphophone 10 years later. In 1888 the Graphophone Company bought the two competing inventors' patents and tried to sell the talking machine in the business world, with no greater success.

In 1890 several companies marketing the phonograph in the United States proposed a far more successful use for this machine: they installed it in public places where anybody could pay a few cents to listen to a piece of music (Gelatt, 1965: 34–5). This use of the phonograph for entertainment was a significant social innovation. Promoters of the 'phonographic juke-box' had, however, to face Edison's determined opposition. He wrote in his house organ *The Phonogram* in 1891 that companies:

> relying only on the profits derived from the 'coin-in-the-slot', will find too late that they have made a fatal mistake. The 'coin-in-the-slot' device is calculated to injure the phonograph in the opinion of those seeing it only in that form, as it has the appearance of being nothing more than a mere toy, and no one would comprehend its value or appreciate its utility as an aid to businessmen and others for dictation purposes when seeing it only in that form.[17]

However, Edison had to admit the obvious: the phonograph for office use was not selling, whereas a 150-dollar machine was earning, on average, 50 dollars a week in a drug store.

The idea of turning the talking machine into a music machine also captured the imagination of Emile Berliner. This inventor of German origin had worked for Bell before developing a microphone which he marketed in Germany. His interest in sound led him, like Edison and Bell, to work on techniques for recording and reproducing it. According to Paul Charbon, his approach 'consisted of looking for forgotten inventions, which he improved and made practical' (Charbon, 1989: 38); in other words, he made others' procedures reliable. His system of engraving[18] was based on the one developed by Léon Scott de Martinville for his 'phonautograph',[19] and inspiration for his reading device came from Cros's machine. That was how, in 1888, he developed a disc machine, the gramophone.

Berliner, like Cooke or Daguerre, appropriated a technology and shifted its use. Like Eastman, he thought of a domestic function. Being extremely fond of music, he imagined using records as an instrument to play music – in particular, famous operas. Fred Gaisberg, Art Director of the company established by Berliner, wrote in his memoirs: 'For many years Berliner was one of the few amongst many known to me in the gramophone business who was a music lover' (Gaisberg, 1946: 25).

Berliner finally opted for the use of a mould to duplicate sound recordings in large series. *A priori* the phonograph, a cylindrical device for the recording and reading of sound, was not designed for this purpose. Nevertheless, when in 1894 Edison made the decision to market his phonograph as an instrument for entertainment, the question of duplication arose. He marketed pre-recorded cylinders, each of which was an original recording (the musicians sometimes played for 24 recordings per day). Later, by means of a pantograph system, 25 copies were produced from an original. The industrial duplication of cylinders was only to be discovered in 1901 with a moulding procedure, but it would already be too late. Use of a disc specifically designed for industrial reproduction would have been adopted and would appear to users to be connected to this new use.

Clearly, technical conflicts and conflicts over usage were interlinked. The machine whose inventor gauged the market accurately triumphed over that of a competitor whose forecasts were wrong. This happened even if, from a strictly technical point of view, the former was not necessarily the better of the two.

The 1890s were a major turning point in the history of communication devices. For the first time a machine was used for entertainment and in the private sphere. As we have seen, it was with the electric telegraph that the private use of telecommunications started to appear, but such use remained minimal. In 1867 Lardner wrote: 'Personal and domestic messages are most generally confined to cases of urgency' (Lardner, 1867: 236). In contrast with the telegraph and the telephone (see below), the phonograph developed as a medium of the private sphere.

A new family sphere

Just as Chappe's telegraph was born at the same time as the modern nation-state, and just as the electric telegraph developed together with the extension of the stock exchange, so the phonograph accompanied a major transformation in private life in the second half of the nineteenth century: the burgeoning of the Victorian family. In so far as the phonograph first spread in the United States and England, it is mainly in these two countries that I shall study the birth of a new family sphere. Unless I specify otherwise, my examples all refer to the United States.

In her study of the 'social origins of private life' in the United States, Stephanie Coontz (1988: 251) considers the years between 1870 and 1890 to be 'the apogee of the private sphere'. The literature of the time describes the family home as a 'refuge', a 'sanctuary', an 'oasis', an 'ivory tower', a 'fortress' and the like. This conception of *privacy* did not correspond to a withdrawal from society, but to a break between the family and involvement in capitalist production which took place outside the home. As John Noyes wrote in the 1870s, 'The two principles as they exist in the world are not antagonistic. Home is the center from which men go forth to business, and business is the field from which they go home with the spoil. Home is the charm and stimulus of business, business provides material for the comfort and health of the home' (Coontz, 1988: 212). This distinction between the public and private spheres corresponded, within the upper and middle classes, to a strict division of tasks between the sexes: the men went out to work and the women stayed at home.

The separation between public and private also appeared in the organization of space. Catherine Hall presents the history of a family of English Quaker shopkeepers from Birmingham. In the 1830s they went to settle in a residential suburb a mile out of town. The lease stipulated that the house could not be turned into a shop or workshop (Hall, 1987: 66). In his monograph on Philadelphia, the urban sociologist Sam Bass Warner considers that it was between 1830 and 1860 that the model of a private sphere imposed itself on the urban organization of large American cities. This conception meant that the individual was first attached to his family and that the community was simply the grouping of families accumulating capital (Warner, 1968: 3–4). Towns lost their coherence, their centre, and social life in them broke up into a succession of groups which rarely managed to structure a complete urban area.

In his monograph on Union Park, a middle-class quarter in Chicago during the years 1870 to 1890, Richard Sennett described the disappearance of all social life outside the home. There were, according to him, very few bars, clubs and restaurants, and it was rare and somewhat exceptional to receive friends. The family circle replaced associative circles by marking the social territory of men and women. It was henceforth towards living room armchairs, rather than towards the local pub, that fathers would head after dinner (Sennett, 1970). Sennett considers that this withdrawal into the home was due to a fear of the town, of the harshness of capitalism. Chicago was then expanding rapidly and was in the process of becoming a gigantic conurbation; capitalist expansion was extremely fast but totally disorganized. The family was an immediately available instrument which men used in trying to protect themselves from the disorder and the diversity of the town (Sennett, 1970).

The home was also a place where individual creativity could be expressed. Numerous books on interior decorating showed housewives how to put a personal touch to their homes. Gwendolyn Wright (1981: 94) aptly remarks on the contradictions which existed between the Victorian ideology that wanted to make the home an individualized place in which the personality of its occupants could be expressed, and the mass organization of the construction of this new habitat (creation of housing estates, industrialized production of materials, and so forth).

This new value attached to the private sphere and the family first appeared within the middle classes. Catherine Hall showed that the ideological trend was born in England in the 1820s among evangelists in reaction to the decadence of the aristocracy (Hall, 1987: 55). In the mid-nineteenth century the family ideal was so widespread that the report presenting the 1851 Census stated: 'Each and every Englishman dreams of having his own house. It provides a well-defined frame for his family and his home, a sanctuary for his sorrows, his joys and his meditations' (Hall, 1987: 70). This middle-class family model, presented as universal, was effectively adopted by the aristocracy and proposed to the working classes by charity organizations. Robert Roberts (1971: 35) gives the following meaning of the word 'home' for a child from the poor quarters of England at the end of the century:

> The home, even poor, was the centre of all his love and interests, a healthy fortress facing a hostile world. Songs celebrating its beauty were on all lips. 'Home, sweet home', heard for the first time in the 1870s had become a second national hymn. In working class houses, it was rare not to see inscriptions such as 'Home is the nest where all is best' on the walls.[20]

Edward Shorter showed that in the United States celebration of the private sphere first appeared in the middle classes. Nevertheless, he considers that the American family was 'born modern'. When the settlers disembarked they immediately wanted their intimacy, their privacy (Shorter, 1975: 242). Then,

> during the last decades of the nineteenth century, the cult of home and motherhood, which had emerged in the 1830s, reached its pinnacle. Novels, poems, lithographs, childrens books, and domestic guides extolled the virtues of domesticity so much that the good family and their suburban home became almost interchangeable concepts. (Wright, 1981: 107)

Within the American working classes the separation between the public and private spheres appeared later. Sam Warner, in a monograph on Boston between 1870 and 1900, described the streets as a centre of social life in the working-class quarters. Labourers met on street corners and in doorways, resting and chatting after a day's work. Musicians played their favourite songs on street organs, and in the Italian community street musicians sang their melodies despite the din of trains and the cries of street sellers (Warner, 1968).

Music at home

In middle-class homes music also occupied an important place, although it was a family activity, generally practised by women. 'What is home without a piano?' stated an English advertisement at the end of the nineteenth century (Ehrlich, 1975: 8). But, in 1843 George Dodd already indicated that the piano was placed in a corner in most upper middle-class homes;[21] it had become a sign of social belonging to the lower middle classes. In 1873, a South Yorkshire miners' leader declared before the Select Committee on Coal: 'We have got more pianos and perambulators, but the piano is a cut above the per-ambulator' (Ehrlich, 1975: 8)!

The piano was not only a status symbol but also the object of an important family activity. John Hullah, in his book *Music in the House* (1877), qualified it as a 'family orchestra',[22] 'for two performers on one instrument can give a very full rendering of almost any Beethoven symphony' (Mackerness, 1964: 173). At the request of music publishers, composers adapted a whole reper-toire of quartets and concertos for the piano and even 'reduced' symphonies for the same purpose. But skilful playing was probably less widespread than it seemed. J.F. Jameson wrote, about the United States, that the 'prodigious frequency of pianos . . . might easily deceive unwary travellers into the unwar-ranted belief that we were a musical people'. However, he or she would be soundly disillusioned if they heard the daughter of the house playing *The Battle of Prague*, a piece which imitates the rumbling of cannons, the din of horses hooves, and so forth (Furnas, 1969: 586).

E.D. Mackerness has shown that, in England, playing the piano in homes led to the production of a large number of so-called royalty songs. The singing of these songs accompanied by the piano constituted a significant part of domestic entertainment. Subjects were varied – religious, patriotic, sentimental ballads, humoristic and so forth – and a huge number of scores was sold. In 1825, two and a half million copies of a song telling the story of the murderer James Rush were sold. In the United States, at the turn of the nineteenth century, the publishing of music scores had become a mass indus-try. From 1900 to 1910 (Buxton, 1985: 31, 39) over a million copies of a hundred different scores were sold. A big hit tune sold up to 6 million copies.[23] It was during this period that the publishers of scores discovered 'ragtime'. They employed a number of black composers to write this music for the first time, and in order to make it accessible to amateur pianists the editors then simplified the original scores. Ragtime was thus adapted to suit the masses (Hobart, 1981: 267).

The piano as an instrument accompanying family romance was widespread at the end of the nineteenth century. Ehrlich (1975: 6–7) estimated the number of pianos in 1910 at 2–4 million in Britain and 4 million in the United States. This indicates that over a quarter of all English homes had a piano, and almost as many in the USA (20 per cent). The piano was thus one of the first instruments of mass entertainment. Contemporaries had, moreover, remarked on this phenomenon. James Buchanan wrote in 1895:

> The progress of invention and discovery . . . and the application of the results to our arts and industries have gained for the entire community an increased and an increasing amount of leisure . . . it is a gratifying reflection that a large portion is being devoted to those recreations and studies that appeal to the higher nature of man. Among these Music now holds an important place.[24]

This mass consumption of music was made possible by the industrial organization of production, notably in the United States (Steinway).[25] In half a century prices declined dramatically. New marketing methods, such as hire-purchase or second-hand sales, were introduced.

On the music mass market, mechanical pianos often known as pianolas appeared at the end of the nineteenth century. Although the technical principle was not new (mechanical organs already existed at the end of the seventeenth century), the wide diffusion of the pianola was a sure sign of the family demand for recorded music.

The end of the nineteenth century was also a period in which the activity of symphony orchestras and operas increased. In the main cities of the United States, 12 major symphony orchestras were created between 1880 and the First World War.[26] In England, the opera season diversified, although the simultaneous growth of the suburbs separated the public from concert halls. There was thus a contradiction between two social movements: while the symphony orchestra reached its peak, the public moved away from the geographical location of concerts.

Thus we witness an effective transformation of musical life at the end of the nineteenth century. Singing accompanied by piano-playing had become widespread in the middle classes and then in a part of the upper working classes. This practice then started to be replaced by that of listening to automatic instruments (the pianola). Moreover, large orchestras were achieving renown and attracting audiences hitherto unknown, while their public was simultaneously leaving the city centres. From a quick economic viewpoint, one could say that in this context a demand for the phonograph existed. However, such an assertion, the result of an *a posteriori* analysis, seems questionable. For contemporaries such as Edison there was nothing obvious about a domestic demand since the first offerers of sound machines had perceived no such demand. It seems more appropriate to talk of a potential niche, the result of changing mentalities and life-styles.

The end of the nineteenth century saw the emergence of the third new representation of communication in a hundred years. A century earlier the vision of communication machines had changed from a romantic one to a new perspective in which they appeared as instruments of state power (Chappe built a state telegraphic network). In the 1830s the new communication machines partook in the development of a new world financial market as the electric telegraph became an instrument of the stock exchange. Debate between

Edison and his licensees, like that in the French Chamber of Deputies in 1837 and in 1850, centred around a conflict between representations of communication machines. For Edison, the phonograph, like the telegraph and the telephone, was a commercial instrument. Using a talking machine for entertainment would be a 'fatal error', just as the deputy Tesnière had considered that commercial use of the telegraph was a factor of 'spoliatory and immoral speculation'.

The domestic phonograph

Edison ended up acknowledging his mistake. By the mid-1890s, all phonograph and gramophone manufacturers offered a machine for domestic use. In the winter of 1895 the Columbia Phonograph Company sponsored an advertisement in American magazines 'picturing a family in a moment of rapt delight: grandfather sitting relaxed in an easy chair, his son and daughter-in-law standing attentively to his either side, and his grandson . . . hopping up and down between his knees. The attention of all four was directed to the horn protruding from a small phonograph on a nearby table.' Roland Gelatt, from whom I have borrowed this description, notes that in all the advertisements at the time the theme of the 'happy family enraptured by the phonograph was unavoidable' (Gelatt, 1965: 69). Penetration of this device into households was rapid. The number of machines in the United States in 1900 is estimated at 500,000; in 1910 at 2.5 million and in 1920 at 12 million (Table 4.1).

Table 4.1   *Penetration rate of domestic goods in American households*

	Piano (%)	Phonograph (%)	Telephone (%)	Automobile (%)
1900	–	3	6	0.05
1910	20	15	25	2
1920	–	50	37	33

Source: Bureau of the Census and Ehrlich (1976) for the piano. For the phonograph, I reconstituted the production series by interpolation from available data (1899, 1909, 1914, 1919). I then finalized the figures by considering that the average life-span of these machines was 10 years. For the telephone, the number of domestic phones was only known in 1920, when two-thirds of all phones were installed in homes. For the automobile, records of registration numbers are available from 1900.

It was only at the beginning of the twentieth century that the mass production and consumption of the phonograph began. In 1910 its penetration rate in households was inferior to that of the piano and the telephone. Even in 1909 the production of pianos (364,000) was still greater than that of phonographs (345,000).[27] Penetration of the motor car was, on the other hand, still very weak. Shortly after the First World War the phonograph, telephone and motor car were all present in American families to a large extent, but the phonograph had the most widespread acceptance and was to be found in about half of all homes. It was the main form of mass media, second only to the press.

In order to enter into the post-Victorian home, the phonograph had to fit in with the furniture, to be presented as a decorative element, to look 'as little like a phonograph as possible'.[28] In 1906 the manufacturer Victor brought out a mahogany phonograph with the same finish as a piano, with a horn concealed inside (Gelatt, 1965: 147). Later, American designers worked on highly stylish models. For example, Columbia proposed the *Donatello*, whose four sides were painted with copies of fifteenth-century Italian art 'at its imperishable best'. Victor chose the style of Louis XVI, without however turning the phonograph into a 'pedestal table for flower arrangements'. It was naturally in the design of Art Deco style horns that gramophone designers' imagination manifested itself most clearly.[29]

If the sale of discs or cylinders is anything to go by, use of the gramophone and the phonograph[30] was fairly extensive. In 1921 a hundred million recordings were sold, four times more than in 1914 (Gelatt, 1965: 212; see also Read and Welch, 1976). That represented an average of eight records per machine (in 1914 the same ratio was only six to one). During the first years, the catalogue was composed essentially of songs, popular ballads and marches played by anonymous musicians. The very limited duration of a recording (about 4 minutes) was well suited to this musical format. The public was the same as that which had played and sung royalty songs; it wanted to have access to sentimental music within the home itself. A Michigan farmer wrote to the magazine *The Phonogram* in September 1905: 'We have a Home phonograph . . . and we may, in view of the following, be excused this one luxury . . . we can't get to town (we are a family of eleven) and when the windows are covered with thick frost, we will listen to "Blue Danube" and thank Edison for his phonograph' (Gelatt, 1965: 161).

A second catalogue was compiled a little later from pieces of operas. This was the golden age of the opera and the great singers of the time enjoyed considerable renown. Moreover, voice recordings were technically far better than those of orchestras. The first of these recordings (1897–1902), intended for a very limited public were produced on a small scale by an Italian, Gianni Bettini, who lived in New York and Paris. Later, it was mainly Fred Gaisberg, Art Director at the Gramophone Company, who built up this catalogue, notably with recordings of the famous tenor Caruso in 1902. These records met with considerable success and Gelatt (1965: 115) estimates that when he died in 1921 Caruso had already earned 2 million dollars in royalties. At the end of 1902 the Gramophone Company launched its red label with 'the most enchanting selection of the world's greatest singers'. These new publishers, in contrast with the first publishers of popular music (notably Edison), embarked on a policy of promoting stars. Their catalogue of classics enabled them to enhance the new machine's value in the eyes of the middle classes (Ehrlich, 1976: 185–6). For the more cultured public, this new way of listening to music changed people's relationship with it. Compton Mackenzie, founder of the first English phonographic review of classical music (*The Gramophone*) wrote in this connection: 'one of the essential merits of the gramophone is its ability to provide the right music for the right mood . . . Brahms is able to seize our pettiest moods and direct them . . . [while Schubert] suits the twilight.'[31] Mackenzie proposed a cultured version of the sentimental consumption of music at home described by the Michigan farmer.

In 1914, on the eve of the Great War, a third catalogue appeared: jazz. Originally designed for a black public (race labels), this music was also to diffuse among the white population. The birth of jazz records was, moreover, accompanied by an extraordinary dance craze; the restraint of the Victorian ball was rejected in favour of freer dancing where young people emancipated themselves from adult supervision. 'The dance mania', wrote Gelatt (1965: 189), 'stimulated the record business as nothing else ever had.' This period was the start of contemporary variety music. It was also the start of the rapid obsolescence of fashions, when publishers' promotional activities increased and when hit tunes had more influence than catalogues.

Media for memories: collections and photographs

If we look again at the music which launched the phonograph, we see that the family collection of records, songs or operas was part of the Victorian family's relationship with the outside world. Just as records were a way of keeping bits of music, souvenirs of tunes or of popular songs listened to (or not), so also collectors kept souvenirs of journeys or of times past.

In the nineteenth century, the taste for collections – which in the preceding century had been limited to the aristocracy – spread to the upper middle classes. 'The art of collection', Walter Benjamin (1989: 222) tells us, 'is a practical form of remembering.' And indeed, if we are to believe Alain Corbin, this practice of collecting went hand-in-hand with the first forms of tourism and notably the Grand Tour that the European (mainly English) nobility and certain artists undertook in Italy in the eighteenth century. To maintain the permanence of memories some visitors, like Goethe, took an artist along with them; others had to be satisfied with buying engravings (Corbin, 1990: 59).

In the nineteenth century some of these collections became encyclopaedic. Thus Thiers, a French politician, wanted to be surrounded by 'an abridgment of the universe, that is to [have in] a space of about twenty-four square metres, Rome and Florence, Pompeii and Venice, Dresden and The Hague, the Vatican and the Escurial, the British Museum and the Hermitage . . .'. He had reduced copies made of the masterpieces of these great museums.[32] Thiers, like other great collectors, wanted to accumulate evidence of his travels and of the main periods in the history of art. Living in these large bourgeois halls, wrote Benjamin, 'was like taking refuge in the middle of a spider web that one had spun oneself and to which the events of universal history were hooked, scattered like the remains of insects emptied of their substance' (Benjamin, 1989:

234). The taste for collecting became an obsession in some people who lived like recluses among a heap of bric-à-brac.

These elitist practices slowly spread to the middle classes, with the fashion of the historical ornament. Edouard Foucaud noted in 1844 that 'thanks to progress in metallurgy, statuary works, reduced with exactitude, are sold very cheaply. Canova's *Three Graces* are installed in the drawing room, while Pradier's *The Maenad and the Faun* are honoured in the nuptial chamber.'[33]

Later, in the 1890s, collecting became more widespread and included post-cards and medals. The private sphere thus consisted of a collection of souvenirs; traces of the outside world were kept in the form of reduced copies of art works or symphonies. These souvenirs also concerned the family's own life: wedding bouquets, christening robes and the like (Corbin, 1987: 499–501) joined the curios brought back from travels, displayed in drawing-room cabinets.

This was also the era in which amateur photography appeared and made it possible to obtain souvenirs of both the outside world and family life. In 1888 George Eastman lent one of the first Kodak's to a shareholder in his company. 'It was the first time', Eastman tells us, 'he had ever carried a camera . . . I never saw anybody so pleased over a lot of pictures before. He apparently had never realized that it was a possible thing to take pictures himself.'[34] The public reacted with the same enthusiasm and, a few months later, Eastman could declare: 'If we go by current signs, it will be the most popular object of this type ever launched on the market.'

The 1890s were thus a watershed in the history of the use of photography. Until then it had served mainly to popularize portraits and was used mostly by professionals. Gisèle Freund notes that, around 1850, Marseilles had four or five painters of miniature portraits, producing about 200 pieces a year. A few years later, a group of 40–50 photographers produced 40–60,000 photographic portraits a year (Freund, 1974: 13). These portraits were realized according to specific norms. The client chose the décor and accessories in a catalogue. The photographer suggested a particular pose and then touched up the photo so that it would conform to the typical image of beauty of the time.

With photography, souvenirs became standardized (Pasquier, 1980: 88). The portraits of ancestors, preserved with care, were hung on the living room walls of the lower middle classes, constituting what Julien Green's Adrienne Mesurat calls 'the cemetery' (Green, 1986: 26). More generally, the photograph album enabled people to see what former generations looked like, thus strengthening the unity of the family group. But it also reflected subjects of interest to the family. Dominique Pasquier (1980: 97) notes that, in English upper middle-class families, the first pages of albums contained photos of the royal family and other celebrities, sold by specialized publishers.[35] The album of family souvenirs was thus a mixture of the public and private spheres. Yet photos which were a reminder of moments in family life were relatively rare. Caroline Chotard-Lioret, who worked on the archives of a bourgeois family, found three albums grouping together about 40 photos taken between 1860 and 1890 (Perrot, 1987: 188). In working-class families, photography was even less common. Often there was only one photo taken by a photographer on the occasion of a wedding or a departure to the front in 1914 (Martin-Fugier, 1987: 195).

With the diffusion of amateur photography, albums became fuller and contained evidence of the numerous scenes of family life. When they travelled for the first time, people could take samples of reality in the outside world. Thus, famous buildings and landscapes took their place in the home. Photography was no longer a substitute for portraits; it became a medium for capturing the past and the outside world.

Pictures born from real life

While photos became a medium for family souvenirs, they were also used by scientists to study the movements of animals. In the United States the photographer Muybridge created a series of successive photos in 1872 which enabled him to reconstitute a horse's gallop. The French physiologist Marey conducted similar experiments to study bird flight with his photographic rifle (1882) and then his chronophotograph (1888). Thus, the first studies on moving images, like those of Scott de Martinville on sound recordings, were undertaken with a scientific objective. But the idea of 'animating pictures' was also present in technical circles.

Edison, it seems, had thought of animating images after the invention of the phonograph. Then, spurred on by Muybridge's research which he discovered in 1888, he and his assistant Dickson took a renewed interest in the question and created a first prototype of the device 'which does for the eye what the phonograph does for the ear' (text of patent quoted by Clark, 1977). Moreover, the model of the phonograph remained present throughout his research. On the first model the photos were placed in a spiral, on a cylinder. In 1889 he used one of Eastman's flexible films and was perhaps inspired by Marey. In 1891 the 'kinetoscope', a device which made it possible to watch a film individually (with an eye-piece) was patented. Remembering his experience with the marketing of the phonograph, which he had initially opposed, Edison installed this new coin machine in shops – soon called 'penny arcades' – in 1894.

Like most of the inventions studied in this book, the majority of inventors worked in parallel without knowing one another. In France, during the same period, Louis Le Prince developed a cinecamera and projector, but he disappeared mysteriously on 16 September 1890 on the Dijon–Paris express train (Toulet, 1988: 34). Some historians have even suggested that he was murdered by Edison's agents! In any event, with this strange disappearance, the reality of the invention of the motion picture surpassed the fiction created later.

From 1894 some users of the kinetoscope in the US wanted to project images. Edison was against the idea. 'If we make this a screening machine' he said, 'it will spoil everything. We manufacture the present machine in large numbers and sell it at a good profit. If we bring out a screening machine, we'll sell maybe ten copies in the entire USA. And those ten copies will be enough for everyone to see the pictures, and that will be it. We mustn't kill the goose that lays the golden eggs (Ramsaye, 1964; Clark, 1977). In spite of Edison's refusal, several inventors were to work on the projection of images, such as Le Roy, Latham and Jenkins in the USA, and Anschütz, Skladanowsky and others in Germany. The image often lacked clarity, until the system developed by the Lumière brothers in France provided a solution to the problem. By means of a device adapted from the presser foot of a sewing machine, they obtained a jerky movement of the film which could coincide with the opening and closing of the shutter.

The Lumière brothers' technical contribution was small. Like Cooke or Berliner, they improved an invention, but above all they created a system of communication, a new medium. What distinguished the cinematograph from Edison's kinetoscope and also from Skladanowsky's bioskope, Anschütz's tachyscope or Latham's eidoloscope, was its content, a link with the public. It is highly significant that Lumière, who patented the cinematograph on 13 February 1895, waited until the end of the year before performing his famous projection at the Grand Café in Paris. In the meantime he built up a stock of film, trained operators and, most importantly, made about a hundred films (Sadoul, 1973: 277).

Lumière's experience as a photographer and artist helped him to imagine the spectacular effect which could be obtained by recording scenes from daily public or private life. Whereas Edison's films had been made without any décor, with white silhouettes against a black background in the tradition of the first systems of animated drawings (zootrope, praxinoscope etc.), Lumière's films were made outside and represented movement. Whether the subject was an official procession, workers leaving a factory or the arrival of a train, people or objects moved from the back of the screen into the foreground. This aesthetic choice, said Maxime Gorki (who was present at one of these first projections) caused 'the picture to be born from life'.[36] The same impression was shared by numerous contemporaries. For some historians of the cinema, Lumière's films constituted the mould from which the seventh art was to develop. Even though they were documentaries, they contained the first seeds of cinematographic narration (Deutelbaum, 1979; Cosandey, 1984).

Lumière's strength, compared to Edison, was that he proposed a system articulating vehicle and content. Yet his system remained unstable as long as a way of marketing it had not been defined. At the start of the cinema, French producers sold their films to travelling shows which screened them. Numerous drawbacks were, however, inherent in this option: the producer's earnings were unrelated to the film's success; the producer had no information on the circulation of copies; some copies were resold to a second circuit of travelling shows; finally, film producers had no feedback on the public's reaction.

In about 1905, Charles Pathé – like Edison, a publisher of phonographic cylinders and of films – wanted to create his own projection halls. His strategy was the classic one of a corporation wanting control downstream, but it also represented the wish to structure what was to become cinematographic operation. Independent operators had also appeared next to Pathé or Gaumont halls. To create some unity between the different cinema-related professions, Pathé imposed a system of film rental from 1907 (Sadoul, 1973, vol. 2: 230–1). Throughout the exploitation of a film, money flowed upstream to the producers, while information was circulated between producers and operators. These broad marketing principles are still relevant to the cinema industry today.

Thus, a medium effectively appears as having three components: a vehicle, content, and a marketing device not only to commercialize the culture but also as a basis for the contract linking the different partners. This contract is essential since a medium requires the articulation within a single system of several economic actors; if this system of cooperation is inadequate, the new medium cannot take off.

Just as Edison had renounced his vision of the phonograph and had devoted himself to the production of cylinders, so he abandoned his kineto-scope very quickly in favour of the cinema. He took full advantage of the strategic position his patents gave him and tried to create a monopoly of cin-ematographic production and film development. After a number of conflicts, he established an oligopolistic structure (the Motion Picture Patent Company) with other major producers and support from Eastman who was the only American manufacturer of cinematographic raw film. Each pro-ducer and each cinema manager undertook to pay a royalty to Edison. This patent war mobilized a good deal of energy among American cinema devel-opers.

In contrast to America, the cinema in France developed without any legal obstacles and was controlled by a number of different people (Lumière, Méliès, Pathé, Gaumont, etc.). From their diverse conceptions, French cin-ema was born and dominated world production until the First World War. In the United States, the most innovative developments were the work of people who were independent of the Edison corporation and who, moreover, finally achieved its dissolution. It was from their ranks that Hollywood's major play-ers were to emerge.

To conclude this short presentation of the birth of the cinematograph, let us look again at the aims of its inventors. Edison tried for a long time to syn-chronize sound and images. He made a number of attempts which were all more or less unsuccessful. In 1891 he wrote: 'When I have completely finished the realization of this invention . . . a spectator sitting at home in his library, linked to a theatre by means of electricity, will be able to see the actors on a screen without losing anything they say' (quoted in IRIS, 1978: 2, 82). Such projects were beyond the technological means available at the time and the effective realization of sound films was to be achieved by telecommunications engineers. It was the radioelectricians of RCA and AT&T, working independently, who were to develop a procedure for sound films in the 1920s.

Edison never interrupted his activities of entrepreneur to realize his dream of the 'total show'. Lumière, by contrast, soon abandoned exploitation of the cinema and returned to his laboratory. He oriented his research to the big screen, colour and relief. For, as André Bazin (1969: 25) says,

> the main myth guiding the invention of the cinema was the conclusion of that which dominated all techniques of mechanical reproduction of reality born in the nineteenth century, from photography to the phonograph. It was the myth of total realism, of a recreation of the world in its own image . . . if the cinema in its infancy did not have all the attributes of the total cinema of tomorrow, this was no fault of its own, and was only because its fairies were technically impotent to give them to it even though they wanted to.

The last years of the nineteenth century were a watershed in the evolution of life-styles. For the first time industrial production turned towards the household consumer market which until then had been supplied by craft production. The communication sector was one of the main areas of this change. In the 1880s, newspapers were selling hundreds of thousands of copies. In the musical field, the production of pianos began to be industrialized. Listening to music at home was to become, in the following decade, the first mass market for a communication machine – the phonograph. The end of the nineteenth century also witnessed a transformation in the communication devices for which a use had been found in the professional world; the photographic camera and, as we shall see in Chapter 5, the telephone were to enter family life.

Thus, in a single century, uses of communication were radically altered. They were first intended for the state, then for the capitalist market and, finally, for the family. Moreover, from the middle of the nineteenth century, a transformation in the family could be observed. While the change from extended families to mononuclear families took place progressively from the eighteenth century onwards, the evolution of the family sphere and the new value given to the home were to emerge later and to constitute the niche for new uses of communication. The first media which found their public in the home were also propagandists of the new life-style. Thus, in 1892 the *Ladies' Home Journal*, a monthly magazine which was one of the main ideological vehicles for the Victorian family model, sold 700,000 copies, or four times more than the largest New York daily (Carman et al., 1952: 374).

Withdrawal into the family did not mean a lack of interest in the outside world. A new collective show was born during this period: the cinematograph.[37] Furthermore, the public and private spheres were articulated in a new way. The theme which appeared at the time in the work of playwrights such as Chekhov or Ibsen accounted for the new mode of communication between the family sphere and the outside world. It was the first time in theatre that the show was focused on the home, but the characters nevertheless had their eyes glued to the windows, waiting impatiently for news from outside.[38] When the theatre was behind closed doors, it opened a window onto the world.

Notes

1 Nicéphore Niepce, 'Notice sur l'héliographie' (1830) in Niepce and Fouque (1841: 167); reprinted, Jean-Michel Place, Paris, 1987.

2 Niepce's first heliographic pictures were lost. The oldest known document dates from 1826; it is sometimes wrongly considered to be the first photograph. The word 'photograph' was first used by Charles Wheatstone (the inventor of the telegraph) on 1 February 1839.

3 Letter from Niepce to Aiton on 16 October 1827 in Jay (1988).

4 Memorandum of 8 December 1827 in Niepce and Fouque (1841: 151).

5 Note of 13 March 1830 in Niepce and Fouque (1841: 162).

6 From the Greek *kalos*, meaning beautiful.

7 Preamble to the law presented by the Minister of the Interior, 15 June 1839.

8 François Arago, report presented to the Chamber of Deputies, 3 July 1839. Another version of this text was presented to the *Académie des sciences* on 19 August 1839.

9 Gay-Lussac, report presented in the Chamber of Deputies session on 30 July 1839.

10 *Le Moniteur universel*, 18 August 1794.

11 André Jammes, 'L'événement Arago' in Frizot et al. (1989: 24).

12 F. Nadar, 'Daguerrotype acoustique', in *Le Musée franco-anglais*, 185, quoted by Perriault (1981: 133).

13 F. Nadar, *Les Mémoires du Géant*, 1864, quoted by Perriault (1981: 133).

14 This idea was also put forward by Tom Hodd in the *Comic Annual* of 1839: 'In this century in which paper that copies visible objects has been invented, is there no future Niepce, Daguerre, Herschel or Fox Talbot to find a kind of paper to echo what it hears?', quoted by Clark (1977).

15 In contrast, such an author as J. Perriault (1981) considers that 'the premature publication of French work in this field caused the Americans to speed up their research.' The American historian of the phonograph, Roland Gelatt (1965), is less affirmative than Perriault, but he does think that Edison may well have read the article in *La Semaine du clergé*.

16 *North American Review*, June 1878, quoted by Clark (1977).

17 Edison, *The Phonograph*, January 1891, quoted by Gelatt (1965: 45).

18 Text of Berliner's patent no. 372.786 of 4 May 1887, quoted by Charbon (1989).

19 According to Jean Cazenoble, Edison's phonograph also resembled Scott's 'phonautograph'. The American inventor was 'content' to replace the Frenchman's roll of paper covered with lamp black by tin foil. Cros also knew of Scott's research (Cazenoble, preface to Clark, 1977).

20 Maurice Agulhon's (1988) study on sociability and working-class leisure activities in France during the first half of the nineteenth century shows that the model of the home was not a common notion. Overcrowding in slums in the nineteenth century was such that sociability among the men was organized around the wine merchants, and more exceptionally family sociability took place at suburban cafés. The counter-model imagined in the middle of the century, by both the Fourierists and bourgeois philanthropists, was that of a group of workers, a 'cabaret with the comfort yet without the promiscuity' (Agulhon, 1988: 70, 90).

21 George Dodd, 'Days at the factories' (1843), quoted by Mackerness (1964: 172).

22 Jacques Attali (1977: 149) also notes that 'the middle classes, not being able to afford an orchestra at home, bought a piano for their children.'

23 Publication of music scores also developed in France. In 1891, for example, the weekly *Gil Blas, illustré* was created. Each issue contained the words and music of a song (Attali, 1977: 149).

24 *New-Quarterly Musical Review*, November 1895, quoted by Mackerness (1964: 230).

25 In 1890, the USA accounted for 35 per cent of world production; in 1910, this figure had risen to almost 60 per cent (Ehrlich, 1975).

26 Baltimore, Boston, Chicago, Cincinnati, Cleveland, Detroit, Los Angeles, Minneapolis, Philadelphia, Pittsburgh, Saint Louis, San Francisco (Mueller, 1951).

27 Information from the Bureau of the Census.

28 Quoted from an article in the magazine *Country Life* 'The phonograph as a decorative element in the home' (Gelatt, 1965: 191).

29 See the catalogue of the reference library of the Fortuny Palace (Venice): *Archeofon*, Milan Electa, 1989.

30 In this paragraph I use the word phonograph to denote all sound machines, except when I contrast it to the gramophone (disc machine) like here; in this case I am referring only to the cylinder machine.

31 Compton Mackenzie, *Gramophone*, I, no. 4 (1923), quoted by Le Mahieu (1982: 377).

32 Charles Blanc, *Le Cabinet de M. Thiers*, Paris, 1871, quoted by Benjamin (1989: 226).

33 Edouard Foucaud, *Paris inventeur, physiologie de l'industrie française*, Paris, 1844, quoted by Benjamin (1989: 241).

34 Letter by George Eastman of 6 July 1888, quoted by Jenkins (1975: 16).

35 In 1867, after Prince Albert's death, 70,000 portrait cards were sold. Some 300,000 portraits of the Princess of Wales, carrying her daughter, were sold.

36 Maxime Gorki, article of 4 July 1896, quoted by Toulet (1988: 137).

37 I will present practices related to cinema consumption in Chapter 9.

38 I have borrowed this idea from Williams (1974: 27).

References

Agulhon M. (1988) *Histoire vagabonde*, vol. 1, Gallimard, Paris.

Attali J. (1977) *Bruits. Essai sur l'économie politique de la musique*, PUF, Paris.

Bazin A. (1969) *Qu'est-ce que le cinéma?*, vol. 1: *Ontologie et langage*, Cerf, Paris.

Benjamin W. (1989) *Paris, capitale du XIXe siècle. Le livre des passages*, Cerf, Paris.

Buxton D. (1985) *Le Rock, star-système et société de consommation*, La Pensée sauvage, Grenoble.

Carman H.J., Syrett H.C. and Wishy B.W. (1952) *A History of the American People*, vol. 2: *Since 1865*, Alfred A. Knopf, New York.

Charbon P. (1989) 'Naissance du transport et de la conservation du son: du téléphone à la machine parlante', in *De fil en aiguille, Charles Cros et les autres*, Bibliothèque nationale de Paris.

Charbon P. (1991)'La première invention d'Edison', *Réseaux*, no. 49, CNET, Issy.

Clark R.W. (1977) *Edison: the Man who Made the Future*, G. Rainbird Ltd, London.

Colson R. (1898) *Original Memoirs of the Creators of Photography*, Editions G. Carré, C. Naud, Paris.

Coontz S. (1988) *The Social Origins of Private Life: a History of American Families (1600-1900)*, Verso, New York.

Corbin A. (1987) 'Le secret de l'individu', in P. Aries and G. Duby (eds), *Histoire de la vie privée*, vol. 4, Le Seuil, Paris.

Corbin A. (1990) *Le Territoire du vide*, Flammarion, Paris.

Cosandey R. (1984) 'Revoir Lumière', *IRIS*, vol. 2, no. 1, Analeph, Paris.

Deutelbaum M. (1979) 'Structural patterning in the Lumière films', *Wide Angle*, vol. 3, no. 1.

Ehrlich C. (1975) *Social Emulation and Industrial Progress: the Victorian Piano*, Queen's University, Belfast, inaugural lecture, February.

Ehrlich C. (1976) *The Piano: a History*, J.M. Dent and Sons, London.

Figuier L. (1888) *La Photographie*, vol. III of *Merveilles de la science*. Reprinted by Lafitte Reprints, Marseilles, 1983.

Figuier L. (1889) 'Le pavillon des téléphones' in *L'Exposition des Paris de 1889*, 9 October, no. 42.

Freund G. (1974) *Photographie et société*, Le Seuil, Paris.

Frizot M., Jammes A., Jay P. and Gautrand J-C. (1989) *1839, La Photographie révélée*, Centre national de la photographie, Paris.

Furnas J.C. (1969) *The Americans: a Social History of the United States*, B.P. Putnam's Sons, New York.

Gaisberg F. (1946) *Music on Record*, Robert Hale, London.

Gelatt R. (1965) *The Fabulous Phonograph: from Edison to Stereo*, Appleton-Century, New York.

Green J. (1986) *Adrienne Mesurat*, Le Seuil, Paris.

Hall C. (1987) 'Sweet home', in P. Aries and G. Duby (eds), *Histoire de la vie privée*, vol. 4, Le Seuil, Paris.

Hobart M. (1981) 'The political economy of bop', *Media Culture and Society*, no. 3, Academic Press, London.

IRIS (1978) *Communications et société. Elements d'analyse 1, 2*, Université Paris–Dauphine.

Jay P. (1988) *Niepce, Genèse d'une invention*, Société des amis du musée Niepce, Chalon-sur-Saône.

Jenkins R.V. (1975) 'Technology and the market: George Eastman and the origins of mass amateur photography', *Technology and Culture*, vol. 16.

Lardner Dr. (1867) *The Electric Telegraph*, James Walton, London.

Le Mahieu D.L. (1982) 'The gramophone: recorded music and the cultivated mind in Britain between the wars', in *Technology and Culture*, vol. 23, no. 3, July.

Mackerness E.D. (1964) *A Social History of English Music*, Routledge and Kegan Paul, London.

Martin-Fugier A. (1987) 'Les rites de la vie privée bourgeoise', in P. Aries and G. Duby (eds), *Histoire de la vie privée*, vol. 4, Le Seuil, Paris.

Mueller J. (1951) *The American Symphony Orchestra: a Social History of Musical Taste*, Indiana University Press, Bloomington, Ind.

Niepce I. and Fouque V. (1841) *Nicéphore Niepce, sa vie, ses essais et ses travaux*, Paris.

Pasquier D. (1980) 'Lewis Caroll, photographe victorien: essai de sociologie historique', unpublished sociology thesis, EHESS, Paris.

Perriault J. (1981) *Mémoires de l'ombre et du son, une archéologie de l'audiovisuel*, Flammarion, Paris.

Perrot M. (1987) 'La vie de famille', in P. Aries and G. Duby (eds), *Histoire de la vie privée*, vol. 4, Le Seuil, Paris.

Ramsaye T. (1964) *A Million and One Night: a History of the Motion Picture*, Simon and Schuster, New York.

Read O. and Welch W. (1976) *From Tin Foil to Stereo: Evolution of the Phonograph*, Bobbs Merril, New York.

Roberts R. (1971) *The Classic Sum*, Manchester University Press, Manchester.

Sadoul G. (1973) *Histoire générale du cinéma*, 2 vols, Denoël, Paris.

Sennett R. (1970) *Families against the City: Middle Class Homes of Industrial Chicago 1872-1890*, Harvard University Press, Cambridge, Mass.

Shorter E. (1975) *The Making of the Modern Family*, Basic Books, New York.

Toulet E. (1988) *Cinématographe invention du siècle*, Gallimard, Paris.

Warner S.B. (1968) *The Private City: Philadelphia in Three Periods of its Growth*, University of Pennsylvania Press, Philadelphia.

Williams R. (1974) *Television, Technology and Cultural Form*, Fontana-Collins, London.

Wright G. (1981) *Building the Dream: a Social History of Housing in America*, Pantheon Books, New York.

5

From Trading in Goods to Trading in Souls: the Telephone

Efforts to establish the paternity of an invention – a focal point in numerous popular histories of technology – derive from the idea that a technological system has only one true inventor. All the others are presumed to be imposters or less brilliant minds. The researcher's role is then to investigate this case for the courts of history. He or she has to choose, among the numerous putative fathers of a technology, the real inventor. Care must be taken to ensure that the traditionally recognized inventor had no precursor, that he or she did not borrow the main idea for the new device from a brilliant but unknown forerunner. Misunderstood geniuses, like accursed poets, have often aroused passionate interest; the historian is in a position to rehabilitate them.

Communicating speech by electricity

If we look at the example of the telephone, we are faced with the question: who invented it? Alexander Graham Bell or Elisha Gray? By an amazing coincidence, they both applied for a patent in Washington on the same day, 14 February 1876. The official history of the telephone has retained Bell's name but there is no certainty that Gray did not have the idea first (Hounshell, 1975). It may even have been Edison, since some contemporaries considered that in 1875 he had already imagined a similar system (Jehl, 1937: 108).[1] Furthermore, we rarely hear about Antonio Meucci, the Italian immigrant to the USA who conducted his first experiments in Havana in the 1850s and filed a patent in the United States in 1871 (von Klinckowstroem, 1967: 229).

Looking back a little further we find Philippe Reis, a German teacher who presented his device to the Frankfurt Society of Physicists in 1861. Often qualified as a musical telephone, his instrument could also transmit speech (von Klinckowstroem, 1967: 228). In France, Charles Bourseul, a telegraph technician, presented a report to the *Académie des sciences* in 1854 and wrote in *L'Illustration*: 'I wondered whether speech itself could not be transmitted by electricity . . . It is feasible; this is how . . .'; and he described the principle of the transmission of sound vibrations by electricity.[2] Could Bourseul, therefore, be considered as the inventor of the telephone? No, since no certainty exists on the matter. Traces can be found even further back of techniques of long-distance conversations. For example, the German Huth wrote a report in

1796 on 'use of the sound tube in telegraphy', which he called a telephone (Libois, 1983: 34). I have already mentioned the English physicist Robert Hooke who, in 1667, studied the transmission of sound by means of a taut string. In fact, the list seems endless, which leads us to wonder about the relevance of the question: 'who was the inventor?'

Significantly, there were connections between all these inventors. Gray, Bell and Edison all knew of Reis's invention.[3] A copy of his device was taken back to the US by Joseph Henry of the Smithsonian Institute and Bell saw it when he visited the Institute in 1875 (Jehl, 1937: 109). In Germany, Bourseul's work became known when it was described in an article published on 28 September 1854 in the *Didaskalia*, a supplement to the *Frankfurter Journal*. One German historian considers, however, that Reis knew nothing of Bourseul's research, although he finds it unlikely that Bell was unaware of it.[4] In his speech to the American Science and Arts Academy on 10 May 1876 (three months after registering his patent), Bell quoted about 30 articles from American, English and French journals concerning 'the acoustic effects of magnetic processes', which included Reis's research but not that of Bourseul (Bell, 1877; Shiers, 1977).

When looking at the social construction of a technology, we should also examine, in order to compare inventions, whether they reached the same stage of maturity. Technical work on the telephone was based not only on a vision of a device and the realization of a prototype, but also on the search for quality and reliability. Huth imagined long-distance sound communication and gave it a name. Hooke and Bourseul laid down the technical principles of the long-distance transmission of sound, but within the framework of two different paradigms: that of the vibration of a string in one case and that of electricity in the other. Reis and Meucci realized the first telephone prototypes. Finally, while Gray and Bell filed their applications for a patent on the same day, Gray's request was only temporary (what is called a *caveat*) and he never proposed a final text. Bell was, in fact, the first, not to present a prototype, but to develop it and to market point-to-point telephonic links, a year after taking out a patent.

The debate on who invented the telephone is thus an endless one. However, as long as a reliable and reproducible object had not been produced, the invention remained incomplete. Just as the outline of a novel or a cinematographic synopsis does not constitute a book or a film, so a technical object does not truly exist until it can function in real life and be reproduced.

Before a device such as the telephone could be invented, some preliminary knowledge of the relationship between sound and electromagnetism was required. In 1837 the American physicist Charles Page discovered that a rod which was magnetized and de-magnetized in very quick succession could emit sounds, and that these sounds were related to the number of charges that provoked them (du Moncel, 1887: 3). Page's work was continued by Rive and Wertheim in Geneva and Paris and was known to Reis, Gray and Bell (Bell, 1877: 1–2; Gray, 1878: 6; von Klinckowstroem, 1967: 227). Thus, they knew that it was possible to transform sounds into electromagnetic vibrations, transport them on an electric wire and re-transform them on the receiving end into audible sounds.

This mobilization of scientific knowledge to attain a technical goal was part of a context in which the utopia of the telephone had already begun to circulate. In 1863, in his account of Reis's experiments, H. de Parville stated: 'Speech will be transmitted like thoughts, like writing. A sovereign will be able to command his armies from one end of Europe to the other.'[5] Whereas the French conceived of the telephone as an instrument of power, the English saw it more as a commercial tool. On the occasion of a dinner given in Morse's honour in 1868, Edward Thornton, a British cabinet minister, declared: 'I hope to see technological progress one day, which will make it possible to transmit oral conversations by transatlantic cable. We will thus be able to witness traders on this side of the ocean discussing business instantaneously with their correspondents on the other side' (Jehl, 1937: 102–3).

Not everyone shared this utopian vision of the telephone. A Boston newspaper wrote in 1865 about a man who was arrested for fraud because he was trying to collect funds to set up a telephone company. It added: 'Well-informed people know that it is impossible to transmit the human voice by wire, and even when it does become possible, it will be of no interest' (Jehl, 1937: 101). Telegraphists were of the same opinion. In 1874 the newspaper *Telegrapher* recalled 'the old joke that used to be current in telegraphic circles that the direct talking plan was once tried between New York and Philadelphia, but had to be given up on account of the Philadelphia operator's breath smelling too strongly of bad whiskey!' (Hounshell, 1975). The two fundamental elements in the invention of the telephone were scientific knowledge (even rudimentary) of the possibilities of transforming sound and electricity, and participation in the telephone utopia. But inventors also had to overcome technical difficulties and the resistance, even the refusal, of sceptics who had no faith in their projects.

We have seen in the cases of the telegraph and the motion picture that these inventions were plural, the sum of a series of micro-inventions. While it is important to identify their genealogies in order to understand how the technologies circulated and were appropriated, this has to be done with the utmost rigour so as not to reach false conclusions. The circulation of ideas and prototypes in no way precluded the existence of parallel circuits which never met or recognized one another. Bell and Gray, who were probably unaware of Meucci's work, conducted their research concurrently.

Gray, like Edison and Bell, worked on multiplex telegraphy (the possibility of transmitting several messages on the same telegraphic wire). During their work Gray and Bell, and probably Edison too, discovered the possibility of transmitting the human voice. However Gray, a technical expert recognized by the telegraph companies, favoured the multiplex telegraph. In contrast Bell, who like Charles Cros was devoted to teaching the deaf to speak, was far more interested in the question of communication by speech. Despite pressure from his sponsors who were persuaded that multiplex telegraphy was a potential future market, he chose the telephone (Hounshell, 1975).

Telegraphists saw in the telephone nothing more than a device to facilitate their work. Thus Alfred Chandler, one of Western Union's managers at the time, saw the telephone as the first stage towards the elimination of handling instruments. He was sure that operators would soon transmit the sound of their own voice by wire and would talk to one another instead of using the telegraph (Hounshell, 1975). For telegraphists, long-distance communication could not be interpersonal; it had to be mediated by human operators who would have the know-how for talking on a telephone.

Bell, by contrast, imagined making the telephone an 'instrument of long-distance communication without any intermediary'. The first advertisement for his new device claimed:

– No skilled operator is required; direct communication may be had by speech without the intervention of a third person;
– The communication is much more rapid [than by telegraph], the average number of words transmitted in a minute by the Morse sounder being from fifteen to twenty, by telephone from one to two hundred. (Casson, 1910: 53–4)

He thus had in mind competing with the telegraph by means of a more efficient instrument to which users had direct access. Faced with the telegraphists' refusal to take an interest in his device,[6] he set up his own operating company. In this venture he was backed by his sponsors and, in particular, Hubbard, an eminent Bostonian whose daughter he had married (after having taught her, for she was deaf and dumb).

In short, Bell, as opposed to Reis, had started his research by working on the telegraph and could therefore deploy technical and practical know-how acquired in that field. Like Gray and Edison, he discovered the possibility of transmitting speech purely by chance during his research. His personal interest in the matter (Reis had the same interest, since he had built an artificial ear) led him, unlike Gray, to opt for developing the telephone rather than the multiplex telegraph. Moreover, unlike telegraphists like Chandler, he imagined use of the telephone without an intermediary, intended for a clientèle similar to that of the telegraph. Finally, this articulation of interests might never have led to anything had Bell not received family capital to launch his own business.

Telephone calls

The business telephone

In terms of usage the telegraph was, for a long time, a sort of 'electrical postal service', used solely for sending messages. In the 1860s it started for the first time to be used for conversations and Bell was to take full advantage of this new trend. Lardner wrote in 1866, with respect to the telegraph:

It often happens that a person desires to 'converse' with another 400 or 500 miles off. An hour is appointed to meet in the respective offices, and they converse through the operator. Cases may be mentioned of steamboats being sold over the wires – the one party being in Pittsburg, the other in Cincinnati. (Lardner, 1867: 242)

In Philadelphia in 1867, the first telegraph exchange allowing for the switching of private lines was set up. Its users were mainly the large banks in town, of which there were 50 in 1872 (Kingsbury, 1972: 84–5). An identical network also intended for banks was built in New York in 1869. Five years later a new telegraph switching network for the use of lawyers appeared (Tarr, 1987: 46). Thus, even before the birth of the telephone, the trend in the commercial and financial spheres was moving from telegraphic messages to telegraphic conversation. It was in this context that the first telephone network, linking five bankers, was built in Boston in May 1877 (Casson, 1910: 53–4). The telephone offered the same possibilities as the telegraph, but with greater speed and efficiency.

Like the telegraph, use of the telephone at the end of the nineteenth century was essentially professional. Western Union, which at the time virtually monopolized the telegraph, had gauged the market accurately. An agreement signed with Bell in November 1879[7] recognized the precedence of his telephone patents and limited the use of his system to 'personal conversations'. The telephone was 'not to be used for the transmission of general business messages, market quotations, or news for sale or publication in competition with the business of Western Union' (Tarr, 1987: 51). This clause of the contract was not, however, to be respected and it was indeed in the commercial domain that the telephone was to find its first market.

An analysis by Sidney Aronson of the telephone directories of the time has revealed that among the 300 lines in Pittsburg in 1879, 294 belonged to professionals. The remaining six were used by entrepreneurs to communicate between their homes and their factories. At Pawtucket (Rhode Island) in 1897, only 11 per cent of the lines were for residential use. We can conclude, like Aronson (1977: 27–8), that 'the early history of telephone usage, then, is largely the story of how commercial and professional communities adopted the new means of communication.'

We have seen that the banking community was the first to be concerned. At the start of the century, George Perkins of Morgan Bank had the reputation of being able to raise 20 millions in 20 minutes. He would prepare a list of names of potential investors and contact them as quickly as the operator could get them on the line (Casson, 1910: 204). The stock exchange also made extensive use of this new instrument, as it had done with the telegraph.[8] At the start of the century, 640 telephone booths in Wall Street provided direct contact with stockbrokers. A single company of brokers received up to 100,000 telephone calls a year.[9] In England, in 1911, a private network with 400 subscribers replaced a telegraphic network between the stock exchange and brokers (Baldwin, 1925: 265–6).

The development of the telephone encountered a difficulty due to it being a network device. 'It is not at all like a piano or a talking machine, which has a separate existence', wrote the historian Herbert Casson. 'It is useful only in proportion to the number of other telephones it reaches' (Casson, 1910: 248). But this connection was not only physical, it was also social, which explains why at the beginning specific professions were dominant users of the network.

Ithiel de Sola Pool notes that doctors accounted for a large proportion of subscribers in New England, while in London many lawyers could be found among the first users (de Sola Pool, 1977: 142).

The telephone gradually linked different sectors of economic activity and became an instrument of intersectorial exchange, to use a contemporary economic expression. In 1910, Herbert Casson wrote: 'It is nothing less than the high-speed tool of civilization, gearing up the whole mechanism to more effective social service. *It is the symbol of national efficiency and cooperation*' (Casson, 1910: 238, his italic). We find in his writing, like that of Théodore Vail, AT&T president, the same prophetic tones as those of the Saint-Simonians concerning the railways. The interest of traders and industrialists in the telephone was manifested in the number of demands by English chambers of commerce which, between 1888 and 1911, repeatedly asked for a large British telephone network (Perry, 1977: 80).

In France, the first uses of the telephone were no different. Catherine Bertho reveals the identity of the first 48 Parisian subscribers (connected in 1879): banks, stockbrokers, telegraph and telephone industrialists, newspapers (Bertho, 1986: 82). Chantal de Gournay's work on the French network in 1884 shows that telephone lines were mainly present in the business and industrial areas of Paris and its suburbs. This situation was to evolve very slowly. After a similar analysis of Paris in 1922, de Gournay (1994: 227) concludes that: 'almost a half century after its invention the telephone remained a tool reserved essentially for profession use.'

The private telephone

Although professional use of the telephone prevailed during the nineteenth century, the first signs of private use started to appear within the upper classes. In 1846, *Punch* magazine wrote that the telegraph 'should be introduced not only into the office but into the domestic circle'.[10] In 1856 Baron de Rothschild had a private telegraph line installed to serve his chateau at Ferrières (Bertho, 1981: 97). Twenty years later, with the development of the autographic telegraph (allowing the transmission of hand-written documents), some American entrepreneurs imagined installing such a machine in all homes (Aronson, 1977: 17). But private use of the telegraph had already started to appear in the 1860s, initially in public places. About a dozen London clubs received a summary of parliamentary debates every half hour, so that MPs could follow them while dining with friends. The same summaries were also displayed in the foyer of the Opera (Lardner, 1867: 238–9). Hence, the use of communication had made it possible to do two things at once.

In the 1870s a telegraphic call service was created in New York by the American District Telegraph Company (ADT). By turning a handle, users could send a signal to a central exchange. The number of turns indicated the service requested: messenger, police, fire brigade, doctor etc. Although it was slow in getting off the ground, the service had 12,000 subscribers in 1885, 900 messengers and 52 offices, and received 6,000 calls a day. Rival companies soon appeared and in the same year there was a total of 30,000 subscribers in New York – a significant figure considering that, during the same period, the telephone network in the United States as a whole had only 150,000 subscribers. This telegraphic call service thus constituted the first telecommunications service for the public at large.[11] Joël Tarr, who has found traces of the (now forgotten) service (1987: 49–50), also tells us that a complete telegraphic service was installed in 1874 at private homes in Bridgeport (Connecticut). A switching device allowed for 'telegraphic conversations' between subscribers. The system was to be transformed in 1877 into a telephone network.

The fledgling telephone found in these first private telegraphic services a demand which it could satisfy. In 1878, the Bell Telephone Company instructed its agents to 'use their best efforts for the introduction of the Telephone into the district Telegraph system' (Tarr, 1987: 51). At the start of the previous year, Bell had installed the first permanent telephone line between the workshop of a certain Williams in Boston and his home in the suburbs (Casson, 1910: 53). Kate Field, in a survey in the USA in 1878, estimated that 500 homes in New England were equipped with the telephone (Field, 1878: 12). However, most of these lines served professional purposes. J.A. Moyer (1977: 351) notes that in the Boston 1887 telephone directory a user could mention, alongside his profession, the fact that the telephone was installed at his residence. In France, in the 1890s, the holiday homes of the Parisian upper classes along the valley of the Seine (Saint-Germain, Le Vésinet etc.) and the Marne (Saint-Maur, La Varenne etc.) were connected to the network. Chantal de Gournay (1994) also notes that towns on the Normandy coast and the Riviera were connected at a very early stage. In the United States, vacation areas seem to have been linked up much later. The authors of the US Special Census of Telephones in 1907 reported the recent development of the telephone in summer resort districts, thus making it possible for 'businessmen to leave their offices for several days at a time and yet keep in close touch with their offices' (quoted in Aronson, 1977: 29).

A first model of private telephone usage thus appeared – that of ubiquity. A businessman was both in his office and in his holiday home with his family. 'Gentlemen in their libraries [gave] orders to clerks in their offices' (Field, 1878: 12). In France the first telephone directories gave instructions on the use of this new communication tool. 'For company directors' wrote Catherine Bertho 'it means being obeyed at the click of a finger or the wink of an eye . . . for housewives, who are company directors in their own way, it means extending the staff of servants, being able to reach obsequious suppliers immediately' (Bertho, 1981: 240). The Bell licensee in Titusville, USA, also described uses of the telephone in a circular: 'In domestic life, the telephone can put the user in instant communication with the grocer, butcher, baker' (Aronson, 1977: 29).

In both the domestic and professional spheres, the telephone served to transmit orders.[12] It was therefore hardly surprising that it spread rapidly in hotels. At the start of the century, the top hundred New York hotels had 21,000 telephones (more than in Spain) and made 6 million calls a year. The Waldorf-Astoria alone, with its 1,100 telephones, made more than 3,000 calls on Christmas Eve to the various luxury shops in the city (Casson, 1910: 199–200). This use of the telephone was similar to that of the telegraph. In 1878 a New Haven brochure described it aptly in the sentence: 'Your wife may order your dinner, a hack, your family physician, etc.' (Fischer, 1988: 38). It was to remain dominant for a long time within domestic telephony.

Nevertheless, at the start of the twentieth century, practices started to diversify. A survey carried out in 1909 by a Seattle operator on a sample of residential telephone conversations gave the following figures: 20 per cent orders for goods, 20 per cent calls from home to the office, 15 per cent invitations, 30 per cent chatting (Fischer, 1988: 38).

The latter function was considered by the operator as 'useless', a point of view shared by most telephone companies. In the Nebraska 1914 directory the following instruction appeared: 'Business or long distance calls shall at all times have preference over social talk.' In Claude S. Fischer's (1988) survey on telephone advertisements before the First World War, the two main apparent uses were professional communication and household management. Interpersonal sociability was rarely mentioned. In the 1920s, the theme appeared more often, but was generally associated with long-distance calls. It was only in the 1930s that the theme of family and friendly communication, of 'telephonic visits' became evident in advertisements.

Telephone operators, like the first promoters of the phonograph, thought first of the business market. When, in the latter years of the nineteenth century, they started taking an interest in the domestic/family market, they still conceived of telephone usage on the same model, that of the sending of orders and invitations, and not as a means of sociability.

Telephone visits

The rural telephone

It was in the agricultural world that the articulation between the two types of telephone usage first appeared. The 1907 American telephone census (Casson, 1910: 199–200) recorded 2 million farmers equipped with telephones, or a quarter of all farms.[13] Some states in the heart of the US were almost totally equipped, like Iowa where 73 per cent of the farms were linked to the network (Aronson, 1971: 164). The primary use seemed to be of a professional order: information on prices, weather forecasts and so forth. Farmers in the Mid-West were already in favour of an agricultural sector functioning on an industrial and international scale. They therefore needed information of stock market prices of grains in Chicago. Use of the telephone was thus closely related to that of the telegraph.

Herbert Casson quotes numerous anecdotes which show the central role of the telephone in the agricultural information system. For example, the

Colorado fruit harvest in 1909 was saved from frost thanks to the telephone. In certain farming states, a political slogan appeared: 'Good roads and the telephone.' In many areas considered unprofitable by the phone companies, groups of farmers installed a network in which several farms often shared the same line. Thus the telephone became part of a local identity, a community feeling. The operator on the exchange who found him or herself at the heart of a communication network was a source of information on local events. During a doctor's rounds the operator would inform him of calls from his patients. The telephone company's information role came to be taken so much for granted that in 1912 the Southern Telephone Company was sued after a local operator had failed to contact the doctor before his patient died![14]

But use of the rural telephone was not linked only to economic activity or to emergency situations. The 1907 Census of Telephones argued that: 'a sense of community life is impossible without this ready means of communication . . . The sense of loneliness or insecurity felt by farmers' wives under former conditions disappears, and an approach is made toward the solidarity of a small country town' (Fischer, 1988: 50). An article on the rural telephone in 1909 claimed that the 'principal use of farm line telephones has been their social use . . . The telephones are more often and for longer times held for neighborly conversations than for any other purpose' (Johnston, 1909; Fischer, 1988: 50).

The urban telephone

At the beginning of the century sociologists also studied the role of the telephone in urban areas. In an article in 1895 F.J. Kinsbury noted that relations between urban and rural areas were transformed by the arrival of the tramway, the bicycle and the telephone.[15] These three new technologies made the development of the suburbs possible. In 1906 F. Rice concluded an article on urbanization in New England by stating that the telephone was the main factor of urbanization (Moyer, 1977: 364). J. Alan Moyer, from whom I have borrowed these two references, analysed the relationship between urban growth and development of the telephone in Boston. Contrary to Rice and Kingsbury's conclusions, he found that the telephone did not play a key role in the decentralization of Boston. This decentralization had already started before its arrival and was mainly due to the development of public transport. The telephone merely accompanied and strengthened the city centre's movement towards the outlying suburbs.

Sam Bass Warner's work on Boston or Max Foran's work on Calgary demonstrated that electric tramways played a determining role in the spread of urban areas. The electric tramway first appeared in the US in the 1880s and developed rapidly thereafter. One of America's main transport historians, George H. Hilton, considers that it was one of the 'most rapidly accepted [innovations] in technological history' (McKay, 1984: 122). In five years, 60 per cent of the rails were electrified. Ten years later (1903) the entire network was electrified and the overall length of lines was two and a half times greater

(Jackson, 1985: 111). With this increased supply, usage increased considerably.[16] In Boston, for example, the number of trips per inhabitant rose from 118 in 1880 to 175 in 1890 (Warner, 1962). The increase in urban transport was accompanied by intense urban growth. Boston, for example, spread by 1.2–1.5 miles per decade between 1870 and 1900.

The development pattern was generally as follows: tramway lines were first extended beyond the city's borders; residential areas were then built around these transport lines. This strategy was systemized in cities like Los Angeles. H. Huntington, one of the tramway magnates, said: 'Lines must precede the arrival of settlers. No line must wait to be asked for. It must anticipate the growth of the "colonies" and be there when the builders arrive' (Lefèvre, 1984: 88).

Yet it cannot be said, as Christian Lefèvre writes, that 'tramways make a city', or more specifically a suburb. The new urban organization was part rather of a mid-nineteenth century American ideal of a home in a bucolic environment. Although this ideological trend was not initiated by the new transport technologies, they did make the dream realizable. Its strength probably explains the swift pace of the urban transport revolution.

During these periods of intense urban transformation, social networks changed dramatically. The telephone provided a means of reactivating sociability beyond the limits of neighbourly relations. Suzanne Keller (1977: 281–99) showed in more contemporary studies that the telephone played an essential role in helping newcomers to settle down in a neighbourhood. In the 1960s Donald Ball wrote: 'In effect, families can afford greater spatial dispersion because of the possibility of maintaining relationships via the conversational linkages available through the telephone' (1968: 59–75) within a single urban area.[17] Thus, in towns and rural areas alike, the telephone was an instrument of social intercourse.

Censuses carried out in 1907 and 1927 provide statistics on telephone usage. In both cases the vast majority of calls were local: 97 per cent and 96 per cent respectively. In other words, in the United States calls were limited essentially to neighbouring farms in the country, or to a single urban area. In two decades, local traffic doubled from 10 calls per month in 1907 to 20 in 1927. A comparison with the postal service shows that local telephone traffic was six times greater than local mail in both 1907 and 1927. Overall telephone consumption (in quantity) had already overtaken that of the post by 50 per cent in 1907 (Barrett, 1940: 136).

This intense telephonic communication was part of local sociability. A survey conducted in the mid-1920s on 500,000 households shows that the telephone was considered as a priority service. Together with the car and radio, it offered the housewife 'the escape from monotony which drove many of her predecessors insane'.[18] A survey by a woman's movement during the same period showed that women would rather have a car and telephone than a bathroom.[19] The account of a salesman for telephone subscriptions in the 1930s indicates (Fischer, 1988: 51) that women's main reasons for wanting a telephone were the following:

1   Conversing with their family and friends.
2   Making appointments and ordering goods by telephone.
3   Calling emergency services.

Men generally placed professional reasons at the top of the list.

Thus, at the start of the twentieth century, the telephone occupied a focal position in the communication practices of American households. In 1910 a quarter of them had a phone and in 1925 this figure had risen to 40 per cent (Bureau of the Census). The telephone was no longer a professional tool only; it had also become a family instrument for true sociability.

The telephone in Europe

Diffusion of the telephone in Europe was much slower than in the United States. Since my approach throughout this book is to deal mainly with the country or areas in which a new communication system first emerged, I shall not report in any length on the European situation. The following brief notes serve chiefly to counterbalance the American evolution.

In 1901 the British Chancellor of the Exchequer, Michael Hicks Beach, declared: 'The telephone does not correspond to the rural mentality.' Indeed, in 1913 a third of all the country's telephones were in London. Beach's opinion was moreover fairly widespread. In 1902 *The Times* wrote: 'the telephone is not an affair of the million . . . An overwhelming majority of the population do not use it and are not likely to use it at all, except perhaps to the extent of an occasional message from a public station' (Perry, 1977: 75). In France, the same attitude was to be found amongst the elite, who until the 1960s considered that the telephone was not a mass instrument intended for households.

The slow development of the telephone in Europe has often been explained by Malthusianism and its advocates. Chantal de Gournay showed that, on the contrary, in France in the 1930s the problem lay with demand rather than supply. In 1935 fewer than 10 per cent of all households were equipped, while the network capacity was far greater. In order to promote the service, the government decided to reduce prices (by installing the line free of charge) and to encourage door-to-door selling (by offering bonuses to civil servants who found new subscribers).[20] The situation was to change radically during the next phase of the French 'telephone crisis', in the 1950s and 1960s, when supply was totally inadequate and long waiting lists became the norm. The demand crisis during the inter-war period requires some explanation. A comparison with the United States has enabled me to put forward some hypotheses which must, of course, be verified.

As far as the rural areas were concerned, agriculture in France during the 1920s was not as modern or productive as it was in America. Farms were much smaller and very few of them operated on an industrial scale. Markets were organized on a local scale, so that farmers had no need for information on national or international prices. For all these reasons, the telephone was required far less for rapid market intervention. Moreover, France's population remained essentially rural and distances between farms, even in wooded areas, were small. The telephone did not yet appear as a necessary instrument in social life. People still used traditional channels – meeting in hamlets and towns, at washing places, in the fields – for social exchange. Moreover, unlike the USA, post was delivered to every farm individually.

As far as the towns were concerned, urban density remained high and sub-urbanization was barely starting in the Parisian region. Telephone demand remained limited to the upper classes or the aristocracy. The Countess of Pange, for example, told in her memoirs how her family had a telephone installed in about 1896, notably because her mother wanted to maintain close ties with her daughter who had just got married and gone to live on the other side of Paris (de Pange, 1968). It was only in the 1950s, with the expansion of the suburbs, that the demand for telephones was to rise sharply and spread to all social classes. For Gabriel Dupuy, the telephone did not appear 'as a sub-stitute but as a means of access for the city-dweller to a certain social and practical control of the urban environment' (Dupuy, 1982: 34).

A universal network

While telephone usage was developing, the lines were being extended to form a network. In 1878, two years after the invention of the telephone, Graham Bell wrote:

> It is conceivable that cables of telephone wires could be laid underground, or sus-pended overhead, communicating by branch wires with private dwellings, country houses, shops, manufactories, etc. . . . Not only so, but I believe, in the future . . . a man in one part of the country may communicate by word of mouth with another in a distant place.[21]

According to a newspaper at the time, 'Prof. Bell's confident expectation [is] that he will shortly be able to send his voice across the Atlantic[22] and talk with men 3,000 miles away as readily as if they were in the next room.'[23] A few years later, the deed of creation of AT&T (1885) indicated that links were to be built between towns in the USA, Canada and Mexico. This text also pro-vided for connections 'by cable and other appropriate means with the rest of the known world'.[24]

This project of global telephony was gradually implemented by telephone engineers. Bell's assistants built a first inter-urban link between Boston and Providence (50 km) in 1880 and three years later they reached New York (300 km). European inventors were also interested in the question. The Belgian François van Rysselberghe conducted experiments during the same period on telegraphic links. In 1882 he tested the Paris–Brussels link. In the winter of 1885-86 he went to the USA where he successfully transmitted a conversation between New York and Boston (1,500km).[25] But it was only in 1893 that AT&T opened this line commercially (Tucker, 1978: 653). For a long time the weakening of telephone signals precluded the establishment of links over longer distances. It was only in 1914 that the New York–San

Francisco line was to be opened, and only in 1956 that AT&T was able to install a first transatlantic line.

In the telecommunications field innovation is not limited to a terminal and connections; these technical components have to be integrated into a system. We shall see in Chapter 6 how an inventor like Marconi designed both the wireless and the system for operating it, but most often these two types of invention were not the work of the same person. Whereas the key figure in the invention of the telephone was indeed Bell, it is to Theodore Vail that the design of the telephone network system can be attributed. To the extent that most later inventions were to take place within Vail's system, his work constituted a strategic phase.

Theodore Vail[26] was managing the American railway postal network when Bell's financiers offered him directorship of the first telephone company. He occupied the post from 1878 to 1887. Then, following a quarrel with his shareholders, he resigned. In 1907 he was again called upon to direct American Telephone and Telegraph (AT&T, the new name given to Bell's company). Vail thus directed the American telephone network twice. In the first phase he developed the telephonic system itself and, 20 years later, he implemented the idea more thoroughly, in a phase of maturity.

Vail defined the telephone as 'a system that will afford communication with any one that may possibly be wanted, at any time' (Vail, 1909: 22). Moreover, he specified the fact that the instrument's value depended on the number of potential connections. This vision of the telephone was expressed in the three slogans of Bell's system: 'A system, a policy, a universal service.'

But Bell's partners who had wanted Vail lacked the capital required to build a large unified telephone network across the United States. Local investors had therefore to be found. The Bell company, as an owner of patents, sold licences for specific areas to local companies. This strategy was, however, hopelessly inadequate to ensure the coherence of the telephone network. The Bell company then undertook technical unification by developing a research policy and specifying the equipment to be used by its partners. To strengthen this central technical control, Vail bought out a telegraphic and telephonic equipment manufacturer, Western Electric, in 1882. The latter was to become the main supplier of local companies (Coon, 1939: 118–35).

Vail thus had access to a set of coherent, although dispersed, networks. To unite them into one large network, inter-urban links had to be established. This was the third strategic axis of the Bell system. When, in 1879, Bell and Western Union negotiated the borders between the two companies' activities – telephonic for the former, telegraphic for the latter – Western Union's directors suggested taking over long-distance calls. Vail refused; he was well aware that this was one of the foundations of a telecommunications system (Coon, 1939: 58–9).

When he returned to business in 1907 Vail strengthened all systems of cooperation. If the telephone was to be 'the nervous system of the business and social organization of the country' (Vail, 1908: 22), it was necessary to centralize research, equipment production, technical management and long-distance links. Local operations could, however, be decentralized (Vail, 1909: 19–20; 1914: 41–3). The main principles of the Bell system were therefore interdependence, intercommunication and universality.

Vail stressed the idea of network universality. He justified it by emphasizing the 'social mission' of the telephone which should never be limited by any borders imposed for 'national, geographic or racial reasons' (Vail, 1911: 26). Claiming to have a civil service mission, he accepted federal government control intended to curb tariffs and prevent the appropriation of excess profit by the operators. But while the Bell system accepted state regulation, in exchange it demanded a quasi-monopoly. In particular, Bell wanted the state to protect it from aggressive competition on the most profitable market segments (Vail, 1910: 32–4).

Financial links between AT&T (which had become the parent company of the Bell system) and its local partners gradually tightened. At first the holding company took a share of the affiliates' capital in exchange for access to patents. Later, AT&T progressively bought the majority of its affiliates' capital. When the Bell patents expired in 1893, numerous independent companies were created. In 1907 they accounted for 49 per cent of all American telephone subscriptions. Vail strove to reduce their share (Coon, 1939: 109). With the help of Moran Bank, AT&T's main shareholder, he bought out independent companies and pressurized the banks that wanted to unite them, so preventing them from creating a rival network (Daniellan, 1939: 70–4). He also suggested that the independent companies link up with his network, on condition that they accepted a subordinate position (Vail, 1911: 29–30). In 1912 these companies' share of the American market was down to 42 per cent and in 1934 to 16 per cent (Coon, 1939: 109).

AT&T's monopolistic strategy was completed by the buy-out of Western Union, the major American telegraph company, in 1909. While Vail thus took his revenge on the company which had almost blocked the young Bell company's development, he also intended creating synergy between the two networks.[27] By working together they would be able to use the same wires (Vail, 1913: 40).

Vail thus appears to be the inventor of a modern telecommunications network. As a manager, he engineered the passage from the transmission of speech between two points, to the organization of a large network. But he also supported technological research, found financial solutions, and negotiated with the federal state. These main strategic principles were to remain at the centre of AT&T's policy. When the company was later faced with fundamental choices, it always used former strategies as a guideline. During the 1920s, AT&T left its radio stations to RCA to obtain the monopoly of long-distance connections; it thereby favoured the network over local activity. When, during the 1980s, it was faced with a very tricky anti-trust lawsuit, AT&T decided to renounce a part of its activities. Some commentators were surprised that the company dropped its local and regional networks and maintained research, equipment manufacturing and long-distance links. Yet, this was exactly the same choice that Vail had made a hundred years earlier.

Notes

1 Francis Jehl was one of Edison's main assistants.

2 *L'Illustration*, 26 August 1854, quoted in *Le Téléphone à la Belle Epoque*, Libro-Sciences SPRL, Brussels, 1976.

3 David Hounshell (1975) noted this regarding Gray and Bell. Edison wrote in a letter in July 1875 that Orton, Western Union's President, had sent him a translation of Reis's article (quoted by Jehl, 1937).

4 Paper presented by Captain Holthof in April 1881 to the Frankfurt Electric Society. Reported in *The Electrician* of 25 August 1883, quoted by Ternant (1884: 91–2).

5 H. de Parville, 'Causeries scientifiques', quoted by Brault (1888: 20).

6 After having seen Bell's device in operation, Orton (President of Western Union) declared: 'It is a scientific toy. It is an interesting instrument, of course, for professors of electricity and acoustics; but it can never be a practical necessity. As well might you propose to put a telescope into a steel-mill or to hitch a balloon to a shoe-factory' (Casson, 1910: 42).

7 This was a compromise agreement which concluded a lengthy case.

8 The first international telephone link, established between Paris and Brussels in 1887, included a specific connection between the stock exchanges of Paris and Brussels (Tucker, 1978: 650–74).

9 During the same period, Standard Oil's New York offices received 230,000 telephone calls a year (Casson, 1910: 205).

10 *Punch*, vol. 11, 1846, p. 253, quoted by Briggs (1977: 49).

11 A similar system existed in London from the end of the 1850s. In 1862 it had transmitted 250,000 messages.

12 Colin Cherry (1977: 112–26) reached the same conclusion in a study of the first uses of the telephone in Australia.

13 In 1913 it was estimated that half of all isolated American farms had a telephone. On the other hand, fewer farms received their mail directly (AT&T, *Annual Report*, 1913).

14 *American Law Review*, vol. 46, July 1912, pp. 596–8, quoted by Aronson (1971: 159).

15 F.J. Kingsbury, *Journal of Social Science*, vol. 33, November 1895, quoted by Moyer (1977: 342).

16 Kenneth Jackson quotes an average of 172 trips for all American cities of over 100,000 inhabitants in 1890.

17 This point had already been noted by H.N. Casson who wrote in 1910: the telephone 'has literally abolished the isolation of separate families' (1910: 199).

18 *Voice Telephone Magazine*, December 1925, quoted by Fischer (1988: 51).

19 *Woman's Home Companion*, November 1925, quoted by Fischer (1988: 51).

20 Memorandum no. 532 by M. Mailley of 27 March 1935, quoted by de Gournay (1994: 230).

21 Graham Bell, brochure of 25 March 1878, quoted in 'Some early telephone prophesies', *Bell Telephone Quarterly*, vol. 15, no. 2, April 1936, p. 120.

22 Bell was nevertheless conscious of problems concerning the weakening of sound. In another conference, he discussed the use of relays (*Providence Daily Journal*, 15 March 1877).

23 *Springfield Republican*, 14 May 1877, quoted in *Bell Telephone Quarterly*, vol. 15, no. 2, April 1936, pp. 125–6.

24 Quoted in *Bell Telephone Quarterly*, vol. 15, no. 2, April 1936, p. 121.

25 Experiments in telephonic transmissions over 1,500 kilometres were reported by *The Electrician* in 1879, then again in 1883. There is no certainty that these experiments were successful, but the reports were nevertheless indicative of the technical community's interest in the matter.

26 Theodore Vail was the nephew of Alfred Vail who worked with Morse in developing his telegraphic device.

27 Following an anti-trust charge, AT&T was forced to abandon its interest in Western Union in 1913.

References

Aronson S. (1971) 'The sociology of the telephone', *International Journal of Comparative Society*, vol. 12, no. 3, September.

Aronson S.H. (1977) 'Bell's electrical toy: what's the use? The sociology of early telephone usage', in I. de Sola Pool (ed.), *The Social Impact of the Telephone*, MIT Press, Cambridge, Mass.

Baldwin G.G.C. (1925) *The History of the Telephone in the United Kingdom*, Chapman and Hall, London.

Ball D.W. (1968) 'Toward a sociology of telephones and telephoners', in M. Truzi (ed.), *Sociology of Every Day Life*, Prentice-Hall, Englewood Cliffs, New Jersey.

Barrett R.T. (1940) 'The telephone as a social force', *Bell Telephone Quarterly*, vol. 19, April.

Bell A.G. (1877) 'Researches in telephony', *Proceedings of the American Academy of Arts and Sciences*, vol. 12, Boston.

Bertho C. (1981) *Télégraphes et téléphones, de Valmy au micro-processeur*, Livre de Poche, Paris.

Bertho C. (1986) 'Naissance d'un réseau: le téléphone parisien de 1879 à 1927', *Revue française des télécommunications*, no. 58, March.

Brault J. (1888) *Histoire de la téléphonie*, Masson, Paris.

Briggs A. (1977) 'The pleasure telephone: a chapter in the prehistory of the media', in I. de Sola Pool (ed.), *The Social Impact of the Telephone*, MIT Press, Cambridge, Mass.

Casson H.N. (1910) *The History of the Telephone*, A.C. McClurg, Chicago.

Cherry C. (1977) 'The telephone system: creator of mobility and social change', in I. de Sola Pool (ed.), *The Social Impact of the Telephone*, MIT Press, Cambridge, Mass.

Coon H. (1939) *American Tel and Tel: the Story of a Great Monopoly*, Longmans, New York.

Daniellan N.R. (1939) *The Story of Industrial Conquest*, Vanguard Press, New York.

Dupuy G. (1982) 'Un téléphone pour la ville', *Metropolis*, no. 52–3, Paris.

Field K. (1878) *The History of Bell's Telephone*, Bradbury, London.

Fischer C.S. (1988) 'Touch someone: the telephone industry discovers sociability', *Technology and Culture*, vol. 29, no. 1, University of Chicago Press, January.

de Gournay C. (1994) 'Paris spurns the telephone', *Réseaux: The French Journal of Communication*, vol. 2, no. 2.

Gray E. (1878) *Experimental Research in Electro-Harmonic Telegraphy and Telephony*, Russel Brothers, New York.

Hounshell D. (1975) 'Elisha Gray and the telephone', *Technology and Culture*, Vol. 16.

Jackson K.T. (1985) *Crabgrass Frontier: the Suburbanization of the United States*, Oxford University Press, Oxford.

Jehl F. (1937) *Menlo Park Reminiscences*, vol. 1, Dearborn, Michigan.

Johnston G.R. (1909) 'Some aspects of rural telephony', *Telephony*, no. 17, 8 May.

Keller S. (1977) 'The telephone in new (and old) communities', in I. de Sola Pool (ed.), *The Social Impact of the Telephone*, MIT Press, Cambridge, Mass.

Kingsbury J.E. (1972) *The Telephone and Telephone Exchanges*, New York.

von Klinckowstroem C. (1967) *Nouvelle histoire des techniques*, Editions du Sud, Paris.

Lardner Dr (1867) *The Electric Telegraph*, James Walton, London.

Lefèvre C. (1984) 'Où les tramways font la ville: Los Angeles', *Les Annales de la recherche urbaine*, no. 21, Paris.

Libois L-J. (1983) *Genèse et croissance des télécommunications*, Masson, Paris.

McKay J. (1984) 'Les transports urbains en Europe et aux Etats-Unis, 1850–1914', *Les Annales de la recherche urbaine*, no. 23–4, Paris.

du Moncel T. (1887) *Le Téléphone*, Hachette, Paris.

Moyer J.A. (1977) 'Urban growth and the development of the telephone: some relationships at the turn of the century', in I. de Sola Pool (ed.), *The Social Impact of the Telephone*, MIT Press, Cambridge, Mass.

de Pange J. (1968) *Comment j'ai vu 1900*, Grasset, Paris.

Perry C.R. (1977) 'The British experience 1876–1912: the impact of the telephone during the years of delay', in I. de Sola Pool (ed.), *The Social Impact of the Telephone*, MIT Press, Cambridge, Mass.

Rice F. Jr (1906) 'Urbanizing rural New England', in *New England Magazine*, January.

Shiers G. (1977) *The Telephone: an Historical Anthology*, Arno Press, New York.

de Sola Pool I. (ed.) (1977) *The Social Impact of the Telephone*, MIT Press, Cambridge, Mass.

Tarr J.A. (1987) 'The city and the telegraph: urban telecommunications in the pre-telephone era', *Journal of Urban History*, Sage, London, November.

Ternant A.L. (1884) *Les Télégraphes*, vol. 1, Hachette, Paris.

Truzi M. (ed.) (1968) *Sociology of Every Day Life*, Prentice-Hall, Englewood Cliffs, New Jersey.

Tucker G. (1978) 'François van Rysselberghe: pioneer of long distance telephony', *Technology and Culture*, vol. 19, no. 4, October.

Warner S.B. (1962) *Street-Car Suburbs? The Process of Growth in Boston. 1870- 1900*, Cambridge, Mass.

Vail T. (1908–1914) *AT&T Annual Reports.*

6

The Wireless Age: Radio Broadcasting

A vast amount of historiographical literature on the wireless exists. As is often the case in this field, these writings have all tried to determine the true paternity of the invention. The results are, unsurprisingly, largely dependent on each author's nationality. Thus, the great encyclopaedias have attributed five different inventors to the wireless. For the *Lexicon der Deutschen Buchgemeinschaft* Hertz is the father; for the *Malaïa SovietskaIa Entsiklopedia* it is Popov. The *Nuova Enciclopedia Sonzogno* has naturally given the first place to Marconi, while the *Larousse universel* mentions him, but second to Branly. Finally, the *Encyclopaedia Britannica* has chosen Lodge (see Joos, 1971; Cazenoble, 1981: 2).

In reality the wireless, like numerous other modern technologies, was developed concurrently in several countries. Moreover, it combined the discoveries of a number of different inventors. As David Landes (1969: 425) writes, 'the array of scientists and technicians who shared in the early development of the wireless reads like a Unesco committee.'

James Maxwell is generally placed at the head of the procession. In the 1860s this English mathematician unified, within the same theory, existing knowledge on the undulatory characteristics of light, electricity and magnetism. Maxwell's theory constituted one of the great paradigms of nineteenth-century physics. It was, however, only confirmed in 1887 by experiments conducted by the German physicist Heinrich Hertz. Hertz managed to produce (and to detect) electromagnetic waves, which were later given his name.

In view of these facts, one might tend to agree with P. Rousseau (1967) that 'the wireless is a typical example of an invention formed entirely by science, in which empiricism and tinkering played no part, and which advanced guided by theory'. In contrast, another historian C. Süsskind (1968), has studied Marconi's experiments and considers that 'once again, a practical invention has a lead over theory' (see Cazenoble, 1981: 7).

It rapidly becomes apparent that neither of these two contradictory analyses is entirely correct, for there is no unilinear model of the articulation between science and technology. More significantly, the sequence of different stages in the history of the wireless was not a foregone conclusion. Hertz's experiments could well have remained confined to academic physics. In no way were they obviously meant to serve in the creation of a new technological system. Similarly, radio broadcasting was not the inevitable result of radiotelephony.

What appears today as a series of naturally articulated steps is, in reality, the history of a difficult passage from one domain to another; from science to technology (and vice versa), from the military to telecommunications, from commercial information to entertainment, and so forth. It is the history of this movement that I shall now retrace.

From Maxwell to Marconi

Science historians generally compare Maxwell to Hertz. The former is said to have formulated the theory of electromagnetic fields and the electromagnetic theory of light; the latter is said to have verified these theories. It seems, however, that such a clear-cut division never existed between these two scientists' work. According to Salvo d'Agostino (1989: 2), 'Maxwell was convinced of having provided some experimental proof of his theory.' Later, English or German scientists were to try to verify parts of Maxwell's theory. Hertz's originality lay in his attempt to demonstrate the English physicist's 'basic theories', i.e. the existence of 'waves with electric force' in a vacuum or in air. Not content to verify certain predictions in Maxwell's theory, Hertz went further and developed an instrumental theory which he compared to the Maxwell system.

The Maxwell–Hertz relationship was therefore more complex than is often thought. It did not consist merely of the passage from theory to experimentation, but rather of a new intellectual development that was compared to a theory. Even in a case which is often analysed as an intellectual filiation, there was a specific development which integrated the initial theory.

In a teleological conception of the history of science, some authors claim that Branly contributed an effective wave-detecting instrument to Hertz's discovery. This view of Branly's research is, however, inaccurate. Branly was a physicist, a specialist in electricity and a meticulous experimenter. He carried out research on conductors and insulators and studied the development of conductivity with respect to different forms of heat radiation and luminous radiation. In 1890 he noticed that under the effect of a spark, a tube filled with iron filings became a conductor or an insulator alternately. Moreover, when the spark transmitter was moved to another room the effect – later to be called the Branly effect – continued.[1]

Branly's interpretation of this phenomenon is not always very clear. Nevertheless, for Jean Cazenoble who has made an in-depth study of Branly, there is no doubt that he explained the effect by Hertzian waves. Branly was thoroughly familiar with Hertz's work, on which he had reported in the *Journal de physique*. Moreover, electromagnetic waves constituted the main subject of discussion among physicists in the early 1890s (Cazenoble, 1981: 67). Thus, Branly integrated Hertz's discovery into his own work on conductivity. He remained first and foremost a physicist who readily admitted that he was not the inventor of wireless telegraphy. In 1903 he declared to a journalist: 'Although I did not perform any wireless telegraphy, my experiments, in the very form I described them, contained the germ of all wireless telegraphy' (Monod-Broca, 1990: 179). This assertion, like many retrospective declarations of this kind, is both true and false. True in that the Branly effect was to be used at the start of wireless telegraphy; false in that this effect had to be used by other inventors, with other perspectives, for wireless telegraphy to exist. Wireless telegraphy did not follow directly from the Branly effect.

Unlike other physical effects discovered during the same period, the Branly effect did not contribute significantly to knowledge in the domain of physics. Nor did it serve as a basis for the development of a measuring instrument. It was nevertheless in the laboratory environment that the effect was first to be used. In 1894 the English physicist Lodge built a Hertzian wave receiver with an iron-filing tube (which he called a coherer). In order periodically to destroy the conductivity of the tube, acquired under the effect of Hertzian waves, he used the movement of a Morse recorder. Lodge's receiver had a purely pedagogic function; it clearly demonstrated the existence of Hertzian waves.

But it was not in physics laboratories that microwave transmission was to be born. Rather than being the outcome of a desire to exploit a scientific discovery, it was the result of a technical project to transmit information without wires. A young Italian, Guglielmo Marconi, had attended Augusto Righi's lectures at Bologna University and observed the experiments in which Righi perfected Branly's and Lodge's work.[2] Aware of the existence of Hertzian waves, Marconi developed a project for transmitting these waves over long distances (Aitken, 1976: 183). He built an experimental device and performed tests in the Villa Grifone on his parent's estate (1894–5). His objective was to increase the distance over which the waves could be propagated, so as to transmit them further than the laboratory. As Cazenoble (1981: 78) says: 'One had to have very rudimentary scientific information on the reality of waves to imagine for one moment that they could leave the laboratory. Their properties of dispersion . . . seemed, in informed physicists' eyes, to confine them there forever.'[3] Thus it was, paradoxically, Marconi's relative scientific ignorance which enabled him to appropriate a scientific theory for the technological project of wireless telegraphy.

Was the invention of wireless telegraphy simply the fruit of chance? Was it the result of an encounter in the young inventor's fertile mind between a technological project and a scientific discovery? The answer is no. It was part of a long tradition of research aimed at freeing telegraphy from the constraints of wires. Cazenoble (1981: 100–8) has shown that from the moment the electric telegraph first appeared, numerous researchers worked on the problem of ridding it of wires (see also Sivowitch, 1971). Morse himself, even before opening his first commercial line, was interested in telegraphy by natural conduction (with transmission by air or water). In 1844 he managed to send a telegraph from one bank of the Susquehanna to the other (1,600 metres). Other experiments were conducted in Europe. Another method, electrostatic telegraphy, was explored in the 1880s, notably by Watson and Edison but the results were disappointing. Telegraphy by electrodynamic induction, on the other hand, seemed more promising. Finally, Bell, Tainter and Berliner worked on the photophonic transmission of speech. Voice vibrations were transmitted by means of a mirror to a light beam and a receiver coupled to a selenium plaque rendered the sound. All of this work was reported in technical journals in Europe and America.

During its course through the second half of the nineteenth century, this wireless telegraphy project was destined to meet up with Hertzian waves. In 1892, two years before Marconi started his experiments, the English physicist William Crookes noted in the *Fortnightly Review* that electromagnetic vibrations could penetrate mediums such as a wall or the London fog. 'Here, then, is revealed the bewildering possibility of telegraph without wires' (Barnouw, 1966: 9). As we have already seen, an inventor is never alone;[4] Marconi was part of a technological research movement aimed at realizing wireless telegraphy. It was this movement which was to appropriate Hertz's and Branly's discoveries.

Independently of Marconi, other inventors also exploited these discoveries. Alexandre Popov, the Russian maritime engineer, built a Hertzian wave receiver in 1895. By means of his device he was able to detect storms (electric disturbances in the atmosphere). He soon thought of using waves for telegraphic transmission, and in the following years he performed several experiments in wireless telegraphy (Petitjean, 1987: 14-16). The British Admiralty similarly envisaged the use of Hertzian waves for communicating between ships. In December 1895 it asked Captain Henry Jackson to study a device for that purpose. In the following year Jackson tested a maritime wireless telegraphy system (Blond, 1989). In the United States, AT&T undertook research in 1892 (two years before Marconi) on the use of Hertzian waves for wireless telephony (Hoddeson, 1981). However, without an appropriate detector this work never produced any positive results.[5]

Thus, at the end of the nineteenth century, a relatively old technological project (wireless telegraphy) furnished the opportunity for a new scientific invention. The passage from theory to application was not direct, but a technological project did capture a theory. This was not only the work of a brilliant young Italian, for the same process took place throughout a technological community. Marconi's superiority probably lay in the fact that he started a little sooner and pursued his research to improve the reliability and efficiency of his system.

'It was distance that counted for Marconi', wrote the historian Hugh Aitken, 'and not only at the Villa Grifone. For the rest of his life it was to remain his technological obsession' (1976: 191). The British telegraph system's head engineer, William Preece, had the same obsession. His dream was the wireless interconnection of the English and French telegraphs (Aitken, 1976: 213) and he had conducted experiments on telegraphy by induction over several kilometres. In 1896, Marconi went to England with his mother, who was British. There he managed, thanks to her family, to meet Preece who gave him his full support.[6] In 1897 Preece gave the first public lecture on wireless telegraphy. A few days later the text was published in London in *The Electrician* and in Paris in *L'Industrie électrique*. The editor of the French journal considered it to be 'one of the most significant scientific events of the year' (Cazenoble, 1981: 30). Clearly, the advantages of wireless telegraphy had not gone unnoticed and the combination of telegraphy and Hertzian waves was in a sense expected. The waves had finally moved out of physics laboratories and become part of a technological project. The next step was to find a social use for the technology.

Maritime communication

In order to make his system more reliable and to market it, Marconi needed funds. His mother's family suggested he start a company and undertook to help him financially. Preece, aware of Marconi's plans, tried unsuccessfully to convince the British government to buy his patent. Thus, despite the Post Office's support for Marconi – and other forms of public support – wireless telegraphy did not become a state monopoly (Aitken, 1976: 218–28; see also Kieve, 1973: 243).

One of the new company's first markets was providing equipment for isolated lighthouses. Marconi was thereby responding to an existing demand, for which Preece had already performed several experiments with his induction device. During the same year (1898) Marconi also covered, together with the press, a number of spectacular events such as regattas.

However, the main social use of wireless telegraphy in these early years was military communication. In 1898 the British army first used Marconi's equipment during the Anglo-Boer war (Aitken, 1976: 232). The Admiralty, as I have already mentioned, showed a particular interest in this type of communication. Coordination in a modern fleet was more complex than it had been with sailing ships; the ships were faster, more mobile, and difficult to distinguish because of the clouds of smoke they emitted. Jackson and Marconi, who had conducted their research independently, started working together in 1897. Their cooperation spawned radio equipment adapted to a maritime environment. In 1901 a hundred radio stations were operational, of which two-thirds were from Royal Navy workshops and based on Jackson's plans, and a third from Marconi's company (Blond, 1989: 14). In 1903 the Admiralty signed a cooperation agreement which gave it access to all Marconi's patents.

During the same period Marconi also developed a commercial use for wireless telegraphy. Preece had already received requests from the maritime insurance company Lloyd's to transmit information on ships. In 1898 Marconi installed the first system corresponding to Lloyd's requirements. A wireless device was installed between Rathin Island and Ireland (Aitken, 1976: 231) with the purpose of transmitting information on boats approaching the British Isles. Thus Marconi used wireless telegraphy to serve the same social usage as Watson had served 60 years earlier with the semaphore telegraph (see Chapter 1).

Cooperation between Marconi and Lloyd's went even further. In 1901 the two companies signed an exclusive cooperation agreement. Lloyd's had a network of over a thousand agents in the main harbours of the world, whose job was to collect and telegraph to London information on the arrival and movement of ships. This network could be mobilized to organize communication with ships. By the end of 1902, 70 merchant ships were equipped with radios and could communicate with 25 coastal stations. In 1907 all the main transatlantic lines were equipped with radios (Aitken, 1976: 235–9).

Communication between ships thus constituted the main function of wireless telegraphy at the start of the century. Like Chappe's first telegraphic link with the Northern army, or electric telegraphy for signalling on the railways, these different uses enabled new telecommunications systems to become operational. They made it possible for the promoter of each invention to start a new activity by responding to an existing demand which had hitherto remained unsatisfied.

The speed with which these three telecommunication technologies (like computers later) got off the ground was partly the result of financing by the military (three cases out of four) or by big companies (railways, maritime insurance). For an innovator, this is a particularly favourable situation as he or she does not have to confront market uncertainty.[7]

The natural monopoly of radio communications

As soon as Marconi wanted to leave the limited, but protected, world of military use, he had to think of another way of marketing his invention. With the army and navy he could simply sell his equipment and leave it up to others to train operators and set up coastal stations. Private ship-owners, on the other hand, had no intention whatsoever of organizing a communication system; they simply wanted to use a service.

Marconi's brief cooperation with the Post Office probably made him aware of the organization and economy of a telecommunications network. He decided to become a network manager and rented his equipment with an operator to merchant ships. He also took over the running of coastal stations. 'Marconigrams' were transmitted on the basis of two tariffs: one for passengers and another, lower one, for ship-owners and crew (Barnouw, 1966: 17).

Marconi's new strategy was also a response to English telegraphic legislation. The only activity which did not contravene the Post Office's monopoly in Britain and its territorial waters was internal corporate communication. Whereas boats were legally forbidden to communicate with the coast, Marconi's operators could communicate with one another. Thus, as Aitken notes, the British telegraphic monopoly unwittingly provided Marconi with a legal base for his future commercial monopoly over wireless telegraphy (1976: 234–5). Thanks too to his exclusive alliance with Lloyd's, Marconi could forbid the latter's ground stations from retransmitting messages from boats using competitors' equipment (except in emergencies). Moreover, Marconi did not hesitate to take action for infringement against those industrialists who used his patents. In this way his network monopoly was strengthened by his technical monopoly.

Independently of the commercial development of his company, Marconi also wanted to continue his technological research. As indicated above, his main preoccupation was covering long distances. In December 1901 he managed to transmit a very short telegraphic message consisting of the letter S across the Atlantic (from Cornwall to Newfoundland). This experiment surprised many of his contemporaries, for physicists imagined that the roundness of the earth doomed it to failure. Once again, Marconi seemed to be guided by a major technological project which he tried to realize without any scientific knowledge. It was only in the following year that two physicists were to provide an explanation for the phenomenon: Hertzian waves transmitted in a straight line are reflected by the ionized layers of the upper atmosphere.[8] Marconi took six years to develop a system capable of transmitting telegrams across the Atlantic.

The articulation of Marconi's technical and social objectives (inter-continental transmission and the creation of a telecommunications network) materialized in 1907 with the creation of a regular telegraphic service between Ireland and Canada. This service was gradually extended to Europe, the USA and Australia. In moving from purely maritime to land communication, wireless telegraphy went from a field in which it was the only medium possible to a sector in which it provided an alternative to an older technique, the undersea cable. The Marconi Wireless Telegraph Company became the competitor of the large English undersea cable corporation, Eastern and Associated Telegraph Companies (Crouch, 1989). In 1909 Marconi offered to build the British Empire's radio network in which 18 powerful stations would be established at different strategic spots (Blond, 1989: 17). An embryo of such a network was built just before the First World War.[9]

Marconi's activities were not limited to England; in 1899 he had already established a subsidiary in the United States. American Marconi developed rapidly, albeit in a difficult environment. The company was seen as wanting to fortify British domination over telecommunications, and a number of rival companies were set up. After conflict over patents and internal management problems, these companies disappeared during the course of 1912. Moreover, American Marconi bought out the main opposition (United Wireless), thereby securing a monopoly (Barnouw, 1966: 42).

During the same year, the *Titanic* disaster endowed wireless telegraphy with a new aura; it became the medium capable of directing rescue operations. In fact, the name *Titanic* and wireless telegraphy were to be linked for a long time in the public mind. While the most modern ship in the world was sinking, a new technology – wireless telegraphy – enabled it to continue communicating with the world. The impact of this shipwreck was such that it was decided at an international conference a few months later to make wireless telegraphy compulsory on all ships.[10] Marconi's position was thereby strengthened and, on the eve of the First World War, he had built up a global monopoly of radio communications. On the seas, he controlled the communications network; on land, his device had proved itself over very long distances.

In 1919 John Griggs, President of American Marconi, wrote to his shareholders:

> The principal aim and purpose of the Marconi Telegraph Company of America, during all the period of its existence has been the establishment and maintenance of trans-oceanic communication. Although the company has done no inconsiderable business in minor branches of the wireless, such as the equiping of vessels . . . yet these by the management have always been considered as incidental to the greater and more profitable business of long distance communication. (Mayes, 1972: 11–18)

During the First World War wireless telegraphy became an essentially military affair. The British and, in particular, American navies took over management of maritime radio communications and controlled industrial activity.[11] In 1919 the American Secretary of State for the Navy, Daniels, suggested that his administration take over control of the radio. 'We would lose very much' he told Congress, 'by dissipating it and opening the use of radio communication again to rival companies' (Barnouw, 1966: 53). 'Since there is a natural monopoly', said the defenders of the bill, 'let it rather go to the state'. In the end the bill was not passed by Congress, but it illustrated clearly that 25 years after its invention, wireless telegraphy had become a new universal telecommunications system.[12] Even though the new technology developed independently of the main telecommunications institutions, it was shaped in the same mould.

From radio telegraphy to radio telephony

While the social use of wireless telegraphy was becoming established, technological research progressed. In the USA in 1900 Reginald Fessenden, an academic who had formerly worked with Edison, undertook research on the transmission of speech. Such a project was only realizable if damped waves used in radio telegraphy were replaced by continuous waves. Supported by General Electric's laboratories (Sivowitch, 1971), Fessenden developed the transmitter he needed and performed his first positive experiments in 1906.[13] He was not alone in undertaking such research; the subject also interested the Swedish physicist, Poulsen, and a self-taught American, Stubblefield, among others (Hoffer, 1971; Decaux, 1979; Dieu, 1987).

Another American researcher, Lee De Forest, who had written a thesis on Hertzian waves, set himself two objectives during the first years of the century: replacing Branly's coherer by a more efficient receiving device, and transmitting sound. De Forest's telegraphic devices, which competed with those of Marconi, began to meet with some success around 1902–3. During his work to find an effective receiver for electromagnetic waves, he learned of Fleming's patent on the diode (1904). Fleming, an English academic and Marconi's scientific adviser, noticed that a two-electrode thermionic tube (a heated filament and an anode, or plate) could detect electromagnetic waves. De Forest, in carrying out different tests to improve the sensitivity of the diode, discovered in 1906 that with a third electrode the lamp could serve as both detector and amplifier. He called this triode an 'audion'.

De Forest's discovery of the triode played a fundamental role in the development of the radio and telecommunications; it marked the starting point of electronics. It was also relatively autonomous with respect to other scientific work conducted during the same period on the electron. The flow of current between the filament and the plate in the diode or in the triode was analysed by the physicist Richardson as the consequence of the movement of particles which he called thermoions, hence the name thermionic tubes. It was only around 1920 that the effect of electrons in this phenomenon was first understood (Decaux, 1979: 370).

While Fleming's and De Forest's discoveries were no longer relevant to the radio alone, it was nevertheless within this framework that their research was carried out. Neither of them had been working on an application for electron physics or trying to open a new technical field. They were simply trying to replace Branly's coherer by a more effective device. The De Forest Radiotelephone Company was not to enjoy the same destiny as Marconi's firm. Following serious financial difficulties, De Forest had to sell his audion patents to AT&T in 1914.

The first American inventors of radio telephony thought spontaneously of radio broadcasting. Fessenden conducted his first experiments at the end of 1906. On Christmas Eve, radio operators on a boat in the Carribbean heard 'a human voice coming from their instruments – someone speaking! Then a woman's voice rose in song. It was uncanny! . . . Next someone was heard reading a poem. Then there was a violin solo.' It turned out that the violin player was Fessenden himself (Barnouw, 1966: 20). For Fessenden this was probably more for the show than part of his project of finding a use for the new technology.[14]

De Forest's situation was very different. As a clergyman's son he had a messianic vision of radio usage. A few months after patenting his triode he had started experimenting with radio broadcasting, and wrote in his diary: 'My present task (happy one) is to distribute sweet melody broadcast[15] over the city and sea so that in time even the mariner far out across the silent waves may hear the music of his homeland' (Barnouw, 1966: 20). In 1908 he went with his wife, a pianist,[16] to Paris where they organized a spectacular presentation from the Eiffel Tower. Their transmission of a sound programme was received 800 kilometres away. In the following year, back in New York, De Forest broadcast an appeal for women's enfranchisement. In January 1910 he broadcast, direct from the Metropolitan Opera, a show starring Caruso. He also produced radio news bulletins and presented election results live.

De Forest's experiments remained marginal due to the lack of receivers (the triode had not yet been industrialized) and, in particular, to the absence of a mode of payment for radio programmes. As an inventor he was, however, just as important as Marconi. Both of them developed the basic technology of the radio and defined its social usage. But whereas Marconi, thanks to the support of his mother's family, imagined a way of marketing his invention, De

Forest never conceived of anything similar. Hence, the development of the radio took place without him.

A new mass media

David Sarnoff, one of the technical managers at American Marconi, was first to define an economic base for the development of radio broadcasting. In 1916 he sent a note on a 'radio music box' to his general manager. 'I have in mind', he wrote 'a plan of development which would make radio "a household utility" in the same sense as the piano or phonograph. The idea is to bring music into the house by wireless' (Graham, 1986: 32). Sarnoff was part of a generation of self-made innovators; he started off at American Marconi as a young telegraphist and climbed his way up to the top. An experience he had as a telegraphist in 1912 probably helped him to discover the broadcasting potential of wireless telegraphy. One afternoon in April he received a message from the *Titanic*. For 72 hours he was the sole link between people on the sinking ship and the rest of America in its state of shock (Barnouw, 1966: 77). Could this not be seen as the role of future radio reporters? In any event, Sarnoff's proposition in 1916 was considered as ridiculous. In January 1920 he presented his proposal again, this time with economic details. He suggested that people who purchased radios should subscribe to the monthly *Wireless Age* which would provide the programmes. Investments would be offset by profits from the sale of receivers and from the press (subscriptions and advertising) (Barnouw, 1966: 79). Less than a year later radio broadcasting was born.

'Sow broadcasting'

It took only 10 years for wireless telegraphy, whose sole use was point-to-point telecommunication, to become a broadcasting system that was one of the main media for mass culture. This shift from one type of technological and social usage to another took place in relation to two developments which we shall now examine. First, the First World War prompted the industrialization of wireless telegraphy. Secondly, in the United States the radio created a communication environment in which amateurs could operate freely.

Wireless telegraphy was a telecommunication tool particularly well suited to war situations – particularly when the front moved rapidly – and to maintaining contact with aeroplanes and tanks. In France, Colonel Ferrié, who was aware of the principles of De Forest's audion, grasped the opportunity afforded by the War and was one of the first to use the component. He had the triode, called a TM lamp ('type militaire'), developed industrially. Soon military receiving stations were equipped with this lamp and from 1917 it was also used in transmitters. By the end of the war lamps were being mass produced in France where factories had a production capacity of 300,000 lamps. According to Bernard Decaux (1979: 374–5), 'French military radio communication equipment was far superior to British or German equipment.' In

1917 the American contingent in Europe adopted French equipment (see Petitjean, 1985).

The Great War also helped to settle a number of conflicts concerning industrial ownership. In 1916 a New York court outlawed the sale of triodes without permission from American Marconi, owner of the diode patent. On the other hand, Marconi could not use the triode without permission from AT&T (owner of De Forest's patent). Furthermore, General Electric had improved the triode in various ways.[17] When America entered the war the government froze all legal disputes concerning patents. AT&T, General Electric and American Marconi all had to cooperate to produce 80,000 lamps for the armed forces.

We have seen that at the end of the war the American navy almost succeeded in securing a legal monopoly over radio communication. When this did not occur, fears were expressed in American military and political circles that the British would use Marconi to control maritime radio communications. It was therefore decided to Americanize Marconi's US subsidiary. Under heavy pressure, the latter agreed at the end of 1919 to sell its interests to a new company, the Radio Corporation of America (RCA). Both AT&T and GE were shareholders (Barnouw, 1966: 48–9) in RCA, and the American government also had a representative on the governing board. By means of this arrangement intended to exploit inter-oceanic links and compete with British undersea cables, the different partners resolved their quarrels over patents.[18]

Although the war had provided new technological and industrial opportunities, these alone could not lead to the new use of the radio that appeared in the 1920s. It was (as we have seen in other examples throughout this book) the social movement at the origin of broadcasting that was to 'capture' it and set it off in another direction. The relative weakness of this social movement in France, compared to the United States, probably explains why broadcasting took so long to develop there. Although France had gained an effective lead during the war in the industrialization of the radio, it was in America that the use of broadcasting was born.

In the USA wireless telegraphy enjoyed lively public interest from the outset. In 1899 Marconi was received in New York as a hero. When he succeeded in 1901 in transmitting a message across the Atlantic, his achievement made national headlines. Later, American newspapers maintained their interest in wireless telegraphy, as Susan Douglas (1986) observed in her studies of the press at that time. She notes that, contrary to articles on other new technologies, 'there were no speculations on wireless sets of the future . . . Rather, the predictions focused on where the messages might go and on what the wireless would do for society and for individuals' (Douglas, 1986: 38). In these texts wireless telegraphy appeared as the means to instantaneous free communication. The user was autonomous, he or she depended on no operator and had no tax to pay. During the first two decades of the twentieth century there was a considerable discrepancy between the effective commercial use of the radio (maritime communication) and the uses imagined by the

media and experimented with by amateurs. Amateur use, which started
around 1906, was to develop rapidly. In 1917 the authorities issued over
8,500 broadcasting licenses and the number of receivers was estimated at
around 125,000 (Barnouw, 1966: 55).[19]

The amateur radio boom was to be sustained by the press and publishing
business. Newspapers, technical manuals, books for teenagers or boy-scout
manuals provided plans and instructions for building a wireless receiver, while
university and college students were taught how to build their own devices. If
we relate the number of wirelesses quoted above to the population likely to
build a receiver (men between 15 and 35 years old), we see that 0.7 per cent of
young Americans actually did so.[20] This high figure gives an idea of the
importance of the wireless phenomenon in the United States.

Yet these amateurs' ambitions remained very modest. Transmitting or
receiving a Morse message over 10 or 15 miles was a 'thrilling experience',
according to one of them (Edgar Love in Douglas, 1986). On the other hand,
professionals complained about amateurs congesting the waves. The latter
were said to be incapable of deciphering more than a few words a minute. Yet,
despite their inexperience, they extended the distance over which they could
broadcast and by 1917 were able to send messages from the East Coast across
to the West Coast. In the following extract from Francis Collins' book *The
Wireless Man*, we see that in 1912 this novelist had already perceived the
new dimension of the radio:

> An audience of a hundred thousand boys all over the United States may be
> addressed almost every evening by wireless telegraph. Beyond doubt this is the
> largest audience in the world. No football or baseball crowd, no convention or con-
> ference, compares with it in size, nor gives closer attention to the business at hand.
> (Douglas, 1986: 49)

Collins had already grasped the fact that these amateurs were busy tilting
usage of the radio from point-to-point telecommunication to broadcasting.

During the years leading up to the First World War a number of amateurs
started broadcasting on a more or less regular basis, either in Morse (e.g. the
weather report broadcast by Wisconsin University for farmers or the time)[21]
or with sound. In California in 1909 Charles Harrold, an academic, broadcast
a news bulletin and music once a week (Greb, 1958–9: 3–13). Near Boston in
1915 a group of students launched a university radio with the same type of
programme (Barnouw, 1966: 33–6). All these experiments were interrupted in
1917 when the government outlawed the use of wirelesses because of the war.

During the war the American navy established a radio station intended to
serve as an instrument for propaganda to Europe (Barnouw, 1966: 51–2). It
broadcast calls for armistice to Germany and promoted President Wilson's
peace plan.[22]

As soon as the war was over amateurs started experimenting with sound
broadcasting again. In 1920 two of them managed to combine their passion
for radios with their company's interests. The first, William Scripps, director
of the Detroit *News*, was a wireless enthusiast. On 31 August 1920 he started

broadcasting a daily news bulletin and recorded music from the newspaper's offices. The day specifically chosen for launching the radio was that of the Detroit primary. His programmes appeared regularly in the *News* but, despite the newspaper's support, audiences were estimated at no more than 500 radio amateurs.

In order to transform broadcasting into a mass media, wireless sets had to be produced on an industrial scale and marketed. Westinghouse was to take this initiative. Another wireless amateur, Frank Conrad, an engineer at Westinghouse, had installed a transmitter in his garage. The company moved the station to its offices in Pittsburg and launched a daily broadcasting service on 2 November 1920, the day of the presidential elections. At the same time Westinghouse, which had gained experience during the war in producing military receivers industrially, decided to market a civil radio set. This plan resembled the one imagined by Sarnoff at RCA, but Westinghouse, relying on Conrad's competence, started earlier. In the following year it created two other stations: one in New York, which concentrated mainly on broadcasting sporting events, and the other in Chicago, which broadcast opera performances in the city.[23] In November 1922 there were still only five stations in the United States; a month later the radio boom began and in eight months 450 new stations appeared (Barnouw, 1966: 91). Growth in such proportions was only possible because a pool of amateurs capable of running these new stations existed. Hence, this social trend provided radio's first audiences as well as its first professionals.

By the 1920s social use of the wireless had changed fundamentally. Its role in maritime communication had declined as it became a mass media. Contemporary commentators emphasized, as Collins (1912) had done, the mass character of radio audiences. *Radio Broadcast* noted in September 1923 that a speech by President Harding was heard by over a million people; 'no president has ever spoken to such a large audience', it said (Barnouw, 1966: 92). Others remarked on different dimensions of the new media. Stanley Frost (1922) noted that, thanks to radio, 'all isolation can be destroyed' (see also Douglas, 1986: 54). In a society in which urban change was rapid and cultures with rural origins had disappeared, radio provided a link with society. Unlike the telephone, it was not used to strengthen ties with family or friends, but rather to become a part of society. It soon became an instrument of home entertainment, like the phonograph, for which it provided a substitute for about 20 years (see Chapter 4). It was an alternative source of music for dancing at home.[24]

Creating a commercial use

In order to become established, the social function of radio had to find an economic base. At first Westinghouse had thought that the manufacturers of radio equipment could pay for the programmes. Indeed, without programmes the manufacturers would be unable to sell mass-produced equipment. Their financing of the programmes was thus a form of investment. This solution, which amounted to organizing the transfer of funds from equipment to programmes, was appropriate for getting broadcasting off the ground. It was, however, inadequate in a period of maturity. In 1922 the journal *Radio Broadcast* launched the debate: 'How to finance radio broadcasting?', which it continued to feed for a number of years. In 1925 it offered a prize for the best essay on the subject (Barnouw, 1966: 154–8).

Two main types of financing were proposed: taxes and advertising. Although the 'European-style' model of a public tax won the *Radio Broadcast* prize, it did not lead to any specific project. On the other hand, David Sarnoff, who had become RCA's MD, proposed a slightly different plan in which taxes on radios would be managed by the manufacturers. The latter would control a public broadcasting service managed by representatives from their own companies and from the public. The Sarnoff plan's main drawback was that it sanctioned the RCA/GE/Westinghouse oligopoly.[25]

The telephone companies and AT&T in particular had a totally different vision of radio's economic base. 'We, the telephone company, were to provide no programs. The public was to come in. Anyone who had a message for the world or wished to entertain was to come in and pay their money as they would upon coming into a telephone booth, address the world, and go out' (Lloyd Espenchied in Barnouw, 1966: 106). Between the idea of making users pay for their messages and that of financing through advertising, there was only a short step which AT&T soon took. At the start, opposition to advertising was fierce. The Minister of Trade, Hoover, declared in 1924: 'If a speech by the President is to be used as the meat in a sandwich of two patent medicine advertisements, there will be no radio left' (Barnouw, 1966: 177). But Hoover changed his mind and in the following year decided that the question of advertising had to be settled by the manufacturers themselves. The debate was to take place among private companies.

Behind the opposition between two types of financing, two different cultures confronted each other. For the telephone companies, radio was simply a succession of messages financed by those who supplied them. The coherence of these different messages therefore had no relevance for them. On the other hand, they imagined connecting the different radio stations to form a network. For them radio took on a national dimension. By contrast, radio manufacturers reasoned in terms of audience size. They saw the motor behind the system as being the sale of receivers, which meant that programmes had to be attractive enough to encourage people to buy. The stations financed by these companies soon invented the basic principles of radio programming. Conflict raged between the 'telephone group' led by AT&T (which had withdrawn from RCA in 1923) and the 'radio group' (RCA, GE and Westinghouse) until a compromise was found in 1926. The 'radio group' set up a company specializing in managing and creating the programmes for radio stations: the National Broadcasting Company (NBC). The latter proposed a national programme, structured into a coherent schedule and financed by advertising. Connections between stations were provided by AT&T. In 1927 a number of independent stations formed a second network which was later to become Columbia Broadcasting System (CBS). The basic principles of the American broadcasting system were thus established and were to remain unchanged.

The history of the wireless, compared to that of other inventions examined in this book, is probably one of the most complex, one of those with the most inventors and entrepreneurs. In the conclusion to his book, Aitken proposes an interpretation through the concept of translation. Hertz translated Maxwell's abstract theory into one that could be verified in a laboratory. Marconi translated Branly and Lodge's physical experiments into a technological telecommunications device. He also translated his device into a marketable service (Aitken, 1976: 330–1).

The above analysis is, I think, interesting but inadequate. By emphasizing the idea of translation it shows that, rather than continuity from Maxwell to Sarnoff, there was a series of ruptures, of changes of approach. On this level, Aitken's interpretation is far richer than that of most histories of radio in which the succession between inventors took place 'naturally' and 'smoothly'. But by focusing on the intellectual activity of translation, one tends to forget everything that is around the translator: two linguistic systems and a text which has to be adapted from one language to another. In other words, importance is given to the interfaces, while the systems to be interfaced are forgotten.

My approach in this book, based on the notion of circulation, is different. It examines how a theory, a technological system or a use, migrates from one continent to another. It pays as much attention to the pilot who led this navigation as to the trends which led a technical object from one state to another. The intention is to articulate a specific study of the inventor's work (micro-analysis) with that of the main trends in social and technological change (macro-analysis). Marconi's main success was unquestionably that of giving a technical use to laboratory experiments. But it is as important to show that he was part of a technological tradition, that the project of wireless communication dated back to the birth of the telegraph, that numerous devices had already been tested and that, in parallel with Marconi's work, other inventors performed the same experiments.

The evolution from technological use to social use is always a delicate operation. Marconi's strength, like that of Chappe or Cooke before him, lay in his identification of the first immediate use (military communication). He was thereby able to procure some revenue without having to define a way of marketing the device. When he later marketed wireless telegraphy he borrowed a method from telecommunications. His link with the telecommunication tradition was therefore twofold: both technological (reaching maximal distances) and commercial (making the transmitter of a message pay for the service).

The road from wireless telegraphy to radio was also highly complex. The inventors of radio broadcasting circulated between four different spheres. They came from Marconi's wireless telegraphy tradition. They sought new receivers for Hertzian waves and found them in thermionic lamps. They were also part of a research trend experimenting with free communication. Finally, they bathed in a social movement, that of a turning inwards of the family to the private sphere, of the organization of entertainment at home. By circulating between these spheres, they were to link up the different contributions. Men like De Forest or Sarnoff knew how to tie all these traditions together, although De Forest was only a precursor. Radio broadcasting necessitated mass production of receivers and the required expertise was developed during the war. But commercial form had to be given to this new social use. It was through the combination of several traditions – those of telecommunications, mass industry and the press – that the radio was finally to find its economic base.

On their long road from Hertz to NBC, waves were in a sense transformed. At each stage of this movement there was a new contribution, an enhancement. The main actors in this process all 'captured' an innovation and integrated it into their own technological or social project, until a stable system was finally attained. A medium was born; its shape changed little afterwards.

Notes

1 For a description of this experiment see P. Monod-Broca (1990).

2 This point on Marconi's education, put forward by Hugh Aitken (1976), is contested by other biographers. Nevertheless, the friendship between Righi and Marconi's parents seems to prove that, in one way or another, Marconi was aware of Righi's research.

3 Aitken (1976) indicates that Righi discouraged Marconi. His attempts to use waves over distances of more than 100 metres were hopeless. By trying a number of experimental devices, Marconi did nevertheless find that a wire on the ground captured the waves at greater distances.

4 Some authors, such as Lloyd Moris (1949), consider that Marconi knew about Crookes' article.

5 Later AT&T hesitated several times before resuming this work. Some experts considered that radio telephony was not realizable at the time. It was only towards 1912 that AT&T started to take an interest in the radio.

6 It was the physicist Campbell Swinton who, after having seen Marconi's experiments, obtained an appointment for him with Preece. In 1908 Swinton was one of the first scientists to describe the principle of television.

7 The navy's interest in wireless telegraphy was also evident in other countries. Alexandre Popov, quoted above, experimented with transmitting to ships. In the summer of 1897 the Italian navy invited Marconi to perform tests off the coast of La Spezia. In France, 130 navy vessels were equipped in 1908 (Petitjean, 1987).

8 The existence of these strata was only proved later.

9 Nevertheless, this project gave rise to a number of controversies. The unsuccessful cooperation between Marconi and the Post Office had left some resentment within the British civil service.

10 In 1908 in an international conference the Germans had obtained the ruling that all stations had to accept maritime traffic, irrespective of its origin.

11 In France, it was rather the army, and notably General Ferrié's services, which acted as a driving force in the development of the radio.

12 In England it was also on the occasion of a war (the Russo-Japanese war) that the state obtained a monopoly over wireless telegraphy (Wireless Telegraphy Act of 1904). The monopoly was attributed to the Post Office but in fact real power lay with the Admiralty (Blond, 1989: 15).

13 Cooperation with General Electric was difficult. Heads of laboratories considered the project as unrealistic and gave it to a young engineer considered as being 'crazy enough to undertake it' (Barnouw, 1966: 20). AT&T resumed its work on radio telephony in 1902 and discontinued it when Fessenden registered his patent (Hoddeson, 1981).

14 Bell also retransmitted concerts to promote his telephone.

15 It is interesting to note that the original meaning of the word *broadcast* was 'to sow'.

16 He later divorced and married a soprano. De Forest was an extremely inventive but unsociable man. A library card was once found in some archives indicating that he had borrowed a book entitled *How to Deal with Women* (I owe this anecdote to Pascal Griset).

17 Edwin Armstrong, inventor of a tuning device for receivers (called a 'superheterodyne') declared in 1923 to the US Federal Trade Commission that 'It was absolutely impossible to build the slightest manipulable device without using all, or almost all, the inventions known at the time' (Landes, 1969).

18 In June 1921 Westinghouse joined this cartel again and became a shareholder in RCA.

19 The number of transmitters was certainly higher; in fact, it was only in 1912 that authorization to transmit was required by law, and many amateurs ignored this formality.

20 There was at the time no manufacturer of wirelesses for the general public.

21 Twenty years earlier weather information had constituted one of the main professional telephone services in rural areas (see Chapter 5). In France, the Eiffel Tower station started broadcasting time signals twice a day from 1910 (Petitjean, 1987: 25).

22 On 29 October 1915, AT&T had already succeeded in broadcasting speech by radio from the USA to the Eiffel Tower station (*AT&T Annual Report*, 1915, p. 31).

23 In France, the first regular transmissions were sent from the Eiffel Tower station from Christmas 1921. In February 1922 the *Ecole Supérieure des PTT* started its transmissions (see Mauriat, 1987).

24 A listener of the Detroit station commented in the *News* (5 September 1920) on one of the first radio programmes: 'We had some of our girl friends up to hear the concert . . . and when "The Naughty Waltz" came on we started to dance. It was great fun' (Barnouw, 1966: 63).

25 Other methods of public financing existed. University radios found patrons and in New York the city financed a station.

References

D'Agostino S. (1989) 'Pourquoi Hertz, et non pas Maxwell, a-t-il découvert les ondes électriques?', in J. Cazenoble (ed.), *Electricité, il y a cent ans*, Editions de l'EHESS, Paris.

Aitken H. (1976) *Syntony and Spark: the Origins of Radio*, John Wiley and Sons, New York.

Barnouw E. (1966) *A History of Broadcasting in the United States*, vol. 1: *A Tower in Babel*, Oxford University Press, New York.

Blond A.J.L. (1989) 'The development of wireless telegraphy as a competitor to cable in the United Kingdom (1894–1914)', *UIT, Conférence de Villefranche-sur-Mer.*

Cazenoble J. (1981) *Les Origines de la télégraphie sans fil*, CNRS, Centre de documentation des sciences humaines, Paris.

Cazenoble J. (1989) *Electricité, il y a cent ans*, Editions de l'EHESS, Paris.

Collins F. (1912) *The Wireless Man*, Century, New York.

Corn J. (1986) *Imagining Tomorrow*, MIT Press, Cambridge, Mass.

Crouch J.H. (1989) 'Historical overview: from pioneers to structures – Cable Wireless', *UIT, Conférence de Villefranche-sur-Mer.*

Decaux B. (1979) 'Radiocommunications et électronique', in M. Daumas (ed.), *Histoire générale des techniques*, vol. 5, pp. 343–433, PUF, Paris.

Dieu B. (1987) 'Un nouveau support pour la parole, la radiotéléphonie' in *La TSF des années folles*, Les Amis de l'histoire des PTT d'Alsace, Strasbourg.

Douglas S. (1986) 'Amateur operators and American broadcasting: shaping the future of radio', in J. Corn (ed.), *Imagining Tomorrow*, MIT Press, Cambridge, Mass.

Frost S. (1922) 'Radio dreams that can come true', *Collier's 69,* 10 June.

Graham M.B.W. (1986) *RCA and the Videodisc: the Business of Research*, Cambridge University Press, Cambridge..

Greb G.R. (1958–9) 'The golden anniversary of broadcasting', *Journal of Broadcasting*, vol. 3, no. 1.

Griggs J.W. (1919) Memo to shareholders in *Wireless Age*, November.

Hoddeson L. (1981) 'The emergence of basic research in the Bell telephone system, 1875-1915', *Technology and Culture*.

Hoffer T.W. (1971) 'Nathan B. Stubblefield and his wireless telephone', *Journal of Broadcasting*, vol. 15, no. 3, pp. 317–29.

Joos L.C.D. (1971) 'Le génie n'a pas de patrie: il y a des Popov partout', *Sélection du Reader's Digest*, November.

Kieve J.L. (1973) *The Electric Telegraph: a Social and Economic History*, David and Charles, Newton Abbot.

Landes D.S. (1969) *The Unbound Prometheus: Technological Change and Industrial Development in Western Europe from 1750 to the Present*, Cambridge University Press, Cambridge.

Mauriat C. (1987) 'La naissance de la radio diffusion d'Etat', in *La TSF des années folles*, Les Amis de l'histoire des PTT d'Alsace, Strasbourg.

Mayes T. (1972) 'History of the American Marconi Company', *The Old Timer's Bulletin*, vol. 13, no. 1, June, pp. 11–18.

Monod-Broca P. (1990) *Branly, au temps des ondes et des limailles*, Belin, Paris.

Moris L. (1949) *Not So Long Ago*, Random House, New York.

Petitjean G. (1985) 'Gustave Ferrié et le développement de la TSF militaire', *Toute l'électronique*, September.

Petitjean G. (1987) 'De l'électricité statique à la TSF', in *la TSF des années folles*, Les Amis de l'histoire des PTT d'Alsace, Strasbourg.

Rousseau P. (1967) *Histoire des techniques et des inventions*.

Sivowitch E.N. (1971) 'A technological survey of broadcasting's prehistory (1876-1920)', *Journal of Broadcasting*, vol. 15 no. 1, pp. 1–20.

Süsskind Ch. (1968) *The Early History of Electronics*. Proc. IEEE Spectrome, August, p. 90.

PART III
GLOBAL COMMUNICATION
(1930–1990)

Introduction

In 1953 Edwin Armstrong, the inventor of FM radio, threw himself out of the window of his New York apartment. His body was found 30 floors below. Twenty years earlier, in 1933 and after 10 years of research, this pioneer inventor of radio had developed FM at RCA's request. Attracted by the new technology, RCA had at first decided not to develop FM but rather to devote its resources to television. However, thanks to Armstrong's persistence and the emphasis he laid on RCA's competitors, the firm eventually accepted the new mode of radio broadcasting after the war. But Armstrong then had to sue Sarnoff for his copyrights and, exhausted after five years of legal battles, he finally committed suicide (Barnouw, 1968: 40–1, 283–4).

Armstrong's dramatic death was also that of the individual inventors of communication machines. Gone were the days of the Bells and Marconis and even the Edisons who had designed communication systems with, at the most, 10 or 20 assistants. Invention henceforth lay in the hands of large institutions. The age of R&D had replaced that of the inventor–entrepreneur. Research and development were carried out by large firms able to afford laboratories with several thousand researchers[1] and to implement a strategy for launching a mass market. Individual inventors did not disappear entirely, but they either worked in less important fields, or their inventions had to be taken over by large firms for them to succeed.

Like the small research teams of the nineteenth century, the large twentieth-century laboratories were to work on different communication fields simultaneously. While Bell laboratories can be found at the origin of the transistor, electronic switching, talking films and high-fidelity sound,[2] RCA developed a new procedure for sound films, a standard for black and white and then colour television, and the 45 rpm record.

This third communication era, which I study in the following section, also started under the sign of a technological innovation: electronics. During the preceding period, all new communicating machines were based on electricity, precision mechanics and sensitized surfaces. With the invention of the triode, a new basic technology was born. Electronics would henceforth be present in all new communicating machines.

Finally, the second half of the twentieth century was characterized by significant transformations in private life. Fragmentation of towns and withdrawal into the home, observed in the preceding period, became more marked. These trends were accompanied by a change in family life-styles seen mainly in greater individual autonomy. The latter was, in turn, to have a significant impact on the use of existing media and the appearance of new media.

Compared to the Bell era, the telephone had undergone profound technological change. We shall first examine in Chapter 7 how electronic technology implanted itself in telecommunications. Chapter 8 then looks at the role of electronics in two new media that appeared in the 1940s: television and computers. Finally, Chapter 9 deals with the evolution of the private sphere and new ways of consuming the media.

Notes

1 For example, Bell laboratories' staff rose from 6,000 in 1950 to 22,000 in 1980.

2 On this relatively unknown aspect of the Bell laboratories' research (which in particular led them to work with a renowned conductor, Stokowski), see McGinn (1983: 38–75).

References

Barnouw E. (1968) *A History of Broadcasting in the United States,* vol. 2: *The Golden Web,* Oxford University Press, New York.

McGinn R.E. (1983) 'Stokowski and the Bell laboratories: collaboration in the development of high-fidelity sound reproduction', *Technology and Culture,* vol. 24, no. 1, January.

7
Telephone Engineers' Technical Options

A telephone network has two main technical functions: transmitting speech and connecting the transmitter with the receiver. The latter, called switching, was first achieved manually before being automated at the turn of the nineteenth century. The present chapter deals mainly with the history of telephonic switching, highlighting the birth of contemporary electronic switching. With respect to transmission, I have focused my investigation on a case of technical failure, that of the waveguide.

The telephone exchange

At the start of telephony, the Americans used the word 'exchange' to denote what the French had called a *'central'*. It would appear that these different linguistic choices represented two distinct approaches to the telephone. With the former, telephones were seen as a means for exchange, for putting two people into contact, whereas the latter evoked the image of a stellate network with a switch at the centre.

These two perceptions of switching defined the technical achievements that telephone engineers were to set as their goals: increasing both the size of telephone exchanges and the flow of traffic. The first exchange (1878) handled 21 subscribers; 30 years later (in 1910), L.M. Ericson installed the world's largest manual telephone exchange in Moscow, capable of switching 60,000 subscribers (Chapuis, 1982: 150). Later generations of automatic exchanges only exceeded this size at the end of the 1970s with the advent of electronic switching. Manual exchanges rapidly became saturated at peak hours and automatic switching was to aim chiefly at enhancing the volume of traffic generally measured in traffic units (TU).[1] The first generation of (rotary) automatic switches never surpassed 600 TU; the second generation (the Crossbars) reached a maximum of 4,000 TU (Pinaud, 1987: 163). Current electronic exchanges have a capacity of up to 15,000 TU.

Towards automation

The automation of telephonic switching is characteristic of industrial developments during the past hundred years. In many labour-intensive industries, machines gradually replaced people. Mireille Nouvion, inspired by the current distinction in sociology and the history of technology between mechanization and automation, distinguishes two phases in the development of automatic switches (Nouvion, 1982: 104). With mechanization, the first phase, operations were of the 'stimulation–response' type. Automation started when information was processed so that action could be organized according to a particular situation. In manual switching the operator created temporary links between two points. The first automatic exchanges did this mechanically, controlled by information (the number) sent by the subscriber. In order to upgrade the process and in particular the routing, the system was then developed further to process information. At first it stored the dialled numbers until they had been connected; later it was able to perform other logical operations such as sorting the numbers according to different routing levels.

Control of the network was finally automated, although this proved to be far more complex. The procedure used was equivalent to the 'reaction control' presented in all books on industrial automation. In telephony, however, this retroactive device was original: it consisted of 'processing information on information processing'.

The mechanization–automation sequence of the telephone resulted, as in other industries, in major staff reductions. The manual system required one operator for about 70 subscribers. With the automatic system operators were no longer required, although maintenance support increased. The first electromechanical systems needed one technician for 1,000 lines; in more developed systems this performance was doubled. Today's electronic switching only requires one maintenance technician for 8,000 lines (Nouvion, 1982).

The long-term nature of technological development is therefore manifested in the constant striving for productivity gains, through mechanization and automation, which characterized the secular evolution of industrial capitalism. In the telecommunications sector, the main objective was to increase the size and capacity of exchanges.

Even though automation appears obvious *a posteriori*, its introduction generated a considerable amount of controversy and resistance. Debates on automatic telephony were central issues at the two first international congresses of telephone engineers in 1908 and 1910 (Chapuis, 1982: 75–9). The head of the Austrian technical services used the results of a detailed economic study to show that, on a local level, the automatic system was usually the most reliable, the fastest and the cheapest. In contrast, the technical director at AT&T favoured a semi-automatic system with an operator for receiving calls but in which all the physical switching mechanisms would be automated.[2]

Technically, there was no reason whatsoever to opt for an intermediary semi-automatic stage. A French engineer, C. Cornet, wrote some years later:

> between the manually operated system which we have installed in almost all French towns and total automation, there have been many intermediary stages marking existing organizations' resistance to progress. The plans and mechanisms proposed to delay the advent of total automation bear witness to the amazing ingenuity deployed by inventors in their efforts to satisfy the defenders of the manual system. Yet every new development introduced by them has also been a new defeat, for they

have all made new concessions to automation . . . Innovations have allowed for the partial automation of operators' work without eliminating it (Cornet, 1922; quoted in Stourdzé, 1979: 29)

The manual/semi-automatic/automatic debate turned into a general debate. What operations could one expect the subscriber to perform? As the French representative at the 1910 conference said, 'the question of knowing whether the subscriber will agree to perform certain movements is not of a technical order, and the answer could vary from one country to another depending on the subscribers.' Although we have no record of users' reactions, we do know what the opinion of the telephone companies and of the press was. While German newspapers were fiercely critical of automation, the Bavarian representative considered that 'subscribers in Munich got used to their new telephones with numbered dials straight away.'

In France, Campana and Jaubert report the following conversation between a telephone operator and a subscriber:

'My dear, what on earth am I going to do when you're no longer there?'
'That's simple, Sir. To get GUTenberg 75 20, for example, you dial the first three letters of Gutenberg, G U T, and then the four numbers.'
'How do I do that?'
'But you do have a telephone with a dial and numbers and letters, don't you?'
'Yes.'
'Well then, just try! Since the telephone isn't connected yet. Dial G U T 75 20.'
'I'm trying . . . There you are . . . Oh my dear, if I could get hold of whoever invented the automatic telephone!'
'Have you got it now?'
'Yes, but . . . must I really stick my finger into these holes seven times?'
'That's it.'
'And one's meant to know all these numbers by heart?'
'It's better if you do,'
'Listen, I'll never have the time for all this. Don't you want to be my telephonist?'
'I'm sorry, that's not possible Sir.' (Campana and Jaubert, 1976: 212–13)

This reluctance regarding the use of dial telephones can be related more generally to the relationship which industrialized societies at the start of the century had with technology. The telephone, like the motor car, was an instrument which the upper classes were loath to handle directly. Their relationship with technological objects passed through an intermediary: the operator or the chauffeur. In France, the inventor of the starter motor had to face the misgivings of car manufacturers who could see no use for an automatic starter when there were chauffeurs to turn the crank!

Whereas the gramophone was from the outset an instrument for the masses and designed as such, photography, the telephone and the car had to be transformed (made more automatic) to become mass consumer goods. Debate on a car or telephone for the masses started at the dawn of the twentieth century. It was settled during the 1920s in the USA, the 1950s in Europe and even in the 1970s for the telephone in France.

A century-old telephone exchange

The acceleration of technological progress often leads to the seemingly obvious conclusion that technological revolutions are becoming more and more frequent, especially in high-tech areas. The technological history of telecommunications shows, on the contrary, that technological changes as such are rare. The electromechanical system, for example, provided the basis of telephonic switching for almost 24 years.

In 1889, 12 years after the invention of the telephone, A.B. Strowger developed the first automatic telephone exchange. As the story goes, Strowger, who had his own undertaker's business in Kansas City, had invented the device to prevent his competitor from receiving all the telephone calls. The latter's wife was the local telephone exchange operator!

The principle of Strowger's device was simple: an arm fixed to an axial rod moved step by step vertically and then horizontally until it had made the required connection. Robert Chapuis (1982) reports the following anecdote on the design of this switch. Apparently, Strowger made the first model with two pencils, pins and detachable collars: 'The collars were stacked in a pile and the pins stuck into the hemisphere of each collar at regular intervals. One pencil served as a vertical rotation axis. A second pencil, at right angles to the first, swept over the circular plane of the pins, on the level at which it arrived.'

This story, like many anecdotes on inventions, is probably untrue. But it illustrates perfectly the fact that switching was a mechanical type of invention in the same tradition as the mechanization of the loom. On this 'step-by-step' technical principle, Strowger successfully created a first automatic switchboard in 1892. The device was upgraded by one of his colleagues and in 1895 they took out a patent. The technical diagram of this device is still, according to Chapuis, 'one of the most well-known diagrams in the history of telecommunications . . . One cannot help being struck by the fact that today, eighty years later [Chapuis was writing in 1978], switches are still built almost exactly according to this model.'

In the following 10 years, various developments appeared such as preselection (instead of one selector for each subscriber the ratio was reduced to 1 : 10) and a common battery for supplying electricity to subscribers' telephones. Chapuis concluded: 'The modern automatic exchange had really been born!' The step-by-step system was to become the most widespread electromechanical switching system in the world. In 1950, 60 years after its birth, it equipped about 55 per cent of all automatic lines worldwide (Jouty, 1953; Chapuis, 1982: 296). The diffusion of Strowger switches continued for another 20 years. In 1974 98 per cent of the English network were thus equipped. In France, the last Strowger exchange was removed in Bordeaux in 1979, after functioning for 51 years!

At the start of this century another electromechanical switching system with a single rotary movement was developed. The selectors and connectors were simpler than those of the Strowger machines. Two versions of this system were industrialized: the Panel in the USA and the Rotary in Europe. In 1939 rotary systems accounted for 25 per cent of all automatic switching in the world, compared to 65 per cent for the Strowger system (Nouvion, 1982: 45).

A third electromechanical switching system, patented in 1917, was to become operational at the end of the 1930s: the Crossbar. The connection was made by activating the vertical rod for an in-coming line and then the horizontal rod for an out-going line. Together these rods formed a matrix.

Historians of the telephone who present these three families of electromechanical switches underline the differences in the connection devices of the three systems. Other observers consider, however, that there was a coherent development: new functions appeared which added to the basic function of connection. For Christian Pinaud (1987: 132), for example, the first automatic (Strowger) switches differed very little from manual systems; moreover, he called them 'automatic anthropocentric switching'. At this stage 'the telephone network can be represented as a direct link from the transmitter to the receiver.' For Pinaud, the major change in telephony in the 1920s was the new awareness that the network was an intermediary technological device and not a prosthesis for human communication. Consequently, the management of traffic had to be optimized.

There was not, in fact, a break in technological time, as Pinaud wrote, but rather a slow evolution of electromechanical technology guided by the search for better performance in processing calls. Moreover, the history of the diversification of switching functions is not that of the three main families of switching systems succeeding one another chronologically. The Strowger system evolved concurrently with the rotary system.

A rotary switch such as the R6 (a French machine installed at the end of the 1920s) differed from the Strowger in that it introduced a separation between the functions 'search and connection of line' and 'reception of a number dialled by the subscriber' (Nouvion, 1982: 124). Later, indirect control switches (i.e. most rotary switches and the second generation of Strowgers in the 1920s)[3] were to distinguish between dialling and selecting functions. A new component (the recorder) saved the dialled number until the call had been put through. The system could then automatically look for an alternative route if the first attempt failed. Unlike the direct control system, it was no longer an automatic switching system with 'lost calls' (Nouvion, 1982: 136–7).

The matrix form of the Crossbar switching device made it possible to know, at every moment, 'the state of all the connecting points: available or engaged. This instantaneous information on the state of all the points of each matrix enabled a new device (the marker) to choose an end to end route for the selector' (Pinaud, 1987: 157). Thus, three main groups of device appeared in this advanced phase of electromechanical switching: control devices (recorders), selecting devices (markers) and connecting devices (matrices). In order to articulate the functioning of these different organs, a whole series of signals had to be transported by cable. In Pinaud's words: this 'wire network is the mirror of the operational logic of an exchange. That is why one says that this mode of functioning is based on a cabled logic' (1987: 157).

The Crossbar's contribution to the overall development of switching was of a different nature. In order to increase the performance of the system, it was necessary to specialize and to coordinate devices rather than simply juxtaposing identical ones. Specialists in switching use an anthropomorphic comparison to summarize this evolution: 'The organs of the old electromechanical systems functioned like a group of isolated and independent artisans doing the same job, whereas those of the new system can be likened to a firm with specialized workers on an assembly line and a large degree of mutual aid' (Lucas et al., 1965: 7).

The development of electromechanical switching was gradual. There were no specific breaks between the different families of equipment based on two or three original mechanical structures. On the other hand, the electrical circuits controlling the connections –the 'nervous system' of a switching system – consisted of increasingly complex devices from the point of view of their implementation. Chapuis, a former switching engineer, has compared this activity to an art 'focused on little things such as wires or relays. The improvements made to them seem minute' (1982: 159). It was through these slow, progressive and obscure developments that the technology evolved.

The inexorable rise of digitization

At any given time there is usually a particular type of technical device accepted by the engineering community. With reference to Kuhn's (1962) analyses of science, we can call this a technological paradigm. We know that Thomas Kuhn distinguishes two states of science: normal science and scientific revolution. Within an established paradigm the 'normal scientist' refines the concept and measures the coherence between facts and theories. When a number of anomalies appears which the existing paradigm cannot explain, a crisis ensues. This crisis is then resolved by a new paradigm which is finally accepted by the scientific community. For Kuhn the evolution of science (normal science – crisis – new paradigm) takes place relatively autonomously within the scientific community. A paradigm is, moreover, less a set of theories than a mode of structuring in the scientific community.[4]

Edward Constant (1973) and the economist Giovanni Dosi (1982) used Kuhn's theory to develop a model of analysis for technological evolution. Constant had an internalist perception of technology; he considered that a technological revolution can only be 'defined in terms of a relevant community of practitioners and has no connotation of social or economic magnitude'. In the technological domain, as in that of science, the paradigm indicates which directions research should follow and which ones it should rather abandon. Dosi talks of a technological trajectory, Constant of normal technology.

This Kuhnian perspective seems well adapted to an analysis of the technological history of the telephone. Telephone engineers' choices did not depend on technological considerations alone. The technological community worked under constant pressure since traffic had to be handled as efficiently and cost-effectively as possible. But to achieve that objective they did have a large degree of autonomy. After internal debate, which was often highly conflictual, the technological community chose a paradigm and stuck to it for a long time. Researchers on switching worked in a framework that was defined by both the economic and social project of telephony, as well as the technological paradigm in which it was situated.

How is a change made from one paradigm to another? For many commentators on Kuhn there was, for example, a sudden epistemological break between 'before' and 'after' the theory of relativity. Sociologists of technology, like Bruno Latour, can easily denounce this type of analysis by showing that scientific progress is constructed every day according to the intellectual and measuring tools of the scientist (Latour, 1985).

The conflict between two paradigms is above all of an epistemological order. A new paradigm is able to integrate into a single theoretical construction, phenomena which were inexplicable for the preceding paradigm. But this theoretical transformation cannot be compared to a political revolution. In the field of technological history, which is of interest to us here, the shift from one paradigm to another was very slow.

According to L.J. Libois (1983), it was in 1934 that the idea first arose of using electronics for switching. The American researcher L. Espenchied imagined building a tree-shaped structure similar to a network of waterways, in which the different calls would be *multiplexed by frequency-division*. This principle proved to be technically impossible to implement. In the 1940s research was resumed, but this time it was aimed at *time-division multiplexing*. Research conducted by Deloraine, Ransom and Adams in the USA and Flowers in Britain was, however, unsuccessful. The components available at the time (vacuum tube) prevented the project from being feasible.

Once they had realized that the question of components was blocking the project of electronic switching, the AT&T laboratories in the USA (the Bell labs) decided at the end of the 1930s to work on solid-state components. After uninterrupted research during the war, they finally developed the first germanium point transistor in 1947. Another eight years were needed to iron out problems. In 1955 the Bell laboratories brought out transistors that were to be the foundation of computers, of digital telecommunications and, more generally, of electronics.

The use of electronics in switching was a central element in engineers' vision of technology. Libois (1983: 151) wrote: 'Electronic switching was in most telecommunications researchers' and technicians' minds like a dream that they'd been trying to realize for generations.' With the development of transistors and computers, this dream could finally become reality.

Between 1947 and 1958 the Bell laboratories built the first models of electronic switches. They experimented with space-division and time-division systems (or in more popular terms, semi-electronic and all-electronic). In space-division electronic switching it is possible to follow the path which, in a switch, links an in-coming and an out-going line. The relays, instead of being electromechanical, become electronic. By contrast, with time-division switching, one can no longer follow the path of the connection. The incoming signal arrives multiplexed in time, with others. It is treated electronically and connected to another multiplex at the exit.

When a new paradigm begins to appear it is not immediately coherent. Several hypotheses may be envisaged simultaneously or, if the technological community agrees on the final goal, there may be disagreement on the means to achieving this end. In 1952, the British head of research on electronic switching, T.H. Flowers, raised the following question at a conference:

> How much attention should be given to semi-electronic systems? Personally, I am totally opposed to heavy spending in this field at present . . . Making a change in two steps will increase the efforts in development and engineering, delay the final benefits of the operation for possibly an entire generation and could well double the expense. (Libois, 1983: 151)

During the 1950s the British Post Office's laboratories built a model of time-division switching. In 1958 they created the first experimental time-division exchange designed to be connected to a network. It was installed in 1962 but encountered numerous problems and was finally abandoned. In Libois's view it was too advanced for contemporary technology. T.H. Flowers had been right too early; in the 1950s he had already seen the advantages of a digital system. He was a perfect example, according to the economist B. Loustalet (1986), of the syndrome of an engineer 'always ready to justify the relevance of long-term technological options which prescribed allocating resources to a technologically ambitious project rather than paying the bill twice'. But who could blame him? Forecasts in this domain are difficult. We shall see later that, in the case of optical fibres, the developmental stage was a lot faster than planned.

The Bell laboratories chose rather to focus their research on space-division switching. The first experimental exchange was installed in 1960 and then removed. It was only in 1965 that a truly electronic switching system (ESS1) was made operational. It was the outcome of a considerable research effort in which AT&T had spent six years longer on the project and invested ten times more (500 instead of 45 million dollars) than originally planned (Brooks, 1976: 279).

Research on electronic switching only started in 1957 in France, where time-division and space-division techniques were studied simultaneously. The national telecommunications research centre (CNET) built a laboratory model (*Plato*) of a time-division exchange and tested it between 1966 and 1969. During the same period it built, together with telecommunications firms, two prototypes of the space-division systems *Aristotle* and *Socrates*. Tested in operational situations, these two prototypes led to the project *Pericles* which was largely coordinated by telecommunications firms. The CNET also installed an operational *Plato* telephone exchange at Perros-Guirec in 1970 (see Lucas, 1971, 1979). It was the first fully electronic switching system used in the world and was later to be produced industrially by Alcatel under the name E10.

In parallel with research on electronic switching, other work was carried out on digital transmission. We know that the core of Graham Bell's invention was the transformation of pressure variations provoked by sound, into an electric current in proportion with these variations. This system of direct transmission was qualified as analogue. Various researchers tried to apply the principles of telegraphic transmission to telephonic transmission. M. Deloraine aptly called these attempts 'telegraphing speech'. The technique was patented several times, for example, by Patten and Minor (1903) and Poisson (1920) (Libois, 1983: 134). But in 1938 Reeves showed that one could 'code a conversation so as to transmit it in the form of telegraphic code in a series of digits. He invented the method of "pulse coded modulation"' (Deloraine, 1974: 133). This system was tested during the Second World War on radio links and developed industrially in the United States in 1962 and in France in 1966.

'Pulse coded modulation' (PCM) consists of sampling a speech signal at very high speed (8,000 times per second). The value of each sample is then coded in the form of an eight-digit binary number. Each speech signal sample, corresponding to different conversations, can be connected to any other one (each sample is transmitted in 3.9 micro-seconds). In Europe a 32-channel primary multiplex was used.

Digital transmission and electronic switching did, of course, tend to combine to form a totally digital solution. That was where the strength of the CNET engineers lay. They felt that time-division switching should be opted for together with a digital network. In their article in 1965, Lucas et al. wrote:

> Electronics is ill-suited to half-measures. Significantly, tests on partial electronization have always encountered problems and have never advanced very far. When the old structure is maintained it constitutes a framework that is too rigid. In contrast, radically new electronic solutions alone can benefit from all the following potential advantages: strength, security, speed and flexibility. (1965: 33)

Several years later, Lucas, after having described the advantages of electronic switching, wondered 'why, with all these advantages, time-division switching is not the only solution chosen'. One of the two answers he found was the following: 'The current telephone network still has very few digital lines and the full advantages of time-division switching can only be found within a digital network' (Lucas, 1971: 155).

The CNET engineers' ambition appears symbolically in the names of Greek philosophers chosen for their projects: *Socrates, Plato, Aristotle.* Not only did they want to make models of a new system; they also wanted to transform the basic technology of telecommunications, to create a new paradigm. In his book L-J. Libois shows, moreover, that the first electronic switching team led by him (the 'research on electronic machines' (RME) division) consisted of engineers and technicians from two different backgrounds.[5]

> They had formerly worked either in the transmission sector (radio links, pulse modulation systems) or in switching. The 'transmitters' were thoroughly familiar with the problems of electronic technology, while the 'switchers' were specialists in complex systems (connection network structures, logical control devices). The latter

were perhaps more inclined to adapt to the new notions of 'programming' that had assumed much importance with the introduction of computerization in switching. (Libois, 1983: 178)

I have already mentioned that telephonic switching is not limited to connecting two telephone lines, and that an exchange is also a system which must receive and process information (it must store numbers, search for a route, exchange information and so forth). Consequently, electronic switching, which developed concurrently with computing, looked to computers for a more powerful and flexible tool for processing information. The cabled logic of electromechanical exchanges was to be challenged by the computer logic of electronic exchanges (called 'recorded program control' by telecommunication specialists).

Computing played such an important role in research on electronic switching that the CNET developed the first European computers built entirely with transistors: *Antinea* and *Ramses*. Huge operational constraints were placed on these machines: they had to be able to function 24 hours a day and to restart automatically in case of failure. The computerization of telephone exchanges led engineers to re-analyse all the traditional functions of switching. 'A new principle emerged, that of the separation of functions . . . Instead of the plurality of devices with multiple functions as in electromechanics, electronic switching led to the conception of a structure with large functional units.' (Lucas, 1971: 157). This specialization of functions had already begun in Crossbar exchanges; here it was perfected. With 'the recorded programme' wrote Lucas:

> the operation of automatic switching equipment can be modified after its installation. The resulting flexibility is unknown in conventional systems where a program does of course exist, but in the form of wiring where any changes are far more difficult to implement than in a semi-permanent electronic memory. (Lucas et al., 1965: 25)

All these elements – synergy of PCM transmission and of temporal connection, computer-aided information-processing in telephone exchanges – show the strength and the coherence of the digital paradigm in telephony. This unification of all telephone techniques around the digital system is a fundamental element in the history of telecommunications. Nouvion (1982) shows how, from the start of this century, there was a process of divergence between switching and transmission. The former was based on standard technology during the electromechanics era; the latter gave rise to scientific and technological progress in signal processing, and hence to the advent of electronics. 'Technical reunification' was to take place in the 1970s, with digitization.

The digital paradigm did not impose itself overnight. The time/space-division issue was widely debated, particularly in France. In reality, the controversy was probably more intense in the industrial than in the technological domain. For a long time the two systems were not compared openly since they were still in their early stages of development. Positions evolved and each technology borrowed elements from the other. In 1965, Lucas et al. added the phrase 'except perhaps for connection as such' to their plea for electronic switching. Clearly, they were not sure yet about the future of the time-division model. In 1979, however, Lucas (1979: 78) wrote 'everybody seems convinced now of the merits of digital switching.' In the meantime, Jacques Dondoux and the CNET research team had demonstrated the superiority of the all-electronic system and had become its determined advocates.[6] Although French telephone authorities opted mainly for the semi-electronic system in 1974, they modified their choice a few years later by adopting the new digital paradigm.

In a CNET report, Lucas (1990: 186–99) showed that research on the space-division system had in fact benefited the time-division system. *Aristotle* (the space-division prototype) made it possible to define the principle of a specific channel for transmitting signalization data, called the 'semaphore channel'. *Socrates* (another space-division prototype) showed the advantage of controlling a telephone exchange by means of two computers operating together. This device for 'sharing the load' (developed by Pierre Lucas) was to be adopted to a large extent in electronic switching.

Sociologists like Nouvion or Pinaud explain the shift from electromechanics to electronics in terms of the technological and economic limits of the former. Since the Crossbar did not lend itself to upgrading, telephone engineers would have been forced to develop another system. We have seen that research on electronic switching started before the Second World War and that the first models appeared in the late 1950s and early 1960s, when the Crossbar was in full expansion. We are thus looking at a change of paradigm by assumption. The technological development appears largely independent of industrial demand.

This position does nevertheless need to be qualified. When technology progresses within a single paradigm, the supply of equipment such as telephone switches is dependent on demand. The shift from one generation of electromechanical switches to another was effectively related to the evolution of telephone traffic. The situation is, however, totally different when there is a change of paradigm. The cost of changing from one system to another is high and the new paradigm modifies the relevance of the outdated system.

Thus, it is not only thanks to the quality of its engineers that France adopted electronic switching. The extreme backwardness of the French telephone system made it far easier to equip a new network with a new technology. Countries like Sweden which were in the fore in this sector adopted the new system far more gradually. As Michel Zitt (1987: 26) writes, a technological tradition (in Kuhn's vocabulary: normal technology) is a steep slope for economic actors. A change of technological paradigm is therefore particularly difficult, with the result that new paradigms do not always manage to impose themselves.

Transmission

We have already seen (Chapters 5 and 6) that one of the main objectives in the development of the telephone and the radio was to cover very long distances. But transmission engineers also tried to increase the volume of traffic. In 1885 the discovery of 'phantom' circuits (by linking two telephonic pairs electrically, a new circuit is created) made it possible to increase transmission capacities by 50 per cent. In 1920 the discovery of current carrier systems in the USA opened the way to frequency-division multiple access. At first four and then 12 channels were transported on the same line in the 1930s.

During the same period very high-frequency radio transmission started being used experimentally in telecommunications. In 1931 a single-channel link was established between Calais and Dover (Sobol, 1984), and then during the Second World War the Allied armies developed 'multiplex' 8-channel telephonic links. Shortly after the end of the war, AT&T defined a system with five radio channels, each with a capacity of 480 telephone channels; this made a total of 2,400 telephone channels per line. In 1973 this figure had climbed to 16,500 telephone channels. With an additional system installed on the same infrastructure, a total capacity of 30,000 telephone channels could be obtained. Within a period of 25 years, the capacity of long-distance lines was multiplied by more than 12, with the same technique of analogue transmission.

The problem at that stage was clear: how to transmit the maximum number of telephone calls by using radio links and an analogue technique. L-J. Libois (1983: 125), from whom I have borrowed the above figures, shows that these results were possible owing to a change of components (from tubes to semi-conductors), to more powerful transmission, and to the upgrading of each of the components of the system. Another system was developed concurrently with radio links, which was as effective and cost roughly the same: the coaxial cable. The first cable of this type was installed in the USA between New York and Philadelphia in 1936. It had a few dozen telephone channels. Some years later, in 1940, AT&T developed a system which could transport 1,800 telephone channels per line. Subsequent progress was even more rapid than for radio links, for in 33 years the cables' transmission capacity was multiplied by 60 (Libois, 1983: 127).

Waveguide versus fibre optics

I have looked at the emergence of the digital paradigm in telecommunications fairly extensively. However, in order to understand the way in which a new paradigm developed, it is not enough to consider the single example of a new innovation which was widely diffused. We must also study an example of failure. For this purpose I have chosen the waveguide, a system in which waves could be transmitted through a hollow copper tube. The technology has now completely disappeared from the collective memory even though it was developed in all the main telecommunications laboratories in the world.

The waveguide was situated at the intersection between the two main transmission technologies of the time. It 'required a material medium and therefore
had the constraint of an underground cable. On the other hand, it used a very
high modulated frequency and both the spacing between repeaters and their
complexity was far closer to radio links' (Herlent, 1973: 280).

The idea of using hollow cylinders to guide the transmission of electromagnetic waves was not new. Lord Rayleigh, the English physicist who
succeeded Maxwell at Cambridge University, published a thesis on the subject in 1897. In particular, he indicated the relations which existed between the
wavelengths used and the diameter of the tube. Raleigh's theoretical work was
not, however, followed up or verified experimentally. During the same period
Marconi developed another mode of transmitting electromagnetic waves.
When, in 1901, he discovered that short waves were reflected by the ionos-
phere (Chapter 6) and therefore constituted an excellent means for
long-distance transmission, research on the waveguide became meaningless.
Marconi oriented developments on the radio towards more powerful transmission with lower frequencies. High frequencies needed for experiments
with the waveguide were therefore not produced at the start of this century.

The situation changed in the 1920s when Marconi became interested in
higher frequencies (up to 500 MHz) within the framework of his work on
microwave links. It was in this context that a new generation of research on
the waveguide was born in the 1930s. Thus, Lord Rayleigh's theory remained
unknown for three decades. It provides us with a pertinent example of an
alternative which was ignored by the prevailing technological development
of the time when it took a different direction – in this case that of Hertzian
waves. Economists like Pavitt use the notion of 'technological trajectory' to
account for the successive choices made by a technology. They state that the
final outcome of such trajectories is, by definition, unknown in advance. But
once a technological path has been abandoned, the cumulative process of
technological progress often makes it very difficult to return to that alternative. The history of motor car engines provides an interesting example in this
respect. Although at the beginning of the century electric cars were faster
than cars with internal combustion engines, it was the latter solution that
was finally chosen. Since then, all attempts to revive the electric car have
failed.

The waveguide was nevertheless 'reinvented' in the USA in the 1930s. Two
teams, who were unaware of Lord Rayleigh's theory and of each other, redis-
covered the laws of electromagnetic transmission in waveguides. George
Southworth of the Bell laboratories presented a paper on his work on
30 April 1936 at the American Physics Society in Washington.
Coincidentally, Wilmer Barrow of MIT (Massachusetts Institute of
Technology) programmed a talk the very next day in the same city at the
American section of the International Scientific Radio Union. A battle over
patents similar to the Bell/Gray dispute could easily have ensued, but the two
men decided to cooperate.

Southworth, who worked on radiophonic high frequencies, had the idea of testing the transmission of these waves in a hollow copper cylinder. When his experiment was successful (March 1932) he tried to find a scientific explanation. The first report presenting his experiment met with general scepticism. One of the leading mathematicians at the Bell laboratories concluded various calculations with the statement: 'the transmission system proposed is impossible' (see Oliner, 1984; Packard, 1984). Southworth worked for two years without any official support and was even deprived of his assistant. He nevertheless managed to get some informal support from a small group of mathematicians.

A few months later the very person who had refused to grant any credibility to Southworth's experiments had to make due apologies; he had made a mistake in his calculations! Mathematicians like Mead and Schelkunoff developed the mathematical theory of waveguides. They proved that there is only one type of wave with the very specific characteristic of having an attenuation that decreased with the frequency.

Southworth's working conditions were not exceptional. He was not an 'accursed' researcher or a misunderstood inventor. In reality, major research institutions, as well as the scientific and engineering community, had difficulty in accepting the development of a new paradigm. Innovators were often obliged to work in secret. Yet the organization of large research laboratories did leave gaps for marginal innovators who could, if they were convincing enough, mobilize their colleagues. The Bell laboratories' management blocked the publication of Southworth's work for two years, fearing that there may be a mistake in the results and 'that AT&T might appear ridiculous'. He was, however, eventually granted the means to continue his technical investigations.

The second 'new inventor' of the waveguide, Barrow, worked in a completely different, academic, environment. A very specific question lay at the origin of his research: 'how can radio communication be used to locate an aeroplane in conditions of poor visibility?' Work on antennae led him to the waveguide. His first experiments, conceived in the context of an inappropriate paradigm – the transmission of sound – were negative. This failure forced Barrow to develop a new theory for the waveguide. Subsequent experiments based on this theory were successful.

The history of the birth of the waveguide paradigm is complex. Unlike the beginnings of Hertzian waves, there was no meeting between a scientific theory and a technical use. Lord Rayleigh's scientific discovery remained unknown. Thirty-five years later, two engineers invented a new waveguide. They adopted an experimental approach, but it needed a theory. Southworth turned to the mathematicians of the Bell laboratories while Barrow developed his own theory. To complete our account we might add that when the two American scientists published the results of their work in 1936, an article by Léon Brillouin appeared in France on the 'transmission of electromagnetic waves in a pipe' (Brillouin, 1936: 227–39). Based on a critique of the American research, Brillouin presented new theoretical elements.

The technological trajectory of the waveguide remained dependent on that of the radio for a long time. Marconi's developments pushed Lord Rayleigh's work into the background. It was only when Marconi took an interest in high frequencies that the waveguide could be reinvented. This case illustrates perfectly Dosi's analysis in which 'technological paradigms have a powerful *exclusion effect*: the efforts and the technological imagination of engineers and of the organizations they are in, are focused in rather precise directions while they are, so to speak, "blind" with respect to other technological possibilities' (Dosi, 1982: 153).

From the 1940s the development of the waveguide encountered another difficulty: how to produce and install tubes at a competitive price. The problems of mechanical stability and parasite waves produced by geometric imperfections in the waveguide had to be solved. After working mainly on the waves, the engineers turned their attention to the guide. The solid copper guide was replaced by a helicoidal guide developed in the early 1950s by the Bell laboratories. Other research during the same period, for example by Jouguet in France, focused on the problem of bends. Finally, progress was also made in producing waves with very high frequencies.

During the 1960s experimental lines were installed in the USA, Britain, Germany and Japan. In France the CNET built an experimental line at Lannion in 1963. A 10-kilometre operational urban line was opened in 1971 between Paris (the Saint-Amand centre) and Meudon. In 1973 the telephone authorities (the DGT) decided to build a 30-kilometre line between Paris and Orléans (Bourgeat and Rolland, 1977: 12-21). At the same time the Americans were preparing a New York-Philadelphia line and the English a 40-kilometre line near London (Baptiste and Herlent, 1974: 331–7).

The waveguide's performance was remarkable. Hopes were placed on it transporting up to 500,000 telephone channels – 12 times more than a radio link and 50 times more than a coaxial cable. In 1972 Y. Herlent concluded a popularized article on the subject as follows: 'We should not consider that the developments which we have presented here constitute disorderly projects for the distant future . . . The waveguide seems to be a future means of transmission that will soon become operational' (Herlent, 1972: 21–2). Five years later, M.H. Carpentier and P. Fombonne (1977: 9) published a forecast on transmission media: 'one might well wonder whether the millimetric waveguide, a dream we have been trying to realize for thirty years, is not already condemned, so soon after its birth.' In fact the Paris–Orléans link was never built. Its fate was to be the same as that of other abortive projects such as the aerotrain or the nocturnal semaphore telegraph.[7] Photographs of the experimental waveguide line in the fields near Lannion are reminiscent of the concrete pillars supporting the Bertin aerotrain in central France.[8]

In view of the failure of these projects, one may be mildly amused at the inaccurate forecasts of Herlent or Bertin; but that would be taking unfair advantage of hindsight. It seems more useful to examine the reasons for which this new technological paradigm was not more successful. As L-J. Libois reminds us, the fact that the attenuation of waves transported by the guide decreases with the frequency 'fascinated the telecom engineers who forecast unusual technical performance for this new means of transmission' (Libois, 1983: 128).

The reason for the waveguide's failure is simple: a different paradigm, that of optical fibres, was adopted for transmission purposes. Thus, competition did not exist only between a new technological paradigm and an old one, but also between two alternative new paradigms (Dosi, 1982: 155). This conflict soon extended beyond the realm of research laboratories. The difference in price between the two technologies – waveguide and optical fibres – was such that network operators chose the latter. As far as their capacity for transporting information and their range (maximal length of network between two repeaters) was concerned, the two technologies had practically the same capacity. The sole criterion for selecting one or the other was therefore cost.

We can see therein the limits of the Kuhnian model for analysing technology. The choice between several paradigms is not made within the engineering community alone. Final decisions, made by the operators, are of an economic nature. The choice is, in a sense, made in two steps: 'It is only once the community has been convinced . . . once the first developments and implementation of a new paradigm have made it possible to establish criteria of cost and efficiency, that economic factors can play their conventional determining role' (Constant, 1973).

Thus, the choice of a new paradigm such as a waveguide is first made within the technological community. If this choice is invalidated by industrial decision-makers, the rejection of the paradigm is delayed by researchers who wish to preserve years of hopes and research work.

The economic choice between two technological paradigms is ordinarily complex. When the former is already widely diffused it benefits from a production tool, while the latter is still in its starting up phase. Considerable costs are therefore involved in adapting to the new paradigm. Furthermore, the two technologies do not always have the same systems and functions. For example, electronic switching was initially more expensive than electromechanical switching but a significant decrease in costs could be expected. Moreover, the new paradigm improved productivity in telephonic operations, allowed for flexibility in management, and opened the prospect for new services.

The waveguide had no specific asset to offset its higher price. Its only advantage was that it had a head start in time. In the early 1970s, when the very first operational waveguide lines were being installed, laboratory research on optical fibres was only starting. Technological progress in the field was, however, extremely rapid, as in that of electronic components.

Optical fibres

The idea of using light to transport information can, as we have already mentioned, be attributed to Graham Bell. Four years after the invention of the telephone, in 1880, he designed the 'photophone' (Mins, n.d.: 7). According to Bell, this device 'made it possible to hear a shadow'. Transmission was achieved by concentrating rays from a source of light, such as the sun, on a reflective surface. The latter vibrated under the effect of sound and these vibrations served as a modulator for the light rays. Despite several successful experiments, problems were encountered in transmitting light in bad weather and the system was never made operational.

Eighty years later, the inventors of the laser[9] tried to use laser rays for transmitting information, and encountered the same difficulties (Tréheux, 1984). Communication by means of light rays had to be guided. Even though the Englishman J. Tyndall managed in 1870 to transmit light by means of water (the luminous fountain) and even though the production of small glass fibres had been launched, the photophone never resulted in an industrial application. At the time, the rapidly expanding paradigm of the telephone prevented that of the photophone from being developed.

As with the waveguide, the first research work on optical communication was interrupted. It was only in the 1950s that research was resumed, first in England and then in the United States. In the first optical fibre created in England in 1958, 99 per cent of the light injected was lost after 20 metres of transmission (Kao, 1981). In the early 1970s decisive progress was made with the discovery of three materials with interesting characteristics in the same area of the optical spectrum: gallium arsenide for transmitting light in infrared, silicon for detecting it and silica for transporting it. Optical fibres made from glass, then silica, had finally found an appropriate technical combination.

From then on progress was extremely rapid. In 1972, the year in which the first pre-operational waveguide links were opened, Corning Glass brought out optical fibres which preserved 40 per cent of the energy injected after 1 kilometre (4 decibels of attenuation). In the following year the attenuation was halved. Because of its fineness the optical fibre, sometimes called a hair of light, became a feasible transmission medium in telecommunications. In France an experimental line was built at Lannion in 1976. Improvements in the manufacturing process made it possible to reduce costs from 25 francs per metre in 1976 to 4 francs in 1980.[10] It then became obvious that the optical fibre had triumphed, especially since it used a very cheap raw material – silica (sand) – in tiny quantities (it had a diameter of a few hundred microns). By contrast, the waveguide required a very expensive raw material – copper – in large quantities (the diameter of a tube was 5 centimetres). The first operational fibre line was installed between the Parisian exchanges Tuileries and Philippe-Auguste in 1980. Other lines were to follow in 1982.

Technological progress in the field was so rapid that the optical fibre's success was unexpected. Only six years after the first laboratory models, experimental lines were installed. The waveguide had taken 25 years to reach the same stage. The passage from the experimental to the operational phase required eight years for the waveguide and only four for the optical fibre. Development of the glass fibre owed its rapidity not only to enhanced performance, but also to the fact that the climate was right for a new paradigm in the field of transmission. This was to be borrowed from a technological domain that seemed far removed from telecommunications. In a sense it illustrated the following idea by Leroi-Gourhan: 'We often borrow what we are about to invent' (Zitt, 1987: 31).

Thus, the waveguide paradigm never succeeded in imposing itself. At the start of this century its scientifico-technological development was blocked by the birth of the radio. During the 1970s another technology, the optical fibre, stopped it at the last minute from being developed industrially. Inventors are thus constantly subjected to competition from new technologies which can ruin years of research.

Notes

1 A traffic unit (TU) is equivalent to the average number of devices or circuits occupied simultaneously during a certain period of time.

2 On the debate in the United States during the start-up phase of automatic switching, see Mueller (1989: 534–60).

3 On the evolution of Strowger equipment see Chapuis (1982: 205–15).

4 'A paradigm governs, first and foremost, a group of scientists, not a scientific field' (Kuhn, 1962).

5 L-J. Libois was, successively, head of electronic switching at the CNET, director of the CNET (1968-1971) and director general of the *Direction générale des télécommunications* (Department of Telecommunications) (1971–74).

6 Jacques Dondoux replaced L-J. Libois as head of electronic switching at the CNET in 1968 and then as director of the CNET (1971–74). He occupied the post of director general of the Department of Telecommunications from 1981 to 1986. On his critical analysis of industrial options in electronic switching in 1974, see the interview with him in *Cadres CFDT*, no. 229, July–August 1981.

7 In 1820 Admiral de Saint-Haouen tested a system between Paris and Orléans, capable of making the semaphore telegraph operational at night. Despite some encouraging results at first, the experiment was considered a total failure.

8 Abortive technologies can remain a sign of modernity: the aerotrain line served as a setting for François Truffaut's film *Farenheit 451* (1966).

9 Abbreviation of light amplification by stimulated emission of radiation.

10 The average price of uncabled fibres given in R. Bouillie, *Fibres optiques: composants de base*, CNET Lannion, undated.

References

Baptiste C. and Herlent Y. (1974) 'Le guide d'ondes circulaire', *Annales des télécommunications*, no. 9–10.

Bourgeat L. and Rolland C. (1977) 'Le point sur le guide d'ondes circulaire', *L'Echo 'des recherches*, April.

Brillouin L. (1936) 'Propagation des ondes électromagnétiques dans un tuyau', *Revue générale d'électricité*, August.

Brooks J. (1976) *Telephone: the First Hundred Years*, Harper and Row, New York.

Campana M. and Jaubert J. (1976) *La Demoiselle du téléphone*, Jean-Pierre Delarge, Paris.

Carpentier M.H. and Fombonne P. (1977) 'Evolution technologique des supports pour la transmission de l'information', in *Congrès de la société des électriciens, de électroniciens et des radioélectriciens (SEE)*, Grenoble, September.

Chapuis R. (1982) *100 Years of Telephone Switching* (1878-1978), vol. I: *Manual and Electromechanical Switching* (1878-1960s), North Holland, Amsterdam.

Constant E.W. (1973) 'A model for technological change applied to the turbojet revolution', *Technology and Culture*.

Cornet C. (1922) '*La Technique moderne*'.

Deloraine M. (1974) *Des ondes et des hommes*, Flammarion, Paris.

Dosi G. (1982) 'Technological paradigms and technological trajectorial', *Research Policy*, no. 11, North-Holland, Amsterdam.

Du Castel F. and Lavallard F. (1990) *Le Centre national d'études des télécommunications*, CRCT, Neuilly.

Herlent Y. (1972) 'Les télécommunications par guide d'ondes circulaire', *Toute l'électronique*, November.

Herlent Y. (1973) 'Le guide d'ondes circulaire', *L'Onde électrique*, September.

Jouty A. (1953) *Un ancêtre qui se porte bien, le système Strowger*, internal note of the PTT Ministry.

Kao C.K. (1981) 'Fibres optiques: historique et perspectives d'avenir', in 'Fibres optiques: technologie, applications', *Revue des télécommunications*, vol. 56, no. 4.

Kuhn T. (1962) *The Structure of Scientific Revolutions*, University of Chicago Press, Chicago.

Latour B. (1985) 'Les vues de l'esprit. Une introduction à l'anthropologie des sciences et des techniques', *Culture technique*, no. 14, CRCT, Neuilly.

Libois L-J. (1983) *Genèse et croissance des télécommunications*, Masson, Paris.

Loustalet B. (1986) 'La recherche-développement dans l'industrie européenne des télécommunications: le système X', Idate, Montpellier.

Lucas P. (1971) 'Perspectives de la commutation électronique', *Annales des télécommunications*, May–June.

Lucas P. (1979) 'Le progrès de la commutation électronique dans le monde', *Annales des télécommunications*, janvier-février.

Lucas P. (1990) 'La commutation électronique', in F. du Castel and F. Lavallard (eds), *Le Centre national d'études des télécommunications*, pp. 186–99, CRCT, Neuilly.

Lucas P., Légaré R. and Dondoux J. (1965) 'Les idées modernes en commutation téléphonique', *Commutation et Electronique*, no. 9, April.

Mins F.M. 'The first century of lightwave communications', in *IFOC Handbook and Buyers Guide 1981–1982*, vol. 4.

Mueller M. (1989) 'The switchboard problem: scale, signaling, and organization in manual telephone switching (1877–1897)', *Technology and Culture*, vol. 30, no. 3, July.

Nouvion M. (1982) *L'Automatisation des télécommunications. La mutation d'une administration*, Presses universitaires de Lyon.

Oliner A.A. (1984) 'Historical perspectives on microwave field theory', in *IEEE Transactions on Microwave Theory and Techniques*, vol. MTT 32, September.

Packard K.S. (1984) 'The origin of wave guides: a case of multiple rediscovery' in *IEEE Transactions on Microwave Theory and Techniques*, vol. MTT 32, September.

Pinaud C. (1987) 'Propagation et duplication de la communication interpersonnelle. Exégèse des figures techniques de la télécommunication ou le message du médium', unpublished doctoral thesis, University Bordeaux III.

Sobol H. (1984) 'Microwave communications: an historical perspective', *IEEE Transactions on Microwave Theory and Techniques*, vol. MTT 32, September.

Stourdzé Y. (1979) 'La généalogie de la commutation', *Colloque Bernard Gregory 'Science et décision'*, CNRS-MIT, Paris, February.

Tréheux M. (1984) '2005 . . . les fibres optiques', *Science et Avenir, L'Explosion de la communication*, special no.

Zitt M. (1987) 'Filiations techniques et genèse de l'innovation', *Technique et Culture*, no. 10, Maison des sciences de l'homme, Paris.

8

The Triumph of Electronics:
Television and Computers

In contemporary thinking on communication one point is often emphasized :
the unification of telecommunications, broadcasting and computing
(Bustamente, 1991). Some authors even go so far as to talk of a 'digital society'. Before studying this question, we need to briefly consider the history of
the basic electronic components of communication devices. The following
chapter presents such an overview and examines the course of the electro-
mechanics/electronics debate in the television and computer fields. Only then
does it attempt to explain the convergence of the three media: telecommunications, computing and broadcasting.

Basic technologies

We have seen that even though the idea of electronic switching started to
appear in 1934, it was only with the birth of the transistor in 1947 that it
materialized. From then on, as P. Lucas said, 'the development of electronic
switching was always a sort of race in which ideas and components took the
lead alternately' (Lucas, 1984: 381). The transistor played another key role in
the development of computing and portable radio sets. In fact, the public at
large identified it so much with the radio set that the latter came to be called
a transistor.

Broadcasting, computing and telecommunications have all been largely
dependent throughout their history on the advent of new families of electronic components. As we have seen, radiotelephony and radio broadcasting
could only be developed with a triode. But the latter was more than just a
detector of Hertzian waves, it was also an amplifier. (A slight variation in the
potential of the control grid[1] produces a significant variation in the current in
the anode circuit.) Thanks to this property, the triode was to become the basic
component of telephonic repeaters which made the first New York–San
Francisco line possible in 1914. The development of electronic tubes was to
take a long time, as engineers left the familiar ground of electricity after a
half-century and ventured into the unknown field of electronics. The vacuum
tube was to serve after the Second World War in the construction of the first
computers.

Amplification effects could also be obtained by means of a transistor (con-
traction of the words transconductance resistor). Semi-conductors such as

germanium crystals or silicon, in contact with metallic points, produced such effects. This new electronic component was to be the foundation of the second generation of computers. As indicated above, it was also used in electronic switching and in the production of portable radio-receivers.

The next technological stage in the evolution of components was the integrated circuit. In 1959 Jack Kilby at Texas Instrument and Robert Noyce at Fairchild, working concurrently, integrated a large number of elementary circuits on a silicon surface. By 1965 it had become possible to integrate several dozen transistor equivalents on a 16 mm^2 chip (MSI or medium scale integration technology). In 1970 the thousand element mark was topped (LSI or large scale integration). This evolution corresponded roughly to Moore's law which in 1964 forecast that the number of components in an integrated circuit would double every 18 months. Integration not only reduced congestion (and costs), it also increased speed and reduced energy consumption. Every time the distances in a circuit were halved, the speed was doubled and energy consumption, as well as the surface, divided by four. Performance was further enhanced by changing the raw materials used. The first circuits were made from germanium, then silicon and finally gallium arsenide today. The latter material has made it possible to increase speed six-fold.

Finally, the microprocessor (the miniature form of the processor, a computer's central processing unit) which appeared in 1971, provided the basis for the future development of microcomputers. Microprocessors were diffused widely and are used today to control the operation of countless electrical devices.

The evolution of each of these families of components was extremely rapid. The broadcasting, computer and telecommunication industries' laboratories had constantly to take new developments into account. Since several years are required to develop a telecommunications system, for example, 'it is necessary' says Jean-Pierre Poitevin:[2]

> to anticipate these developments and to design future telecom systems with the most advanced technologies available. It is even becoming increasingly necessary to use technologies which do not yet exist at the start of the project. Consequently, the material realization of the first models has to be replaced by CAD to simulate the operation of future components and predict their availability or even their existence. At the same time designers cannot anticipate too far in advance as this might delay the production of new equipment or even make it impossible. It is important to aim accurately and to do so as early as possible; otherwise options might have to be modified, developments interrupted mid-way, design recommenced. . . . (Poitevin, 1986: 41)

The above example clearly illustrates the complexity of the technical options facing an innovator. He or she is dependent on a number of technologies, each of which evolves at its own pace. Innovation takes place in an uncertain environment; the success or failure of the innovator's system is not only related to the technological devices developed, but also to his or her ability to anticipate other technological changes.

The 'all-electronic' option in television and computers

The issues involved in controversies over paradigms are not always the same. In the case of telephonic switching studied in Chapter 7, debate remained confined to the telecommunication engineering community and did not affect telephone usage directly. The new technology did lead to reduced costs in the telephone service and to the preparation of new services, but on the whole the debate remained internal. With television and computers, the situation differed considerably. Electromechanical techniques were used at first and the electronic paradigm had difficulty imposing itself. It was, however, to modify the external characteristics of these two communication systems profoundly.

Two ways of scanning

It was in the 1920s, at the beginning of the development of broadcasting, that the first television prototypes started to appear. Several television patents had, however, been taken out at the beginning of the century. A number of rudimentary experiments were performed by Max Dieckmann and Ernst Ruhmer in Germany and by Georges Rignoux in France. They never succeeded in transmitting more than a letter such as E or H. Most systems were based on the principle of image analysis (used notably for the telephonic transmission of photographs). Images were scanned line by line by means of a Nipkow disc (a spirally apertured rotating disk). Light shone through the apertures onto a photo-electric cell which produced an electric current. The latter was transmitted by radio to the receiving end where the image was recreated by reversing the transmitting mechanism. Because of the type of image scanning device used, this procedure was called a mechanical system. During the same period the English physicist Campbell Swinton suggested creating a television system by scanning images with an electron beam. In Russia the engineer Boris Rosing created a receiver based on the same principle (Abramson, 1987: 35–7).

Thus, two television paradigms appeared in the 1910s. 'Mechanical television' was the first to become operational. In 1925 Charles Jenkins in the United States and John Baird in England first demonstrated their television system publicly. The American historian David MacFarland finds it 'ironic that a man such as John Baird of Great Britain should be the one to stumble onto the right combination of factors that would give him the honor of being the first to send "true" television pictures (that is, pictures of animate objects, and with gradations of light and dark)' (MacFarland, 1975: 49). In effect, Baird's originality probably lay not in his device itself, but in his project for an enterprise.

In 1925, when neither the BBC in England nor NBC or CBS in the USA had yet been created, John Baird set up the world's first television company, Television Limited, with a capital of £500! (Briggs, 1961: 519). A few months later he performed his first public demonstration and attracted investors. He also wrote to the British Post Office to obtain a frequency for experimental broadcasting, but for a number of years a conflict with the BBC prevented him from actually doing so. Nevertheless, Baird launched an advertising campaign on the theme 'Television For All' and 'Practical Television in the Home' (Briggs, 1961: 533), and in September 1929 experimental programmes were started. The images were still rudimentary and only comprised 30 lines (Abramson, 1987: 140) but by 1930 sound and image synchronization was achieved. The Prime Minister MacDonald, one of the first TV viewers, thanked Baird for this 'wonderful miracle' that had 'put something in his room which would never let him forget how strange the world was – and how unknown' (Briggs, 1961: 549). MacDonald's enthusiasm was not, however, shared. In January 1931 Baird had sold less than a thousand sets (Briggs, 1961: 154). Yet he created the first TV programmes in cooperation with the BBC: theatre with a play by Pirandello and a live broadcast of the Derby. The *Daily Herald* journalist commented (4 June 1931): 'We had found the stepping-stone into a new era in which mechanical eyes will see for us great events as they happen and convey them to us at our homes' (Briggs, 1961: 552).

Development of the electronic option was concurrent with that of mechanical television. Vladimir Zworykin, who had been Rosing's assistant at the St Petersburg Technological Institute, emigrated to the United States after the First World War. Influenced by his teacher, he 'was firmly convinced not only that television was coming but that, when it came, it would be electronic television' (Zworykin, 1962: 69). In the Westinghouse laboratories, where he strove to realize his intuition, Zworykin, at the end of 1923, demonstrated the feasibility of an all-electronic solution with a camera and a receiver. Yet despite this early success, he never managed to convince the directors of Westinghouse who asked him to 'go to work on something more useful' – in this case sound movies (Abramson, 1987: 81).

In 1927 a young inventor from the West Coast, Farnsworth, created the first model of electronic television. He managed to transmit a few drawings, notably the dollar symbol (Barnouw, 1968: 39). It seems that the goal of individual inventors – making their fortune – was manifested in the choice of this first message. Both Farnsworth and Baird were the last representatives of the inventors–entrepreneurs who wanted to control the development of their new technology.

At the end of the 1920s the defenders of the electronic solution were in the minority and mechanical television predominated. Baird started broadcasting regular programmes with the BBC. In 1928 Westinghouse demonstrated the mechanical system publicly, thereby impugning Zworykin's claims (Abramson, 1987: 122). In the preceding year the Bell laboratories, which were by far the major communication research centre of the day, had tested a mechanical television system with 50 lines. Contemporaries spoke of 'excellent daguerrotypes which have come to life and started to talk' (Abramson, 1987: 99). RCA and CBS also each set up (in 1928 and 1931 respectively) an experimental station using the mechanical system.

Despite the initial success of mechanical television, Farnsworth and

Zworykin persisted with their research. Zworykin, who worked on a largely personal basis, travelled to Europe in 1928 to study his colleagues' work. He was particularly interested in research carried out in Paris by the Belin laboratories on television (cathode ray) tubes. He even poached Ogloblinsky, Belin's chief engineer, who joined him in the USA in the following year.[3] By restructuring, RCA was able to take over a part of the production of radio sets from its parent companies, General Electric and Westinghouse. Within this new context, Zworykin managed to persuade Sarnoff, RCA's managing director, to set up an electronic television research laboratory. This reversal in RCA's choices can probably be explained by Sarnoff's desire for autonomy regarding the parent companies' technological policies. The mechanical television experimental broadcasts from RCA at the time were in fact performed with General Electric equipment. By gambling on electronic television, Sarnoff was also playing for technological independence (Stern, 1964: 287). Suddenly Zworykin's research became more credible. In 1929 he developed the television tube (kinescope) and two years later the camera tube (iconoscope) (Zworykin, 1962: 71–2).

During the same period the company EMI, a product of the restructuring of the British record and radio industries, launched a research programme on television. RCA was a 25 per cent shareholder in the new company. After a few initial attempts at mechanical television, the EMI researchers opted for the electronic solution. They were familiar with Zworykin's work and had access to all RCA's patents and expertise. Their choice was not, however, an obvious one; images from the first electronic scanning tubes were of a poor quality and the temptation to revert to the mechanical solution was very strong. 'Instead' wrote Shoenberg, the research director, 'we decided that the potentialities of the electronic scanning tube justified a great effort to overcome the problems it presented at the time' (Briggs, 1961: 569). At first the researchers focused their attention on reception. They continued to use a mechanical device since an agreement with RCA prohibited them from undertaking autonomous research in this field. They nevertheless remained convinced that the future lay in an all-electronic solution. In 1932 two of them, Tedham and McGee, built a scanning tube (similar to the iconoscope) almost clandestinely, without informing their managers. In the following year EMI decided officially to base the entire sector on the electronic system.

Baird, on the other hand, remained convinced of the superiority of the mechanical solution. After a trip to the United States in 1931, he declared that he saw 'no hope for television by means of cathode ray tubes' (Abramson, 1987: 176). Yet he was slowly to change his mind. In 1933 EMI demonstrated its television device to the BBC. The quality was far superior to that of the Baird system and it had three times more lines per image and twice as many images per second (Briggs, 1961: 570). Faced with such a vast difference in quality, noticed immediately by the guests at the demonstration, Baird accused EMI of being a foreign agent. Even though the latter denied this accusation by asserting that all its equipment was produced in its own laboratories, the Post Office, unlike the BBC, was swayed by Baird's argument.

Baird was furthermore to deploy the same tactics that he had used some years earlier to obtain the right to broadcast – he took full advantage of contradictions between the Post Office and the BBC. But he also decided to reorientate his research and employed A.G.D. West, formerly chief engineer at the BBC and EMI, with the mission to develop a 120-line television tube. Contracts were also signed with Farnsworth in the United States to buy his electronic camera technology.

In 1934 the British government set up a commission of enquiry to define the state's position with respect to television. Competition intensified between Baird and EMI. Everyone seemed to agree that low-definition television (30 lines) used by Baird for his experiments with the BBC was outdated. In January 1935 the commission proposed a minimal definition of 240 lines and 25 images per second. A few months later Baird announced that he would achieve this quality with a mixed system (mechanical for transmission and electronic for reception). EMI bet on a 'high-definition' (405 lines) standard, made possible by electronics. It was the time when RCA sold its shares in EMI, giving the latter its financial autonomy to add to its technological independence. The American historian Abramson considers that EMI then had 'the most advanced television system in the world. By this time they had passed up every other company, including RCA' (Abramson, 1987: 225).

In November 1936 the BBC opened a permanent television service. Unable to decide between the two industrialists, it alternated Baird's and EMI's equipment on a weekly basis. The superiority of the EMI system soon became obvious and the BBC opted for it definitively in February 1937.

By the start of the Second World War, British television had effectively taken off.[4] It had been offering regular TV programmes for a number of years and between 20,000 and 25,000 sets had been installed (Briggs, 1961: 620). In the United States regular programming only started in 1939, when the total number of sets barely exceeded 10,000 (Barnouw, 1968: 128).

We cannot assess the mechanical/electronic television conflict without discussing Baird in more depth. He was a highly controversial character. His stubbornness has often been condemned, but such criticism appears unwarranted for two reasons. It is far too easy, now that the electronic paradigm has triumphed, to point a finger at those who persistently tried to pursue an alternative solution. At the time, when electronics was still in its infancy, the mechanical solution seemed to make the most sense. All major companies agreed on that point until 1929. Moreover, Baird did undertake research on the electronic solution in 1932. Other historians have criticized the pretentious side of Baird, his desire to be first in everything (he took out patents on colour television, stereoscopic television, image recording on discs and large screen TV). I think, on the contrary, that John Baird's extraordinary dynamism should be celebrated. He led television from the laboratory experiment stage to its first life-size realizations. It was unquestionably he who understood that one of television's characteristics as a medium was its ability, like the radio, to broadcast events live. (For a long time the mechanical system was undeniably superior to the electronic system for reporting outside events.) Baird was part of the tradition of inventors–entrepreneurs: the Cooks, Bells and Marconis. From the outset he wanted to enter the broadcasting market; that was his strength but also his weakness. In the first third of the twentieth century a new medium could not be launched in the same way as in the nineteenth century. It was not so much the complexity of electronics compared to conventional electricity that made the work of individual researchers impossible. After all, in 1939 Farnsworth developed an electronic television system of such quality that RCA felt obliged to buy his patents (Stern, 1964: 290). It was rather the impossibility for an individual, or more precisely for a medium-sized company, to manage all the technical and commercial problems involved in launching a new medium. That is what T. Vail was referring to when he said: 'A good idea can arise in a man's mind anywhere, but when it has to be integrated into a whole that is as complex as the Bell system [we could also say as television], no single individual can successfully implement his idea.'

A company such as EMI was, by contrast, able to play this role. It started entering the television field when the medium's characteristics had already been defined by Baird's and the BBC's experiments. Like everybody who worked with television, EMI encountered the limits of the mechanical system. Once the company became aware of Zworykin's research it was able to take the gamble of electronics and to rely on engineers who were as obstinate as Baird but had opted for the electronic system. In the twentieth century it was far easier for large firms like EMI or RCA, than for individual inventors like Baird, to take advantage of the technological or use-related opportunities that lie at the core of innovation.

The slow maturation of the computer paradigm

The birth of computing was surrounded by the same type of hesitations concerning the definition of a new paradigm and the appearance of intermediary technical devices. A first generation of calculators was developed before the war: analogue machines. At MIT, V. Bush built a machine in the 1930s based on the principle of seeking natural or artificial devices with variations analogous to those to be calculated. This principle of equivalence constituted an original calculation method but never spawned any further developments (Breton, 1987: 61–2). It was rather digital machines, in the same tradition as Pascal's and Leibniz's, which gave birth to the computer. During the 1930s and 1940s two opposing paradigms of digital calculators prevailed: electromechanical calculators and electronic calculators. The conflict resembled the one surrounding the telephone 20 years earlier and whose outcome influenced the technical choices of telephony.

It was, moreover, a telephone engineer who developed the first electromechanical calculator. George Stibitz of the Bell laboratories noticed in 1937 that a telephone relay, the basic component of exchanges, which could assume two states (open or closed) could also serve as a component in a binary calculator (two possible states: 0 and 1). Three years later, the complex calculator, a scientific machine intended for Bell laboratory technicians, was brought out. It was a simple calculator which could add two eight-digit decimal numbers in a tenth of a second and multiply large numbers in one minute. Six successive generations of this equipment were built for the defence forces during the 1940s. The last model comprised 9,000 relays and occupied over 100 square metres of floor space (Breton, 1987: 66–7).

During the same period H. Aiken at Harvard University, in cooperation with IBM, built another electromechanical calculator: the ASCC (automatic sequence controlled calculator).[5] It was more sophisticated than previous machines in that it was controlled by a program. Data and instructions were stored on punched cards or tape. The ASCC could add in 0.3 seconds and multiply in 4–6 seconds. It was inaugurated in 1944 and functioned until 1959. After a conflict between Harvard and IBM, the university continued its work in this field until 1952 and built four successive generations of the ASCC. In 1948 IBM brought out the SSEC (selective sequence electronic calculator) which, despite its name, was a mixed, partially electronic and partially electromechanical machine. Between 1948 and 1952 IBM opened the use of its calculator to outsiders. In Germany, a similar electromechanical calculator project was led by K. Zuse.

In the USA and Britain another paradigm developed concurrently during the war: the electronic calculator. Both the manufacturers (IBM) and the academic establishment (Harvard and MIT) were relatively reserved concerning the use of electronic techniques for the production of calculators. The English computer scientist A.D. Booth summarized contemporary positions on the subject when he wrote: 'It is excessive to say that the pre-War years were the era of generalized electronics. Electronics existed already but were not yet in use' (Ligonnière, 1987: 269).

Despite such reservations, researchers at Iowa University developed the ABC (Atanosoff Berry computer) in 1942. This machine, which used triodes, was organized around the principles of Boole's algebra and of binary arithmetics. It was, however, neither programmable nor automatic. A more ambitious project was launched between 1943 and 1945 in another university (the Moore School in Philadelphia): the ENIAC (electronic numerical integrator and computer). The project leaders, J. Mauchly and J.P. Eckert, had received considerable military funds since ballistic calculations required powerful automatic means of calculation. The ENIAC was an enormous machine weighing 30 tonnes and comprising 18,000 electronic tubes. Like the ABC, it possessed a system for synchronizing the internal operations of the machine by means of an electronic clock. Different operations could thus take place simultaneously. The main advantage of electronics compared to electromechanics lay there. Whereas the ABC system only supplied 60 pulses per second, the ENIAC worked at 200,000 pulses per second. This new performance enabled the ENIAC to perform 30 million elementary operations per day, equivalent to the output of 75,000 people working manually.

Mauchly and Eckert's machine, thanks to its electronic capacities, was a high-performance calculator. Its other principles remained similar to those of earlier calculators in that it was programmed externally; in order to be repeated a programme had to be reintroduced.[6] Like the ASCC and unlike the ABC, the ENIAC was a universal machine, capable of performing any calculation. Stibitz's machines and the ABC used binary modes of calculating, whereas the ASCC and the ENIAC did not. In Britain it was also in a military context that the electronic calculator *Colossus* was developed by the mathematician A. Turing and the telecom engineer T.H. Flowers during the war.

Thus, in 1945 two paradigms of digital calculators coexisted. The two systems were fairly similar in their architecture, and the electronic system owed its superiority essentially to the rapidity of its calculations. But these machines were still calculators rather than computers in so far as they were unable to process information. At the time, data processing was performed mechanographically. The evolution from calculators to computers took place at the end of the 1940s, at the convergence of two research trends: Mauchly and Eckert's electronic calculator and von Neumann's mathematical and logical research. The latter had synthesized the principles of early computing in a text in 1945 known by the name of the 'First Draft' (von Neumann, 1973). The computer could be distinguished from large calculators by the fact that it no longer only calculated; it also processed information by means of pre-recorded universal algorithms. The second basic principle of the computer was that it had an internal control unit.

Von Neumann's role in the definition of the computer's basic principles is highly controversial. Goldstine, who was the military sponsor of research on computing, considered von Neumann to be 'the first person . . . who understood explicitly that a computer essentially performed logical functions' (Goldstine, 1972: 191). Eckert and Mauchly, on the other hand, considered that they had defined the principles of computing before von Neumann (Burks, 1980). If this debate was of such importance to the founding fathers of the computer, it is because the 'First Draft' presented the basic principles of computing in a widely circulated general document.

In any event, the theories formulated by von Neumann were more suited to an electronic than an electromechanical machine. Thus, the computer had to be an electronic system.

Telecommunications, computing and broadcasting in the process of unification

Since electronics constitutes the basic technology of television, computing and contemporary telecommunications, it seems logical that close links should exist between upstream products (the components) and downstream products (televisions, computers, telephone exchanges). Together these constitute what Bertrand Gille (1978: 16) has called a technological path. But relationships between the various systems become more and more complex with time. While the construction of computers necessitates new components, the development of such components relies on computer-aided design. This interdependence of technologies constitutes, in Gille's terminology, 'a technological system'. Gille has chosen an example of nineteenth-century technology as an illustration: 'While the steel industry used steam engines, the latter needed increasingly resistent metals to withstand high pressure and over-heating' (Gille, 1978: 18).

Telecommunications and computing

In the communications field, the articulation between technologies dates back to the infancy of the various devices. We have already noted that Lee De Forest's triode served as an amplifier for radio and television, in telecommunications and in computing. But the links between telecommunications and computing were to appear with the birth of the latter. In 1937 Claude Shannon, before being employed by the Bell laboratories, presented his doctoral thesis at MIT. In it he linked electromechanics and binary calculations. He showed notably that any complex mathematical operation could be automated by means of relay circuits used in telephony. One simply had to use binary numbers and to respect Boole's algebraic principles. In the same year, but totally independently from Shannon, G. Stibitz of the Bell laboratories built the first relay calculator along identical principles. In 1940 he conducted a first experiment in 'telecalculation' when he consulted his calculator situated 300 kilometres away, in New York, by means of a terminal linked to it telephonically (Ligonnière, 1987: 231).

The passage from electromechanics to electronics was also manifested in the cooperation between telecommunications and computing. As we have seen, T.H. Flowers, a researcher at the British Post Office laboratories, led the team which built the first English electronic calculator, *Colossus*, during the war (Ligonnière, 1987: 500ff). Later, during the 1950s, he led British research on electronic switching. We have also seen that French researchers at the CNET developed the first entirely transistorized European computers for the requirements of research on electronic switching.

Telecomputing was first used with the start of 'electronic computing'. In the early 1950s the American network SAGE (semi-automatic ground environment), responsible for aerial detection (calculation of the trajectory for intercepting enemy aircraft) consisted of several computers linked telephonically (Breton, 1987: 142). The use of computers on a time-shared basis was to develop in the 1960s, and computing networks in the following decade. A universal transmission standard made it possible to generalize telecomputing in the form of telematics.

Satellites

Relations between telecommunications and broadcasting date back to the start of the radio. We have seen that in the early 1920s AT&T used its telephone network to connect its radio stations. When in 1926 it left them to RCA, it maintained its transmission activities. Later, each new innovation in transmission was used by both the radio and television. Thus, AT&T installed the first coaxial cable for telephonic transmissions in 1936 and tested television broadcasting by the same means in the following year (Abramson, 1987: 241). The same was true for point-to-point Hertzian links. The link installed in 1945 in the United States served both the telephone and the radio. In 1950 (Libois, 1983: 105–6), AT&T was already able to transport a TV channel by means of radio links.[7]

The development of satellites provides another example of the articulation between telecommunications and broadcasting. After a number of limited experiments in 1960, the first experimental satellite, *Telstar I*, was launched two years later by NASA. It was an orbiting satellite, revolving on an elliptical orbit with its apogee over the northern hemisphere. For half an hour it was visible from both the East Coast of the United States and the west coast of Europe. One of its first experimental uses was the transmission of a television image received in France at the Pleumeur-Bodou station (the famous 'radome') (Libois, 1983: 117–19). In 1964 the first geostationary *Syncom* was launched. Situated 36,000 kilometres away, it revolved at the same speed as the earth, which meant that it remained stationary for an observer on the ground. Unlike an orbiting satellite, it was constantly operational. When television coverage of the Tokyo Olympics was provided via *Syncom III*, contemporary commentators recognized the event as the start of 'global communication' (Hudson, 1990: 157–8). The first commercial satellite, *Intelsat I*, launched in 1965, could serve either for telephony (240 channels), or for television (one channel). All telecommunication satellites in the 1960s and 1970s were to serve separately or simultaneously for the telephone and television (Libois, 1983: 120).

In the 1980s the idea of specializing satellites was born. A consortium of companies led by IBM launched the Satellite Business System (SBS) in 1980. This satellite's main objective was the transmission of inter-firm data. France, the first European country to have developed a space industry, launched *Télécom I* in 1984 and *TDF 1* a few years later. The former was designed for the exchange of information, while the latter made new TV channels available to the general public. But *TDF I* was a failure. Moreover, use of *Télécom I* also proved to be less significant than expected. This satellite finally found its market in radio and TV broadcasting. Fortunately, flexibility in the use of satellites made such reorientation easy to implement.

The 'all digital' solution

Telecommunications and broadcasting, on the one hand, and telecommunications and computing, on the other, had thus been closely related for a long time. But computer scientists also took an interest in images at a very early stage. In 1950 a computer was coupled to a cathode ray tube for the first time. The image calculated by the computer was used in the SAGE system by the American airforce. In 1960 General Motors launched a system for the design of motor car prototypes. In the same year J.E. Sutherland developed a computer program of the same type at MIT. These systems allowed for conversational graphic visualization in which the user could manipulate all or part of the image; he or she could execute translations, rotations or changes in scale. In 1963 the first program for 3-D design appeared. In 1965 a Bell laboratories' program made it possible to delete hidden parts. During the same period, owing to General Electric's work for NASA, the surfaces covered by an aeroplane in flight could be calculated and colours could be visualized. All this research work was to be used in computer-assisted design (CAD), in flight simulators and finally in computer-animated drawing. In 1969 Ken Knowlton produced the first film in computer-generated images, entitled *Incredible Machine* (see Queau, 1986: 201ff).

During the same period television also took a few steps towards computing. From 1978 images were digitized in order to achieve special effects such as compression or rotation, used chiefly in TV credit titles. The serial *Mannix* provides one of the earliest examples of this technique. Such procedures were used more extensively in videoclips which were the first form of TV production to be based on the new techniques. But the passage from analogue to digital images has not remained limited to special effects. In image production, digital technology has started spreading. What will its future impact on broadcasting and reception be? Current research shows that digitized radio and TV broadcasting will enhance the conditions of reception and make it possible to increase the number of channels available by radio link. In the sound domain, a first step forward was taken with the diffusion of the compact disc which offers households a means of listening to digitized sound. Digital radio might constitute a second step.

As far as television is concerned, controversy existed in the early 1990s between those who thought we should opt for digitization without delay, and those who held a more long-term view. The latter felt that it would be better first to improve the analogue technique and to aim for high-definition TV (more than 1,000 lines) progressively.[8] The defenders of both opinions could find support in the examples studied in this book. Partisans of digital television could point to Baird who did not want to bet on a technology of the future, while supporters of a gradual approach could take the case of Flowers who opted for electronic switching too soon. Today it appears that the digital solution has finally won.

Yet most specialists agree that digitization in broadcasting can only increase to the extent that computers process data, sound and images. The digital telephone network is in the process of becoming the Integrated Services Digital Network (ISDN); with this transformation the telephone network can now transport voices, data and images alike. Not only do telecommunications, broadcasting and computing overlap, we also have a technological system which is becoming more and more coherent, in which digital electronics are the unifying factor. These digital communication techniques provide a good example of what Christopher Freeman calls a 'technological revolution'. He distinguishes this notion from radical innovation by the fact that it 'not only leads to the emergence of a new range of products and service; it also has an impact on all the other sectors of the economy by modifying the structure of costs as well as the conditions of production and distribution throughout the economic system' (Freeman, 1986: 96). Freeman gives two examples of these technological revolutions: the railroad and electric energy. A technological revolution is not only characterized by the basic aspect of the new scientifico-technological paradigm, but also by its ability to diffuse throughout a significant part of economic activity.

Some observers consider that the technological convergence between telecommunications, computing and broadcasting will lead to fusion between these sectors. I feel that this view seriously underestimates the cultural peculiarities of each one of them. In the 1920s, AT&T gave the radio over to RCA, maintaining only its links between stations. In France, RTF also acquired its autonomy with respect to the PTT. It seems unlikely that the new capacity of telecommunications networks to transport images will change this situation fundamentally. On the other hand, it may well modify the border between software-related and hardware-related activities. Telecommunications and computing also have very different positions on the question of standardization. Since T. Vail, telecommunications have always been defined as a universal service whose main objective has been that of enabling any two persons linked to the network to communicate. By contrast, computing has developed in a far more competitive environment with the idea of providing a specific service. We could compare the two industries with the transport sector: while the telecommunications tradition is somewhat like that of the railroad, the computing culture is closer to that of the motor car.[9]

Notes

1 A triode consists of a heating filament (a cathode) which emits electrons towards a plate (an anode). A third electrode (a grid) is introduced between the two others.

2 Jean-Pierre Poitevin was director of the CNET from 1982 to 1990.

3 During the 1920s French research on television was very advanced. In 1926 Edouard Belin (inventor of a system of transmitting photographs by telephone), together with Fernand Holweck (a former assistant of Marie Curie) and Ogloblinsky, demonstrated television reception on a cathode ray tube. This research was, it seems, discontinued in about 1929. The first experiments with television in France were performed within the framework of the mechanical system by two rival teams, led by René Barthelemy and Henri de France, in 1931.

4 In France, the first official television programme was shown on 26 April 1935 using a mechanical procedure (180 lines) developed by René Barthelemy. In 1938 the electronic system with 455 lines was adopted. Programmes were broadcast daily, but on the eve of the war the public was still non-existent (only about 200 TV sets).

5 For Harvard the machine was called Mark I, and for IBM, ASCC.

6 On the ENIAC's history, see Burks (1980) and Mauchly (1980).

7 In France, the first television radio link was installed in 1951 between Paris and Lille.

8 The term high-definition television was also used in the 1930s. At that time it denoted TV with 400 lines as opposed to 30 or 60 lines.

9 IBM's attempt at the start of the 1980s to get a foothold in telecommunications by buying out the telephone equipment manufacturer Rolm was a flop. As for AT&T, it has tried – relatively unsuccessfully until then– to break into the computer market. The recent takeover of the world's fifth largest computer manufacturer, NCR, did, however, enable it to reach a critical size in this field.

References

Abramson A. (1987) *The History of Television, 1880 to 1941*, McFarland, Jefferson.

Barnouw E. (1968) *A History of Broadcasting in the United States*, vol. II: *The Golden Web*, Oxford University Press, New York.

Breton P. (1987) *Histoire de l'informatique*, La Découverte, Paris.

Briggs, A. (1961) *The History of Broadcasting in the United Kingdom*, vol. II, Oxford University Press, London.

Burks A.W. (1980) 'From ENIAC to the stored-program computer: two revolutions in computers', in N. Metropolis, J. Howlett and G.C. Rota (eds), *A History of Computing in the Twentieth Century*, Academic Press, New York.

Bustamente E. (1991) 'Telecommunicaciones y audiovisual en Europa, encuentros y divergencias', Telos, Madrid.

Freeman C. (1986) 'Technologies nouvelles, cycles économiques longs et avenir de l'emploi', in J-J. Salomon and G. Schmeder (eds), *Les Enjeux du changement technologie*, Economica, Paris.

Gille B. (1978) *Histoire des techniques*, La Pléiade, Gallimard, Paris.

Goldstine H. (1972) *The Computer from Pascal to von Neumann*, Princeton University Press, Princeton, New Jersey.

Hudson H.E. (1990) *Communication Satellites: their Development and Impact*, The Free Press, New York.

Libois L.-J. (1983) *Genèse et croissance des télécommunications*, Masson, Paris.

Lichty L. (ed.) (1975) *American Broadcasting: a Source Book on the History of Radio and Television*, Hastings House, New York.

Ligonnière R. (1987) *Préhistoire et histoire des ordinateurs*, Robert Laffont, Paris.

Lucas P. (1984) *Histoire du CNET*, Ronéo, CNET.

MacFarland D. (1975) 'Television: the whirling beginning', in L. Lichty (ed.), *American Broadcasting: a Source Book on the History of Radio and Television*, p. 49, Hastings House, New York.

Mauchly J. (1980) 'The ENIAC', in N. Metropolis, J. Howlett and G.C. Rota (eds), *A History of Computing in the Twentieth Century*, Academic Press, New York.

Metropolis N., Howlett J. and Rota G.C. (eds) (1980) *A History of Computing in the Twentieth Century*, Academic Press, New York.

von Neumann J. (1973) 'First draft of a report on the EDVAC contract', Philadelphia, 30 June 1945, in B. Randell (ed.), *The Origins of Digital Computers, Selected Papers*, Springer-Verlag, Berlin.

Poitevin J.-P. (1986) 'Composants: le rôle stratégique du CNET', *Revue française des télécommunications*, no. 60, November.

Queau Ph. (1986) *Eloge de la simulation. De la vie des langages à la synthèse des images*, Editions du Champ-Vallon, Seyssel.

Randell B. (ed.) (1973) *The Origins of Digital Computers, Selected Papers*, Springer-Verlag, Berlin.

Salomon J.-J. and Schmeder G. (1986) *Les Enjeux du changement technologique*, Economica, Paris.

Stern R. (1964) 'Television in the thirties', *American Journal of Economics and Sociology*, vol. 23.

Zworykin V. (1962) 'The early days: some recollections', *Television Quarterly*, vol. 1, no. 4, November.

9

Private Communication

As we have witnessed several times throughout this book, the development of communication is based on the inter-relationship between technological and social movements. At the start of the nineteenth century, communication was first controlled by the state, then by the market; at the turn of the century, it entered family life; finally, during the second half of the twentieth century it pervaded the economic and private spheres and is now, in that sense, truly global. A study of the flow of information in the corporate environment would probably exceed the dimensions of this book. I will therefore limit this chapter to an observation of the changes in private communication which constitute a progression of the trends considered in Chapter 4.

From public to private sphere

The individualization of the private sphere

In his analysis of public and private life in the eighteenth and nineteenth centuries, Richard Sennet noted that the English club, originally a place of conviviality and exchange, became an establishment where people socialized in silence. His observation of Parisian cafés at the end of the century led to the same conclusion: for the first time there was a large number of people in the cafés who rested, drank, read, etc., but remained separated by invisible partitions (Sennett, 1974). Edgar Allan Poe was one of the first authors, in the 1840s, to describe this solitary crowd. In 'The Man of the Crowd' (Poe, 1971: 102), a convalescent is seated at the window of a café, observing the passers-by:

> By far the greater number of those who went by had a satisfied business-like demeanour, and seemed to be thinking only of making their way through the press. Their brows were knit, and their eyes rolled quickly; when pushed against by fellow-wayfarers they evinced no symptom of impatience, but adjusted their clothes and hurried on. Others, still a numerous class, were restless in their movements, had flushed faces, and talked and gesticulated to themselves, as if feeling in solitude on account of the very denseness of the company around. When impeded in their progress, these people suddenly ceased muttering, but redoubled their gesticulations, and awaited, with an absent and overdone smile upon the lips, the course of the persons impeding them.[1]

Charles Baudelaire, who translated Poe, was also interested in crowd phenomena and studied them through the stroller figure, who 'fitted in with the crowd'. For him 'it is an immense pleasure to feel at home in a crowd, in its swaying movement, its transience and its infinity. Being away from one's home and yet feeling at home everywhere; seeing the world, being at the centre of the world yet hidden from it' (Baudelaire, 1961: 1160). Thus the stroller takes his private sphere with him throughout his wandering in the town. This intense personal experience is a source of pleasure. 'For Baudelaire', wrote Walter Benjamin, 'the crowd is a veil in front of the stroller; it is the lonely person's ultimate drug' (Benjamin, 1989: 463). Sennet spoke of 'day-dreaming' with respect to this 'public private life' where 'the silent spectator has nobody in particular to look at and is protected by his right to be alone' (Sennett, 1974).

Private life in public places was manifested not only in the streets and cafés but also at the theatre. In the eighteenth century, there was no separation between actors and their public. Some spectators even had seats on the stage. The public participated spontaneously and enthusiastically in the show and did not hesitate to shout out to the actors.

In the 1850s the stage and the public became two distinct areas. Nevertheless, the spectators still laughed or cried noisily and spoke to one another freely during the show. Twenty years later social conventions had changed; silence became the norm, at least in theatres frequented by the upper classes. Applause was reserved for the end of the performance. This practice of quiet and disciplined listening finally reached popular theatres at the end of the century (Sennett, 1974).

The passage from collective listening to the juxtaposition of a series of individual listening experiences was probably far less sudden than Sennet suggests. He makes no mention of the role of boxes in the new organization of the theatre. The latter were, in fact, a form of extending the family drawing room into the theatre. Spectators with a box could turn away from the show and converse among themselves.

In *Illusions perdues*, Balzac characterized the opera box as follows: 'In it one can see and be seen'.[2] The occupants of boxes were more interested in the public than in the show. Not only did they stare at the people sitting opposite them, they also tried to see what effect they or their companions were having on the other spectators. This game provided the subject matter for numerous conversations. The men moved from box to box, carrying out a series of mundane visits and hawking rumours and gossip concerning everyday life or the show (Balzac, 1988: 186–200). The theatre environment thus appears as the juxtaposition of private drawing rooms all facing one another.

The practice of extending one's drawing room into the theatre lasted for most of the nineteenth century. Frédéric Henriet, in his 'monograph on the spectator at the theatre', described stage boxes as being 'like a small drawing room where one feels totally at home if one moves right to the back of the box, and totally conspicuous if one moves under the shower of light . . . from the footlights and the chandelier. One is then the sighting point for all opera glasses' (Henriet, 1892: 23).[3]

Henriet distinguished three types of public. In 'inferior' theatres, he said, the working-class public 'is impressionable, convinced . . . it becomes impassioned, punctuates the show with "murmurs" and "diverse movements" very similar to a Chamber of Deputies session. It takes sides with the characters to the extent of sometimes butting in at the most moving moments' (Henriet, 1892: 30). In cultured theatres, the middle-class public listened quietly and attentively. The aristocracy and upper classes, on the other hand, continued to behave as if they were in their drawing room, even if they no longer moved from box to box as in Balzac's day.

> See [these women] burst into their box ostentatiously, scraping their chairs, vying with one another in their exchange of polite remarks, sitting down, changing places with their silky rustling of fabrics, talking loudly . . . To make sure that their obtrusive arrivals have the desired effect, they always plan them for after the curtain has been raised. And since there is nothing more boring than listening to a play when one has missed the introductory scene, they then indulge in futile chatter. (Henriet, 1892: 19–20)

Boxes were rented whole, sometimes for a full year at a time. In this 'home reconstituted at the theatre', the social rules of the private sphere prevailed (Martin-Fugier, 1987: 209). Thus a woman who would never watch a show alone in an orchestra seat, received her friends in her box with the same etiquette as in her drawing room.[4]

The theatre box constituted a new mode of articulation between the private and public spheres. It was a first attempt at 'privatizing' the theatre. This formula owed its success to a mirror effect, peculiar to the Italian theatre, where the box public created their own show; they watched and were seen. Sometimes plots built up which rivalled those being acted out on the stage. Although, as Sennett showed, there was no more confusion whatsoever in the public sphere between the stage and real life, ambiguity did reappear in the private sphere that was on show. This ambiguity probably played a large part in the nineteenth-century upper classes' fascination for the theatre.

Unlike the box, which amounted to transporting the private sphere into the public sphere, the theatrophone was intended to do quite the opposite: to take the show into the home. The first promoters of the telephone organized a number of experiments in broadcasting operas and concerts by telephone. Graham Bell performed a number of demonstrations of this type in the United States. It was probably in France, during the Electricity Exhibition in 1881, that the promotional effect of the theatrophone was most effective. Two halls at the Palais de l'Industrie were equipped with telephones for listening to the Opera and the Comédie-Française. The experiment was a resounding success, with the result that the number of Parisian telephone subscribers doubled in 1882 (Carré, 1983: 72).

Use of the telephone for listening to theatrical plays or concerts nevertheless remained limited.[5] It is important that this failure be explained, for 15 to 20 years later the phonograph was successfully to propose music at home. Many things changed in those two decades. As we have seen, watching a play in the 1880s was a highly sociable event in everyday life. The public who could afford a box and a theatrophone was used to watching shows in company, in a group, whereas the telephone offered it a means of listening individually. Furthermore, the major urban exodus towards the suburbs was only beginning in the USA and was to intensify at the turn of the century with the electric tram. During the 1880s the public was still geographically close to the numerous concert halls and theatres which existed at the time. Finally, records were not yet a satisfactory substitute for concerts since they contained only very short extracts.

At the start of the twentieth century the theatre was transformed when a critical trend with regard to Italian-style theatre emerged.[6] André Antoine wrote in 1890:

> The circular shape generally adopted condemned two-thirds of the spectators on the upper levels to be placed literally and without any exaggeration directly in front of one another. They could only follow the action on the stage with difficulty, by bending their necks ... The privileged spectators in the boxes ... and baignoires, closed into confined, dark and over-heated spaces, lost even more of the show. (Bablet, 1963: 14)

Theatres built in the early twentieth century, like that of the Champs-Elysées (1913), took this criticism into account. Boxes disappeared and seats were arranged so that everybody could see (Pougnaud, 1980: 110). But a new way of watching shows – anonymously and silently – imposed itself simultaneously. The spectator was alone in the public, facing the actors. This modification in the relationship between spectators and the stage was intensified by the new architecture of theatres. It was also related to the transformation of the actors' social role. Whereas in the eighteenth century artists were seen as servants, during the next century they were to become divas who imposed their personality on the public. People no longer went to the theatre to be entertained, but to expose themselves to art.

The cinema: the last collective show

Unlike the theatre, the cinema remained an essentially popular form of entertainment for a long time. In France films were shown at fairs until 1908. 'There were', wrote Jean-Paul Sartre in *Les Mots*, 'vulgar manners which shocked serious people; it was entertainment for women and children' (Sartre, 1972: 102). In contrast with theatrical performances of the same period, film shows were punctuated by comments, bursts of laughter, cries of fear and whistling. The spectators participated intensely in the show.

As a contemporary critic noted in *Mercure de France*, in September 1907, most cinema-goers had never even been to the theatre (Abel, 1990). Their experiences of shows came mainly from café-concerts or music halls. Nevertheless, the presence of children made the cinema the 'family show *par excellence*' (Laurens, 1906; Abel, 1990: 31).

American research on the sociology of the cinema confirms Sartre's description. Silent films before the First World War were essentially a collective social experience (Hansen, 1983). Robert Sklar considers that during the entire period the cinema was essentially a popular show, attracting many immigrants, and that halls were equipped mainly in working-class suburbs

(Sklar, 1975: 14–17). However, monographs by other American historians on the setting up of halls in New York and in a small town in the South help to qualify Sklar's thesis. Cinemas were in fact also found in middle-class areas (Allen and Gomery, 1985: 202–7). Another study on the development of a major cinema chain in Chicago between 1919 and 1925 gives some indications of the strategy employed by its promoters. They built or bought large halls so that no point in the city would be more than 15 minutes away by tram (Allen and Gomery, 1985: 202–7).

Thus the cinema, originally an essentially working-class show, became a form of mass entertainment during the 1920s. In 1922 every American over the age of five went to the cinema almost twice (precisely 1.75 times) a month. This figure rose until 1930 when, with a figure of 3.5 times a month, consumption had doubled compared with 1922 (Figure 9.1). In the year 1930 the cinema attracted the largest number of people, proportionately speaking, in the United States (Bureau of the Census).[7] Interpretation of this figure is, however, tricky. A cinema historian, David Robinson, considers that it was the advent of sound films which 'revived the spectators' enthusiasm' (Robinson, 1973) and led to a rapid growth in attendance between 1927 and

Figure 9.1   *Monthly cinema attendance in the USA by population over the age of 5 years (Bureau of the Census)*

1930. Yet, while the first widely shown musical film was *Jazz Singer* in 1927, sound films were only to occupy a major place in cinemas from 1929 onwards.[8]

The increase in the number of cinema-goers until 1927, and the major part of that growth in 1928, was therefore not owing to enthusiasm for sound films but to the growth of the silent cinema public. This progression was amplified in 1929 and 1930 by the attraction of sound films, but it was short-lived. A survey in 1929 showed that 56 per cent of all spectators preferred silent films (Cuel, 1979: 5). Hollywood companies nevertheless imposed sound by henceforth producing sound films only and rapidly withdrawing all silent ones from circulation. In 1931 cinema attendance decreased. The Depression most probably played a role in this trend. In 1933 nearly a third of all cinemas closed down, while the price of a ticket had also been reduced by nearly a third (Sklar, 1975: 162). Lower prices were, moreover, probably one of the reasons for an increase in attendance from 1934. It was to peak again in 1936 and 1937 and remain stable (around three cinema visits per month per inhabitant) until 1948.

The effects of the Depression aside, the cinema public in the 1930s changed fairly substantially. 'At the time of silent films' wrote Robert Sklar 'it was acceptable for the public to comment out loud on the film . . . People sharing the same emotions could therefore form a bond, so creating a community of spectators that had originally been strangers.' At the time of sound films, however, such behaviour was repressed by the other spectators. 'The talking audience for silent pictures became a silent audience for talking pictures' (Sklar, 1975: 153).

The year 1930 was thus a major turning point in the sociology of shows. While at the start of the nineteenth century 'noisy listening' was the rule at the theatre, it gradually became the exception and, at the end of the century, only concerned the working classes and a fraction of the aristocracy. The silent cinema revived this manner of consuming shows, which again disappeared with sound films. 'Silent listening' then became the new social rule. The shift from 'noisy listening' to 'silent listening' was not an insignificant change; it effectively marked the end of a means of communion, of participating in the show. Although it was fairly rapid, this modification nevertheless took place in stages. At the start of the 1950s French cinemas still displayed the sign: 'Talking is forbidden during sound films.'[9]

'Silent listening' was probably one of the reasons for the working classes deserting the cinema. Shortly after the war, when cinema attendance was high (see Figure 9.1), the industry commissioned its first sociological studies on audiences. Contrary to prevailing ideas on the subject, the cinema did not have a mass public with undifferentiated social characteristics (Sklar, 1975: 269), but an audience in which the middle classes predominated.[10]

The cinema's reorientation towards the middle classes also appears if we look at the price policy applied to films. From 1948 to 1950 the price of entrance tickets rose by 37 per cent (Bureau of the Census)[11], an increase which led to lower attendance among the working classes. Moreover, family

Table 9.1   *Trends in cinema and television in the USA, 1949–50*

	Decline in cinema attendance (%)	Increase in cinema price (%)	Television sets (%)
1949	23	24	2
1950	15	11	11

outings to the cinema, which had been a habit during the inter-war period, became rare as families were less able to afford them. Thus the imposition of silent listening and higher prices together generated a new cinema consumption that was less frequent and less collective (Table 9.1).

Cinema attendance in America declined by 33 per cent between 1948 and 1950, which corresponded roughly to the rise in the price of entrance tickets. At that time the number of television sets was still small, which proves that, contrary to an often held belief, it was not the arrival of television which caused cinema audiences to decline sharply (decrease of 50 per cent in five years). A part of the public, and notably the working classes and families, had already deserted the cinema. Was this trend provoked by the higher price of tickets, or did the cinema profession, on the contrary, devise its price policy to offset the departure of its public? It is difficult to say. Either way, a public was ready to receive television, and it was to be given the opportunity to resume its previous habits of 'noisy and collective listening' at home.

'Living together separately . . .'[12]

Family viewing of television was to be part of a tradition which emerged with the piano and the phonograph and developed more intensely during the inter-war period with the radio. The BBC, for example, had made the family aspect of the radio one of its golden rules. C.A. Lewis, the first British radio programmer wrote:

> Broadcasting means the rediscovery of the home. In these days when house and hearth have been largely given up in favour of a multitude of other interests and activities outside, with the consequent disintegration of family ties and affections, it appears that this new persuasion may to some extent reinstate the parental roof in its old accustomed place, for all will admit that this is, or should be, one of the greatest and best influences on life. (Lewis, 1942; Frith, 1988: 32)

Moreover, numerous illustrations of that period show families gathered together around their radio.

This family aspect of the radio was taken for granted to the extent that, when French manufacturers commissioned a market study on the new transistor radio set at the end of the 1950s, the answer was that the only demand was for replacing existing radio-receivers. But the marketing men were wrong; the late 1950s and the 1960s were to be a period in which the transistor boomed.

Figure 9.2 *Number of radio sets per household in the USA (excluding car radios) (Bureau of the Census)*

As before, I shall examine the development of the transistor radio market in the countries in which it originated: the USA and Britain. The portable transistor radio was brought out in America at the end of 1954 (Winston, 1986: 197), the post-war year in which American consumption of radio-receivers was the lowest. At that stage all households already had about two sets on average.[13] Yet consumption was to increase four-fold between 1954 and 1962 and seven-fold between 1954 and 1972.[14]

A study of the number of radio sets indicates that this phenomenon was not the result of replacement purchases. Figure 9.2 shows that while American families systematically had two sets in the 1940s and 1950s, from 1959 they were to start having several sets per family. Within a period of 10 years the national average rose from two to four sets per family. A profound transformation was taking place within the family, for with the transistor the radio became not only mobile but also individual. Whereas in the 1940s the family had gathered together around the radio, in the 1960s each family member pursued his or her own activities while listening to a separate radio. An identical evolution appeared in the other industrialized countries. In England it took place at the same time as in the US; in France it was a little later.[15]

A French observer, J. Ormezzano, remarked in 1957:

> The transistor is a more important revolution in family life than the television . . . The radio or television which were barely transportable and often unique could but impose themselves, dominate the home from a choice position. Lord of the family unit, they attracted, imposed themselves, subjugated by virtue of their very presence. They united the family in a unity that was formerly found around the hearth. The transistor introduced not only freedom, but also fragmentation, the dispersal of the family unit. Everyone took their transistor into their own little corner . . . It never prevented them from working, or talking, or moving around; it punctuated daily life . . . It accompanied people like a piece of clothing or a dream. (Ormezzano, 1957; Fize, 1990)

Teenage music

The 1950s also saw a revival of the record, with the development of LPs (33 rpm) in 1947 and singles (45 rpm) in 1949. These new products broke into the market around 1953 and provoked a boom of the electrophone. From 1952 to 1955 the production of record players increased five-fold. For the first time in 1954 the level of activity in this field was comparable with that of 1919.[16] Growth of the electrophone was accompanied by the development of the record market. The latter, which had remained stable between 1946 and 1954 (around 200 million records), tripled within five years.[17]

The record industry boom coincided with the birth of a new type of music: rock 'n' roll. It was in 1955 that Bill Haley recorded *Rock Around the Clock* which, according to Lillian Roxon, was 'the "Marseillaise" of the teenage revolution' (Ewen, 1977: 554).[18] It remained at the top of the hit parade for eight weeks running. Elvis Presley soon became the main star of this new music. In 1956 he sold 10 million records, the highest annual sales ever achieved by a singer.[19] It is difficult to distinguish the extent to which record sales during this period could be attributed to rock music, but we do have an indicator. In 1955, rock accounted for 16 per cent of records in the 'Top 50'; in 1957, this figure had risen to 60 per cent (Gillet, 1983).

Rock was not consumed in the same way as popular variety music in preceding years. As the critic Howard Junker (1970) notes:

> the main point in pre-rock culture was that society acted as though it were homogeneous . . . In short, it was theoretically possible for everybody to appreciate the common culture. The whole family, from six to sixty years old, listened to *Your Hit Parade*. [This programme] worked very well, until the kids demanded music that the family could no longer stand. (Buxton, 1985: 62)

The transistor and, to a lesser extent, the record player were the instruments that made this type of individual listening possible.

Rock was music designed for dancing, hence the importance of rhythm; irresistible and implacable rhythm which *had* to make one sway. It was dancing music no doubt because it was also highly social music, associated with significant transformations in society. Remi Hess has shown that the waltz became prevalent during the French Revolution. It was during that period that the couple started to assert itself, to appear in public places. In contrast with dancers during the time of the *ancien régime*, waltzers freed themselves from their social status, they could move freely amidst other couples in the ballroom. 'People were no longer side by side. They were no longer face to face. They were in each others' arms'(Guilcher, 1988; Hess, 1989: 317).

Rock music, which some critics consider to have 'changed the world' (Loder, 1986), has produced similar analyses. Many observers consider it to be related to the emergence of adolescence as an autonomous age-group, in conflict with the adult world. As protest music it was 'written by youngsters, to be played and sung by youngsters, and to be directed exclusively to youngsters' (Ewen, 1977: 556). The themes of the songs were mostly related to teenage preoccupations: parties, adolescent passion or feelings towards adults (Gillett, 1983). Surveys in the US and Britain on adolescents' spare-time activities showed that from the end of the 1950s rock was the main form of entertainment and that it structured young peoples' consumption. Mark Abrams (1959) estimated that in 1959 teenagers' purchases accounted for 42 per cent of British record consumption and that 25 per cent of teenagers between the ages of 16 and 24 had danced in the week preceding his survey.[20]

The survey carried out by P. Jephcott in Glasgow in 1965 showed that rock music was at the centre of teenagers' leisure activities. 'The young's interest in pop determined the television programmes they watched, the magazines they read, the cafés they went to, the "necessary tools" – transistor, record player, tape recorder, guitar – they sought to own' (Frith, 1978: 38).

During the 1950s music was often listened to in public places where the juke-box was used as an active medium for diffusing rock.[21] There were close on 500,000 of these machines in the United States, accounting for about 40 per cent of all record sales (Gillett, 1983). Later, listening was focused more on the home, notably among teenage girls whose culture became, for Frith, 'a culture of the bedroom, the place where girls meet, listen to music and teach each other make-up skills, practice their dancing' (Frith, 1978: 64).

The most common explanation put forward for the success of rock music among teenagers is economic. During the post-war years teenagers' budgets increased considerably. In the United States their average weekly spending money rose from 2.5 dollars in 1945 to 10 dollars in 1960 (Levy, 1960; Buxton, 1985: 73). In England Mark Abrams' study of teenagers shows that their income rose by 50 per cent between 1938 and 1958, while that of adults only increased by 25 per cent. Their discretionary spending doubled (Abrams, 1959). However, this sharp rise in young people's spending potential provides only a partial explanation. It is often combined with the extension of schooling.

For Paul Yonnet (1985: 181) rock music allowed teenagers to form an autonomous social group, refusing the organization of their lives by adults.

'Rock was their true class consciousness.'[22] Yet the conclusions of an English study by the Schools Council in 1968 contrasted sharply with this argument which placed rock at the centre of teenagers' lives. Only a small minority of teenagers considered that this was effectively so. More interestingly, when the same questions were put to adults their answers indicated that they in fact grossly overestimated the role of music in teenagers' lives (Table 9.2). These figures indicated, and numerous other surveys confirmed, that music was probably less important in itself than as an instrument dissociating teenagers' world from that of adults. 'Music – played on transistor radios, record players, portable cassettes – becomes the easiest way for the young to maintain and display their control of their rooms, clubs and street corners, of their pubs and discos . . . Music is the context for, rather than the focus of, youthful leisure' (Frith, 1978: 48).

Table 9.2 *Percentage of persons considering that music was important for themselves, their children or their pupils*

	Boys	Girls
Children	20	35
Parents	41	64
Teachers	38	71

Source: Frith (1978: 39)

Unfound adolescence

The social characterization achieved by means of this music, the fact that it was at first refused by adults, has led many analysts to explain the rock phenomenon in terms of the conflict between generations. The intensity of this conflict was reflected in 1955 in Richard Brooks' film *The Blackboard Jungle* based on a book by Evan Hunter published the previous year. After intense conflict with his pupils, a teacher tried to initiate dialogue by playing his own jazz records to them. The class responded by creating an uproar and throwing their teacher's records across the classroom. In the film it is the implacable rhythm of Bill Haley's *Rock Around the Clock* that is used to express the teenagers' rejection of their teacher's 'swinging' jazz music (Gillet, 1983).

A number of surveys has shown that the generation gap was far wider in the 1950s than 20 years earlier. Music was only a symptom of this phenomenon. The conflict between generations was also reflected in political opinions, religious practices and sexuality. By contrast, Edward Shorter considers that American sociological studies in the 1950s 'point to a delightful harmony between parents and children: nobody challenges or rejects, and sample after sample of high school students or college freshmen declare how much they like their mother and father, agree with the way they were brought up, and so forth'. An analysis of literature from the 1960s has provided similar conclusions (Shorter, 1975: 273).

To choose between these two theses (conflict or harmony between the generations), it seems useful to examine historians' points of view. John Gillis studied the history of teenagers in England in the nineteenth and twentieth centuries. Until the mid-nineteenth century all children, with the exception of those in the upper classes, started working very early. Moreover, children traditionally had a large degree of autonomy. It was during the Victorian era and mainly in the middle classes that adolescence started appearing as a specific age. Young people were under the dual authority of their parents and educational institutions. For Gillis, the invention of adolescence was an effect of the reform of secondary schooling in England in the mid-nineteenth century (Gillis, 1974: 105). Public schools then became closed areas which took over the education of the children of upper class families.

From the early twentieth century the concept of adolescence, the specific organization of an age-group directly dependent on adults, was to spread down to the working classes. During the same period youth movements were created to take care of teenagers outside their school time. A specific legal system was established for the youth with specialized courts and prisons. Thus, society attributed a particular status to those who were no longer children and were not yet adults. The imposition of adolescence as a specific age did not, however, take place smoothly. Resistance to this new way of supervising the youth was found in the working classes in particular. Two opposing teenage figures appeared: those who conformed and those who rebelled.

If adolescence and juvenile delinquency did originate at the start of this century and not in the 1950s, as is sometimes claimed, was there a transformation in the youth after the war? For Gillis, the 1950s and 1960s marked the end of adolescence. The youth found a part of the autonomy they had lost a century earlier and the boundaries between school and home became less impervious. In the middle classes the patriarchal attitude of parents declined, young girls were no longer chaperoned. It was probably in relationships between the sexes and in the political field that transformations were most apparent. Separate education for girls and boys was abolished. Young people became sexually active earlier and married younger than in the preceding period. In England in 1931 only 7 per cent of young men between the ages of 15 and 24 were married. By 1951 the figure had risen to 12.5 per cent and to 15 per cent by 1957. For women, the percentages were 14, 27 and 30 per cent respectively (Gillis, 1974: 189–90).

Political activism in the 1960s also indicated the end of adolescence; the youth had gained enough autonomy to be able to participate in political debate. Moreover, in a number of countries the state recognized this evolution by lowering the voting age.

Gillis's conclusions are shared by a number of sociologists. Kenneth Keniston (1965: 395) considers that 'the values and behaviors of the youth culture are rarely explicitly anti-adult, but they are rather non-adult.' He talks later of a 'gentleman's agreement' between generations that did not want to interfere with each other. R.W. Connell (1972) has drawn the same conclusions from a general study on political socialization in the family. He thinks that the old and new generations develop their opinions concurrently, rather than successively, through similar experiences in a similar life-style. Michel Fize's work on the French family shows that there is often a large degree of ambiguity in adult–adolescent relationships. Young people claim to 'feel good with their parents' and yet to be over-supervised by them (Fize, 1990: 72). Such contradictions have to be situated in the long evolution towards what Fize calls 'family democracy'. For him, the liberal and egalitarian functioning of the family started in the late 1960s. Yet it seems that Fize has difficulty dating the evolution for, on a number of occasions, he notes manifestations of it in the 1950s.[23] He rightly remarks that this family change first took place in the middle classes and that it started in the English-speaking countries. In short, Fize tends to confirm Gillis's analyses.

The transformation of adult–adolescent relations also comprised another element: the fact that the image of youth became the ideal image for an entire society. Max Horkheimer already noted in 1941 that in our fast-changing society, where age is viewed with suspicion, the main figure is no longer the father but the child who now represents reality (Horkheimer, 1941; Ewen, 1976).

To return to music, it was not only a means for teenagers in the 1950s and 1960s to situate themselves beside their parents. It was also a means to becoming independent as distinct individuals and simultaneously to show their belonging to a particular peer group. During a survey conducted by Simon Frith in 1972 in a small British town, the following answer often appeared: 'I like what I like, no one changes my opinions on music' (Frith, 1978: 40).

When they were launched, the transistor and long-playing record benefited not only from a new form of music (rock) but also from a profound change in private life. The family did not disappear but it was transformed; the home was maintained but as a place in which individual practices were juxtaposed. Music was particularly well adapted to this new 'juxtaposed home'. Family members could all listen to the music they wanted to in their rooms. Record players or tape recorders became affordable goods for teenagers who had more and more money to spend. Rock provided the opportunity to mix the collective and individual dimensions of their lives, not only within the family but also in peer groups. The choice of records was individual but through it a teenager could belong to a specific, more or less ephemeral, group.

The communication bubble

The individual consumption of music, born with the transistor, was to find a new modality 20 years later in the walkman. I shall present the use of this new facility briefly, for very little empirical research has been conducted on the subject. The main objective of these few pages, like those which I will then devote to telematic message services, to the VCR, zapping and mobile telephones, is to indicate some thread in the evolution of private communication which first started to appear at the end of the nineteenth century and finally took shape from the 1950s onwards. The sociology of new communication machines is still too embryonic for us to be able to draw definitive conclusions today.

The walkman appeared in Japan in 1979 and conquered a very large market both in the United States and Europe. In France almost a third of all homes (31 per cent) have one today. Possession of a walkman varies markedly according to age: 67 per cent of young people between the ages of 15 and 19 have a walkman, while only 4 per cent of adults over the age of 65 have one (French Ministry of Culture, 1990).

Contrary to most preconceived ideas, the walkman is not only a device for listening to music outdoors. It is also used in the home. One of the rare surveys conducted in France on the subject, by Marie-France Kouloumdjian, shows that the walkman is part of the 'juxtaposed home'. It allows teenagers to remove themselves from adult supervision while still living with their parents. As one interviewee said, 'being alone, knowing that the whole family is there' (Kouloumdjian, 1985: 16). Like the transistor, this new teenage practice has not developed without adult opposition, for the little machine changes parent–child relationships. 'He doesn't answer anymore when I call' remark the parents. But adults themselves also use the walkman and, in contrast to teenage habits, they do so mainly at home. This juxtaposed use of the walkman has caused collective sound, the reference point of family life, to disappear.

The walkman, as its name indicates, is also used outside, on trips on foot or in a vehicle or during the exercise of an individual sport (roller skating, skiing, etc.). It thereby becomes a sort of prosthesis which changes people's relationship with music. The musical instrument no longer offers an auditive environment alone, it also creates new links between the body and music. A roller skater with a walkman moves to the rhythm of the songs he or she hears. But this solitary activity, in which sport and dancing sometimes overlap, can even take place in a crowd. Thus we find, more than a century later, a practice similar to that of Baudelaire's stroller: the pleasure of being alone in a crowd, of being at home away from home. Use of the walkman has often been compared to a communication bubble. The image is accurate provided that we note that with this bubble one can simultaneously withdraw into oneself and handle certain social interaction with one's surroundings.

The ambiguity of walkman-related behavioural patterns can be compared to another practice in the 1980s, that of telematic message services. The user is both at home and elsewhere, he or she can instantaneously change his or her place of dialogue by going from one message service to another. But, as Yves Toussaint has shown, in this game of communication where each interlocutor uses a pseudonym, the user does not only want to assume a new identity, to use his or her mask to behave differently. 'It is less a question of hiding than of showing oneself with even more realism than in ordinary life.' 'For most users of message services' continues Toussaint, 'it is the abolition, the elision of their social masks which finally allows them to be authentic'

(Toussaint, 1989: 75–6). The anonymous users of a communication device try to participate in a permanent carnival and to simultaneously be 'totally sincere'. By means of a pseudonym one can reveal other facets of oneself and thereby display one's true identity more effectively. Josiane Jouët, in her monograph on the message service 'Axe', shows the same type of contradiction: 'Axians' want to create a convivial electronic community. Their communicational model is not that of random contact in an anonymous crowd, but, on the contrary, that of a group of friends who meet in a café (Jouët, 1989: 49–66).

Personal television

Like the phonograph and the radio, television was born as a family medium. Some sociologists have seen it as the equivalent of the hearth in rural families. 'The active role of the log fire in the shaping of family life, in the manifestation of its organization and in its daily social production, has shifted to the television . . . It is henceforth the time and place of the television which structure the family's daily life, from meals eaten together and their time, to the children's bed time' (Lafont, 1982: 208). This family characteristic of television may seem strange, from a historical point of view, in so far as the radio and the record became individual media in the 1950s. Indeed, during the 1960s American TV audience specialists started wondering whether we were heading towards personal television. Some of them still think that such a tendency will be the main change during the next few years. By having several sets in the home, family conflicts can be avoided.[24] However, this vision automatically takes as a reference the existing model of change from the radio to television and is, in that sense, partially wrong. In fact, we should rather place all broadcasting media into the contradictory context of the functioning of family life. While listening to the radio is becoming more individual, family listening focuses itself on the televisual media. As Alain Le Diberder and Sylvie Pflieger (1987) note, 'television is aimed at a group, the household, and not at an individual. Even if the multiplication of television sets causes a rupture in this model, it does not really threaten it.'

The possession of several TV sets has therefore developed far more slowly than in the case of the radio. In the United States, homes had an average of 1.1 televisions in 1960, 1.4 in 1970, 1.7 in 1980 and 1.9 in 1988.[25] In Britain, only 15 per cent of British homes have more than one television. But the second (or third) set is used far less than the first one. According to a British survey conducted in 1987 (AGB Research), 88 per cent of all viewing in the home was done on the main set. The secondary sets were used at different hours to the main one (meals, late evenings). They nevertheless functioned simultaneously to the main set for a third of the viewing time over weekends and 27 per cent of viewing time on weekdays.[26] A French survey shows that possession of more than one set is more frequent in homes with teenagers: 38 per cent of all teenagers live in a home with more than one TV set, whereas this figure drops to 24 per cent if the overall population is considered (French

Ministry of Culture, 1990). Teenagers also tend to consume television in a more individualistic way.

Even though television is a focal point in most homes, this does not necessarily mean that TV shows unite the entire family. The expansion of television programming is enabling each member to find the programmes intended for him or her at a specific time of the day.

Use of the VCR has the same impact.[27] In their research on the video, Baboulin et al. (1983: 106–107) consider that 'use of the VCR helps to harmonize family relations, rendered conflictual by television, by making viewing more individual and eliminating confrontation . . . Regulating family life implies the management of differences rather than the elaboration of a problematical consensus. [This is] the ambiguous – individual and social – function of the VCR.' As one of their interviewees aptly put it: 'We each go our own way, together. . . .'

Another peripheral device of the television, the remote control, is associated mainly with individual viewing.[28] The authors of French research on 'zapping' distinguish the occasional 'dropping out' of a TV viewer waiting for a programme or fleeing the ads (15–20 channel changes per day) from true zapping (over 100 changes per hour for some individuals). Intense zapping is mainly done alone, very rarely in company. The zapper sees the programmes in such an individualistic way that in the end his or her construction makes sense only to him or herself. Moreover, this practice requires a great deal of concentration since the zapper has to constantly take micro-decisions, change channels, work out what he or she missed on a particular programme, anticipate action on another programme, and so forth (Bertrand et al., 1993). There is in zapping, as in message services, a complex game between that which is marked and that which is shown. The programme displayed 'on the screen, screens' all the others. Chantal de Gournay and her colleagues note with respect to zapping, like Josiane Jouët with respect to message services, a certain nostalgia which seems somewhat surprising in these champions of electronic modernity. As the users of message services try to rediscover the sociability of yesterday's café, so zappers, by trying to reconstitute the coherence of a TV metaprogramme, feel nostalgia for the time when there was only one channel. By zapping, they no longer have to choose one programme rather than another. They can, just as at the beginning of television, 'see everything'.

Nomadic communication

The two tendencies characterizing the use of communication over the past 30 years – individual reception and transportable devices – diffuse from one medium to another and pervade new media in particular. The (social) novelty in the 1990s is the mobile telephone. Even if the car radio-telephone has existed for a long time, it was limited to an exclusive part of the population. From the mid-1980s mobile communication has developed widely in the professional world with the cellular phone technology. While there were only

90,000 subscribers in the United States in 1984, this figure had already risen to 3.3 million by the end of 1989. In Europe, the mobile telephone was first developed in the Scandinavian countries (600,000 phones in 1987) and then in Britain (450,000 terminals in 1987 and 700,000 in 1988).[29]

Radio-message systems inform users of a call either by means of a sound signal or by a visual message. At the end of 1987 there were 6.5 million subscribers to this system in the USA and 400,000 in Britain.[30] In 1990 a device (known as Pointel in France) appeared, giving pedestrians the possibility of making, although not receiving, a telephone call. For the user there is a certain continuity between this simplified mobile telephone and the use of a cordless telephone at home (400,000 users in Britain in 1987).

The success of mobile telecommunications systems is unquestionable. Some British experts forecast, moreover, that by the year 2000, 20 per cent of all subscribers will use mobile devices. In a number of countries demand exceeds technical supply. The lack of terminals and particularly available frequencies has resulted in the creation of user waiting lists. A bottleneck of this type indicates that a demand truly exists, not only among professionals but also in the public at large.

Mobile communication is the culminating point of a long transformation of the public and private spheres. The private sphere has become the main locus of entertainment, of consumption of music and shows. This area has itself broken up into several small juxtaposed cells. However, the withdrawal into the private sphere does not mean the disappearance of the public sphere. In the 1950s, in the United States, open-air cinemas provided an interesting case of articulation between these two worlds. Teenagers took their dates to the drive-in movie in their first car. Without leaving their car, they passed from the sound bubble of the car radio to the visual bubble of the cinema. Today, the users of walkmans and cellular phones, like Baudelaire's stroller, transport their private sphere with them. They are in an anonymous crowd, listening to the music they like; they are absent from their home or office yet in potential telecommunication with the whole world. Message services also link the public and private spheres for the user is both at home and in a network of conversations without any geographical roots. The current social evolution is probably less that of the hypertrophy of the private sphere (split into individual micro-spheres) than the possible setting into motion of private spheres within a reorganized public sphere where the individual is constantly here and elsewhere; alone and linked to others. Edgar Allan Poe's man of the crowd was alone; the twentieth-century stroller with a walkman or cellular phone remains alone, communicating not with passers-by but with those to whom he or she is connected. We are witnessing the superposition of two types of sociability: one is immediate (often atrophied), the other is mediatized.

Notes

1 This text, like other citations from novels, should not be taken as an ethnographic description, but as a historic reference point of a new awareness of the crowd phenomenon. A sociologist like Gustave Le Bon made one of the first scientific analyses of this question at the end of the nineteenth century.

2 This novel is situated in around 1820. It was first published in 1839.

3 It was only in the 1890s that the lights in the auditorium were turned out during a play (see Chenais, 1990).

4 On the same subject, Maurice Descotes quotes the report of a critic writing in 1904: 'Barely twenty years ago one would never have seen a lady in the stalls of the Théâtre-Français' (Descotes, 1964: 313).

5 A contemporary like Louis Figuier was persuaded that the theatrophone would attract a mass audience. He imagined that Parisian buildings would soon have 'the opera on all floors', just as they already had water and gas (Figuier, 1885: 282). Yet the theatrophone was only successful in Hungary. The 'Hirmondo telephone' created in Budapest in 1893 had up to 6,000 subscribers. Its programmes were focused far more on current events than on broadcasting shows (see Briggs, 1977: 50–5).

6 What is often inaccurately called Italian theatre is in reality a combination of two types of arrangement: an Italian type of stage which offered the spectator a classical perspective in the centre of the hall, and a French type of hall in which the public was seated in a horse-shoe (see Chenais, 1990: 123, 137).

7 In absolute figures, the highest attendance was in 1946. Many histories of the cinema note this date, but without taking into account population growth.

8 Although most studios started producing sound films in 1928, some of them continued producing only silents. Paramount, for example, only switched to sound films exclusively in 1930 (Sklar, 1975: 153). Robinson estimates that in 1929 'three-quarters of all full-length films made in Hollywood had at least some sound sequences, and every fairly large cinema had sound equipment' (Robinson, 1973). A monograph on Milwaukee shows that at the end of 1928 all major cinemas were equipped for sound films. Yet by 1930, 25 per cent of all small cinemas in the suburbs could still show only silent films (Allen and Gomery, 1985: 196–7).

9 Quoted by R. Icart at the INA seminar 'Communication audiovisuelle et société', on the birth of sound cinema (18 January 1982).

10 A survey in 1931 on the structure of consumption in American homes shows that employees and labourers spent twice as much on the cinema as self-employed professionals (Ewen, 1976).

11 The rise in cinema prices was evaluated by means of the following ratio: box-office takings/annual attendance. On the evolution of attendance in France, see Bonnell (1978).

12 I have borrowed this title from Baboulin et al. (1983).

13 Information from the Electronic Industries Association and Bureau of the Census.

14 The figures are: 1954, 6.1 million; 1962, 24.8 million; 1972, 42.1 million. I have not included car radios which were already fairly common in the USA (60 per cent of all vehicles were equipped in 1955).

15 In England, the production of radio-receivers doubled between 1959 and 1961, from 1.4 to 2.7 million. In 1960 two-thirds, and in 1962 100 per cent, of all production was transistorized (Central Statistical Office). In France, the production of transistor radios was as follows: 260,000 in 1958, 820,000 in 1959, 1.7 million in 1960 and 2.2 million in 1961 (Syndicat général de la construction électrique).

16 The figures are: 1919, 2.3 million; 1952, 0.8 million; 1954, 2.7 million; 1955, 3.9 million (Bureau of the Census).

17 Sale of records in millions of copies are as follows: 1954, 213; 1955, 277; 1956, 377; 1957, 460; 1958, 511; 1959, 603 (figures from *Billboard*).

18 *Rock Around the Clock* sold 16 million copies throughout the world.

19 In 10 years Presley sold 115 million records (Ewen, 1977: 559). According to P. Yonnet, Presley sold 500 million records in 30 years. The Beatles did even better, with 1 billion records and tapes (Yonnet, 1985).

20 A major survey conducted by James Coleman (1961) in the USA produced similar results.

21 It was only at the end of the 1930s, when the radio had already been substituted for the phonograph in most homes, that the juke-box spread in public places. There were 30,000 in 1934 and 300,000 in 1939, when only 30 million records per year were sold (Frith, 1988: 16).

22 To illustrate his thesis he uses an *a contrario* argument: the countries in which rock music is forbidden are those where the youth are in a state of moral and physical dependence vis-à-vis adults.

23 He quotes numerous sociological studies from the late 1950s (Alain Girard, Paul-Henry and Marie-José Chombart de Lauwe, the General Inspector Hatinguais) who demonstrate this transformation of the family.

24 'Multi-set trend poses research questions', *Printers' Ink*, 13 November 1964.

25 Figures from *Statistical Yearbook* (1989). At the end of the 1980s, 30 per cent of all televisions sold were portable.

26 In France, 30 per cent of all homes are equipped with several television sets (BIPE). In Japan, statistics show 1.8 sets per household.

27 In the United States, VCR sales took off in the 1980s. In 1984, 10 per cent of all homes were equipped; in 1990, 65 per cent (*Statistical Yearbook*). In Japan, 80 per cent of all homes were equipped in 1989. In France, this figure is 30 per cent (BIPE, 1989).

28 In France, half (55 per cent) of all TV sets are equipped with a remote control (BIPE, 1989).

29 Information from 'World Mobile Communications' Conference, November 1988, London, and 'Telephones that get up and go', *The Economist*, London, 16 September 1989. In France, the market is more limited: 40,000 subscribers at the end of 1987, 98,000 at the end of 1988, 170,000 at the end of 1989 (France Télécom).

30 The number of subscribers in France was 120,000 at the end of 1987 and 220,000 at the end of 1989.

References

Abel R. (1990) 'The blank screen of reception in early French cinema', *IRIS*, no. 11, Summer.

Abrams M. (1959) *The Teenage Consumer*, London.

Allen R. and Gomery D. (1985) *Film History Theory and Practice*, Alfred A. Knopf, New York.

Aries P. and Duby G. (eds) (1987) *Histoire de la vie privée*, vol. 4, Le Seuil, Paris.

Bablet D. (1963) 'La remise en question du lieu théâtral dans la société moderne', *Colloque Royaumont*, CNRS, Paris, June.

Baboulin J.-C., Gaudin J.-P. and Mallein P. (1983) *Le Magnétoscope au quotidien: un demi-pouce de liberté*, Aubier-Montaigne, Paris.

Balzac H. (1988) *Illusions perdues*, Folio, Gallimard, Paris.

Baudelaire C. (1961) 'Le peintre de la vie moderne' in *Oeuvres complètes*, La Pléiade, Gallimard, Paris.

Benjamin W. (1989) *Paris capitale du XIXe siècle*, Le Cerf, Paris.

Bertrand G., de Gournay C. and Mercier P.-A. (1993) 'The Global Programme', *Réseaux – French Journal of Communication*, no. 1 vol. 1, London, Spring.

Bonnell R. (1978) *Le Cinéma exploité*, Le Seuil, Paris.

Briggs A. (1977) 'The pleasure telephone: a chapter in the prehistory of the media', in I.de Sola Pool (ed.), *The Social Impact of the Telephone*, MIT Press, Cambridge, Mass.

Buxton D. (1985) *Le Rock: star-système et société de consommation*, La Pensée sauvage, Grenoble.

Carré P.A. (1983) 'Paris, capitale électrique', *Revue des télécommunications*, no. 4, Paris, July.

Chenais R. (1990) *Les Racines de l'audiovisuel*, Anthropos, Paris.

Coleman J. (1961) *The Adolescent Society*, New York.

Connell R.W. (1972) 'Political socialization in the American family: the evidence re-examined', *Public Opinion Quarterly*, vol. 36, no. 3.

Cuel F. (1979) 'Don Juans et fous chantants', in *Dossier du muet au parlant, Cinématographe*, no. 47, Paris, May.

Descotes M. (1964) *Le Public de théâtre et son histoire*, PUF, Paris.

Ewen D. (1977) *All the Years of American Popular Music*, Prentice-Hall, Englewood Cliffs, New Jersey.

Ewen S. (1976) *Captains of Consciousness: Advertising and the Social Roots of the Consumer Culture*, New York.

Figuier L. (1985) *Le Téléphone*, Librairie illustrée, Paris.

Fize M. (1990) *La Démocratie familiale: evolution des relations parents-adolescents*, Presses de la Renaissance, Paris.

French Ministry of Culture (1990) *Les Pratiques culturelles des Français (1973–1989)*, La Découverte/La Documentation française, Paris.

Frith S. (1978) *The Sociology of Rock*, Constable, London.

Frith S. (1988) *Music for Pleasure: Essays in the Sociology of Pop*, Polity Press, Cambridge.

Gillet C. (1983) *The Sound of the City: the Rise of Rock and Roll*, Souvenir Press, London.

Gillis J. (1974) *Youth and History: tradition and Change in European Age Relations: 1770-Present*, Academic Press, New York.

de Gourmont R. (1907) 'Epilogues: cinématographe', *Mercure de France*, September.

Guilcher Y. (1988) 'Toute forme de danse n'est pas possible à n'importe quelle époque', *La Recherche en danse*, no. 4.

Hansen M. (1983) 'Early silent cinema: whose public sphere', *New German Critique*, no. 29.

Henriet F. (1892) *Monographie du spectateur au théâtre*, Laurens, Paris.

Hess R. (1989) *La Valse. Révolution du couple en Europe*, A.M. Métailié, Paris.

Horkheimer M. (1941) *The End of Reason*.

Jouët J. (1989) 'Une communauté télématique: les axiens', *Réseaux*, no. 38, CNET, Issy, December.

Junker H. (1970) 'Ah: the unsung glories of pre-rock', *Rolling Stone* 72, December.

Keniston K. (1965) *The Uncommitted, Alienated Youth in American Society*, Harcourt Brace and World, New York.

Kouloumdjian M.-F. (1985) *Le Walkman et ses pratiques*, Multigraphie, CCETT, Rennes.

Lafont H. (1982) 'Les téléâtres', *Autrement*, no. 36, Le Seuil, January.

Laurens J. (1906) in 'Le cinématographe: les sujets', *Photo-ciné Gazette*, 1 September.

Le Diberder A. and Pflieger S. (1987) 'La consommation de la télévision de demain', *Futuribles*, no. 106, Paris.

Levy A. (1960) *Operation Elvis*, André Deutsch, London.

Lewis C.A. (1942) *Broadcasting from Within*, Newnes, London.

Loder K. (1986) 'The music that changed the world', *Rolling Stone*, no. 13.

Martin-Fugier A. (1987) 'Les rites de la vie privée bourgeoise', in P. Aries and G. Duby (eds), *Histoire de la vie privée*, vol. 4, Le Seuil, Paris.

Ormezzano J. (1957) 'L'image et le son: la révolution du transistor', *L'Ecole des parents*, no. 7.

Poe E.A. (1971) 'The Man of the Crowd' in Poe's *Tales of Mystery and Imagination*, Everyman's Library.

Pougnaud P. (1980) *Théâtres: quatre siècles d'architecture et d'histoire*, Editions du Moniteur, Paris.

Robinson D. (1973) *World Cinema: a Short Story*, London.

Sartre J.-P. (1972) *Les Mots*, Folio, Gallimard, Paris.

Sennett R. (1974) *The Fall of Public Man*, Alfred A. Knopf Inc., New York.

Shorter E. (1975) *The Making of the Modern Family*, Basic Books, New York.

Sklar R. (1975) *Movie-made America: a Cultural History of American Movies*, Random House, New York.

de Sola Pool I. (ed.) (1977) *The Social Impact of the Telephone*, MIT Press, Cambridge, Mass.

Toussaint Y. (1989) 'Voile et simulacre sur les messageries', *Réseaux*, no. 38, CNET, Issy, December.

Winston B. (1986) *Misunderstanding Media*, Routledge and Kegan Paul, London.

Yonnet P. (1985) *Jeux, modes et masses*, Gallimard, Paris

10

Final Reflections

During the two centuries in the history of communication covered in this book, one period in particular is noteworthy for its fertility: the last quarter of the nineteenth century. It was during those years that the telephone, the phonograph, mass photography, the cinematograph and the wireless were born. We have seen that this was no historical coincidence, for the various inventions were all inter-related. They were, first and foremost, linked technologically. For example, the phonograph was a product of research on telephonic and telegraphic repeaters; the motion picture was initially envisaged as a device similar to the phonograph and adopted the same film used in photography. But these inventions also had similar uses. The telephone was used to broadcast concerts, while the phonograph was first marketed as a telephone answering machine. The phonograph and motion picture were both, during a short period of their history, a type of juke-box before becoming, respectively, a private and a public sphere medium. As a result of this inter-relationship between technology and usage, some inventors envisaged the development of integrated media such as a telephone for both conversing and listening to the opera. Similar projects were, however, never completed; the convergence of various media did not lead to any multi-media systems. Yet in a number of cases a technology or its use shifted and in so doing provided an important element in the fertilization of new media.

A century later, when we are talking of a communication society, of the convergence of telecommunications, broadcasting and computing, we also find ourselves in a potentially fertile period where numerous new communication systems could well be developed. Technologies which have even more in common with one another than those of a century ago indicate that we are heading for an integrated network, on the one hand, and a 'multi-media station' on the other. The former will connect all homes and enterprises by supplying them with a telephone (and videophone), radio, television and telematic data. The latter, a derivative of the microcomputer, will be used to read texts, listen to recordings and view images. According to the scenarios forecast, each 'station' will be autonomous or connected to a network. Behind these projects lies the idea that information is analogous to energy and that networks and computers are there to transport and process it.

A study of the late nineteenth century can probably help us to understand current developments and make us wary of certain technological fiction. It seems highly unlikely that a large unified network with a single terminal comprising the telephone, television and data will come into being. For cultural reasons (peculiarities of professional traditions), but also political and economic ones (risk of a gigantic information and communication monopoly abusing its dominant position), such a scenario remains unfeasible. Yet the famous technological convergence introduced by digitization causes technologies and uses to shift, which in turn favours the appearance of new systems. Technological integration will result far more in the movement of borders between the various media than in the removal of these borders.

Within the framework of thought on future communication, the project of substituting telecommunications for transport was widely debated a few years ago. Telework had become possible owing to new networks, and white-collar workers could practice their professions at home in their suburbs or provinces. Voluntarist experiments were conducted but, surprisingly, they were a total failure. The transfer of the workplace into the private sphere had taken into account neither the richness of sociability at the office, nor the reorganization of the private sphere for accommodating professional activities. The alienation of the monotonous travel–work–sleep life-style was replaced by solitary confinement in the private sphere. Nevertheless, the emergence of new communication tools (microcomputers, Minitel and more recently the fax) have helped to make the borders between the professional and private spheres far less impervious. Executive staff (and not employees as in the preceding example) can now work partly at home. In her study on the personal computer, Josiane Jouët (1987) has shown clearly that one of the main uses of this tool at home is word-processing. Executives use their PC to produce professional texts – at home.

All too often the inventors of new communication systems reason in terms of substitution, when they would do better thinking along the lines of a shift of uses and technologies. Take for example telematics, imagined at first as a substitute for paper. It immediately became a subject of controversy as the press saw in this nascent medium a future competitor. Yet, while the electronic telephone directory has remained the main function of the videotext, the electronic newspaper has been largely unsuccessful (Charon, 1991: 304–7). Telematics are used to provide information and perform transactions (bank, transport etc.) on the one hand, and as a means of corresponding (message services) on the other hand. There has thus been an effective shift compared with the original design.

Similarly, in current debate on the television of the future, the assumption is made too often that it will have the same function tomorrow as it has today. Controversy surrounds technological solutions (analogue or digital) and standards (European or Japanese), but rarely usage. Will this new television, oriented towards high definition, finally and definitively 'repatriate' the cinematographic image into the private sphere? Or will the multiplication of channels and the arrival of the individual small TV screen lead to the fractioning of audiences, similar to those of the radio? These are two possible shifts in the way new television might be used.

At the turn of this century the various communication devices are hardly likely to merge into a large integrated system. Communication is rather like a kaleidoscope, allowing innovators to compose and recompose new media. More than ever, a large number of communication devices can now be envisaged, but tomorrow's innovators will have to change their outlook often if they are to find successful configurations. They will need to be as mobile as the media they are preparing.

References

Charon J-M. (1991) *La Presse en France, de 1945 à nos jours*, Le Seuil, Paris.
Jouët J. (1987) *L'Ecran apprivoisé, télématique et informatique à domicile*, Collection Réseaux, CNET, Issy.

Index